The Heritage Seekers

American Blacks in Search of
Jewish Identity

by

ISRAEL J. GERBER

JONATHAN DAVID PUBLISHERS
MIDDLE VILLAGE, N. Y. 11379

THE HERITAGE SEEKERS
Copyright © 1977 by
Israel J. Gerber

No part of this book may be reproduced in any manner
without prior written permission from the publisher. Address all inquiries to:

Jonathan David Publishers, Inc.
68-22 Eliot Avenue
Middle Village, New York 11379

Library of Congress Catalogue Card No. 77-2907
ISBN 0-8246-0214-5

Library of Congress Cataloging in Publication Data

Gerber, Israel Joshua, 1918-
    The heritage seekers.

    Bibliography: p.
    Includes index.
    1. Original Hebrew Israelite Nation in Jerusalem.   2. Afro-
American Jews.   3. Israel—Emigration and immigration. 4. Lost
tribes of Israel—Miscellanea.
I. Title.
BM205.G44   296.6'7   77-2907
ISBN 0-8246-0214-5

Printed in the United States of America

TABLE OF CONTENTS

In Memory of
HELEN K. LEYDEN
Devoted to Her Family
and
Dedicated to Worthy Endeavors

PREFACE

This book came to life in a corridor of New Science Hall at Johnson C. Smith University when Dr. Stephen Klepka, Professor of History, pushed a letter into my hand. "Read it, Rabbi," he urged. Intrigued by the Israeli postage stamps, I promised to return the letter as soon as I had read it. "Keep it," he said, grinning. "I don't need it. They are *meshugah* (crazy)."

Although I had left my congregation and did not expect the title to follow me into the academic world, Dr. Klepka liked to call me "Rabbi," rather than "Doctor," as did other faculty members and students. A non-practicing Catholic priest, he had served parishes in predominantly Jewish neighborhoods where he became acquainted with Yiddish and Hebrew expressions which he injected with delight into our conversations. *Shalom* was his usual greeting, and he never missed an opportunity to extend best wishes to me on Jewish holidays.

The letter he gave me was written by Shaleak Ben Yehudah, Chargé d'Affairs of the Original Hebrew Israelite Nation in Jerusalem. It urged him to settle in the State of Israel, because, Shaleak claimed, it was the homeland of the black people. Because he was teaching in a predominantly black college, the letter apparently was sent to him on the assumption that he was black. Dr. Klepka, however, is white.

The Original Hebrew Israelite Nation in Jerusalem consists of a group of black Americans who claim to be descendants of the founders of the Jewish people, the Patriarchs Abraham, Isaac and Jacob. Throughout the book, they are called Black Hebrews or Hebrew Israelites.

Dr. Klepka's letter from Israel aroused my interest. From innocuous news items that appeared sporadically in some periodicals, I knew that these particular blacks, like other groups from different parts of the globe, claimed Israel as their homeland and had actually emigrated there; but the fact held no particular significance for me. They were in Israel—so what? Now, with a direct communication in my hand, they became real.

I began a search for information and wrote to them in Israel. In their lengthy replies, it was assumed, as with Dr. Klepka, that I, too, was black, and I was also urged to settle in Israel. Assisted by the Ford Foundation, the Institute of Jewish Studies, and the Blumenthal Foundation to whom I am most grateful, I traced the Black Hebrews from Chicago to Liberia, to Israel—where a number of them are living today— and back to Chicago where most of the returnees reside.

This book deals with their search for a meaningful existence, their claim to being Jews or Hebrews, their motivations for going to Liberia and then moving into the State of Israel, and also the development of black Jewish sects in the United States, back-to-Africa movements, and other related information. There is no intention to be judgmental; rather, to present the facts and their psychological and sociological aspects. On the basis of the data presented herein, the reader will interpret, evaluate and formulate his own conclusions concerning the various participants in the narrative.

Interest in the subject has been evinced in the United States, in Israel and in Africa, wherever Black Hebrews were mentioned. Many conversations recorded within these pages were reconstructed from first-hand reports supplied orally, as well as from published articles and documents.

Thanks are also due to Ruth Slesinger and Robert Conn who read the material in preparation and made valuable suggestions in organizing the mass of accumulated data. Many others are deserving of sincerest appreciation for assisting in bringing this work to completion. Their anonymity does not in any way detract from their contribution. Special mention, however, should be given to June Garfinkel, educational chairman of the Institute of Jewish Studies, for her active support when the project was launched, and Dr. Walter Yates, Dean of Hood Theological Seminary, who was ever ready to extend assistance.

Certainly my wife, Sydelle Reba, is deserving of my greatest admiration. She felt keenly the competition of this venture, yet good-naturedly shared in it and contributed the title of the book. For her it meant spending many lonely hours while I was abroad and even when I was at home she was still alone. She relinquished attending activities because I was unable to share them with her and fulfilled responsibilities that were clearly mine. Her constancy only heightens my thankfulness for a loving mate who has always had my unbounded esteem and adoration.

ISRAEL J. GERBER

Charlotte, North Carolina

January 21, 1977

Chapter I

THE PLAN

"Brothers and sisters!" Ben Ammi Carter exclaimed to his small congregation of black people. "The American government does not wish to free the blacks. The American people do not wish to free the blacks. Even our black leaders are faithless."

It was a Friday evening in Chicago in 1966. The followers of Ben Ammi Carter were gathered for their Sabbath worship in an upstairs apartment at 4456 South Cottage Grove Avenue. They listened attentively. With each phrase their leader uttered, they nodded their heads and mumbled *Amen*. The group called itself *B'nai Zakin Sar Shalom*, meaning "Descendants of the Elders Prince of Peace," because they all believed themselves to be direct offspring of the ancient Hebrew patriarchs Abraham, Isaac and Jacob. They observed the Jewish day of rest.

Eyeing his listeners closely, Carter spoke in a clear but solemn voice about the future of black people in the United States. He despaired of the future. Then, with hands upraised, palms open, his long, thin fingers moving like flickering candles, he proclaimed, "Brothers and sisters, *Elohim*, the Lord High God, has commanded me to lead you out of the American wilderness."

"*Hallelujah! Hallelujah!*" The congregation stirred and exchanged happy but bewildered expressions.

Leaning toward his eager listeners, Carter lowered his voice and went on. "There is only one solution to our predicament. Only in Africa can we be truly free. Let us return to Africa."

A woman stirred by his oration demanded, "But how can we do that, Brother Carter?"

Smiling benignly and with hands clasped prayerfully, Carter responded, "That's a good question, sister. We know black people must go to Africa to be free. We must separate ourselves from American racism. But we can't just keep talking about it year after year. Now . . . now is the time to do something. Now is the time to move."

Heads bobbed in agreement. "*Amen. Amen.*"

Having touched a responsive chord, Carter continued. Defeat and disillusionment were their fare, he said. They were oppressed, the butt of intolerance and bigotry. If ever they were going to live better they must leave this so-called bastion of democracy that excludes them from full participation. It was their only hope; the ultimate option that they might still be able to live as free people on the continent from which they came.

The meeting place of the congregation was called the Alpha Beta Israel Hebrew Center, in use contracted to A-Beta. Like their Greek-Hebrew-English name, their Sabbath service was also a strange mixture. Unlike any other mutation of Judaism in the 20th century, it consisted of random readings from the King James Version of the Bible[1] and exhortations from their leader, Ben Ammi Carter, punctuated by cries of *Amen* and *Hallelujah* from his listeners. The language and forms of worship resembled, more than anything else, the fundamentalist Christian churches that had nurtured the worshippers before they joined the Black Hebrew movement.

Other groups of black people who profess Judaism also exist in Chicago, together comprising the second largest community of black Jews in the United States. They are also found in Philadelphia, Washington, Cincinnati and in other cities mainly along the eastern coast. New York City, with approximately five strong black Jewish congregations and a half-dozen small ones, is the largest.[2] Estimates of their total number in the United States range from 12-15,000 to over 100,000. James

Benjamin, former executive director of the now-defunct *Hatzaad Harishon* (The First Step),[3] believes that 10,000 live in the New York City area and 100,000 are scattered throughout the country. Rabbi Solomon J. Sharfman, Chairman of the Synagogue Council of America's Committee on Black Jews, mentioned the figure of 40,000 on a television program that brought together black and white rabbis, and the NEGRO ALMANAC offers 44,000.[4]

Diverse, varied and decentralized, the black Jewish movement in America is far from consistent in ideology and belief. While almost all regard themselves as Orthodox Jews, some profess various interpretations of Judaism, while others approximate Christian belief. *Christianity Today*[5] divides the black Jews in the United States into three categories: those who predict that they will return to Israel at some distant future date; those who believe that blacks are true Jews but accept Jesus as a prophet; and, those who call themselves Black Israelites or The Original Hebrew Israelite Nation or Black Hebrews, whose immediate goal is to establish themselves as a living community in the land of the Bible. With some variation, the second and third categories describe the constituency of Congregation *B'nai Zakin Sar Shalom*.[6]

Carter's group went its own way, having little if any contact with the white Jewish community and little association with other black Jews. Others in the black community, however, were already working with the mainstream Jewish establishment. Under the leadership of the Chicago Board of Rabbis' Committee on Black Jewish Brethren, the leaders of four black groups, Rabbis Robert Devine, James Hodges, Naftali Ben Israel and Richard Nolen, banded together on November 7, 1967, as the United Leadership Council of Hebrew Israelites (ULCHI). Two of the Council's objectives were "to bring into focus national unity among Hebrew Israelites (Black Jews)" and "to boldly proclaim the message of the Restoration of the Nation of Israel." These black leaders, together with the committee of white rabbis, formed the Chicago Fellowship of Multi-Racial Jews to plan and to implement programs for the black congregations. A memorandum issued by an investigative committee noted that A-Beta did not become associated with these groups because of its "confused motivations and erratic leadership." For several years, the memo explained, members of A-Beta were said to have had as their aim settling in Liberia where they hoped to develop a black Jewish colony.

Ben Ammi Carter, a handsome tan-skinned man with grey-green eyes, finely chiseled features and a trimmed black beard, had worked at Howard Foundry on North Koster Street. Earlier he had been a bus driver. He began his study of Judaism in about 1960 with a self-styled rabbi who calls himself Levi Israel (his real name is Fred Lang) of Congregation *Beni Zakin Ba Sholom* (Descendants of the Elders Come in Peace), housed in the former Broadway Strand Theatre at 1643 West Roosevelt Road in Chicago. After a year and a half, Carter left Levi Israel to study with Rabbi Abihu Reuben of the Congregation of Ethiopian Hebrews. Neither teacher ordained him, but Carter claimed that in 1961 Rabbi Reuben gave him the name Ben Ammi, meaning "Son of My People." Two years later in 1963 he became leader of the group that met at Alpha Beta. They called him *Abba*, Father, and *Yo-etz*, counselor. Responding to his personality and authority, the Congregation *B'nai Zakin Sar Shalom* gave him the title *Moreh Tzedek*, Righteous Teacher.

On this Sabbath, Carter held the congregation's attention with the flowing oratory he had learned by preaching to the street vendors and shoppers on a corner of Maxwell Street. The people were animated by the Righteous Teacher's exhortation. This proposition, as others before, would undoubtedly soon be laid to rest, yet it was satisfying to hear the plan revived from time to time. There was relief in reciting their complaints, but it was pure pleasure to indulge in fantasies of a life free of adversity in Africa. They could talk freely of attaining goals they knew would never be realized. It was a major factor in helping them keep their personalities intact.

Carter then placed before his followers the plan that changed their lives. As Moses had sent 12 men ahead to examine the land of Canaan, they would dispatch a committee of three to explore their promised land. First, they would need to ascertain which country most suited their needs and purposes. Then, if the members concurred, the representatives would embark on an investigative trip. Their expenses would be paid out of the congregation's treasury and by raising additional funds.

Carter appointed Brother James T. Greer[7] and Brother Charles Blackwell to share this responsibility with him. They agreed to meet the next night at his home to start deliberations. Carter promised the congregation a report on the following Friday night.

Visibly affected by what had taken place, the members clapped their hands; the men slapped each other on the back, while the women hugged and kissed. They were full of hope. A young woman shouted, "At last we're on the move."

This was not the first time the present followers of Ben Ammi Carter had considered moving to Africa. In 1958, fearing that a war between the United States and Russia would unleash atomic destruction, they considered escape to Africa, but were unable to finance the move. Instead, they embarked on a farm project in southern Illinois, away from large cities. Once there, however, many rethought the decision, realizing that atomic warfare could easily engulf them there, too, and decided to move back to Chicago.

Carter's urgings to move to Africa had already been proposed by many black leaders as the only solution to the problem of their people. They advocated Pan-Africanism, a term that defies definition. Basically, it seeks an acknowledgment of the right of black people to repatriation and self-determination in Africa. It advocates the moral justification of exiles of African descent to agitate for African independence. As a response to the discrimination, degradation, inequality and injustices blacks suffer because of skin color, Pan-Africanism sought to unite black people everywhere into a spiritual oneness to work toward a solution to eliminate their flagrantly inhuman treatment.[8] Defensively, the excluded blacks determined that their best response to the existing situation would be to separate themselves from the dominant white society.

In addition to Carter, two civil rights workers, Stokely Carmichael,[9] who was instrumental in developing the phrase "black power," and James Meredith,[10] who was shot while on a voting rights march in Mississippi, are more recent proponents of the concept of Pan-Africanism. Blacks will never be completely free, they contended, until they are in full control of economically viable land in Africa. Real estate is the springboard for their liberation, for as Malcolm X had stressed, revolution is based on land because ideas, by themselves, are insufficient to rouse people.

Another aspect of the same phenomenon was the westward migration of blacks to Kansas and Oklahoma.[11] In the early months of 1879, a cumulation of circumstances caused approximately 50,000 blacks to migrate to the North, with most of them moving into Kansas, John Brown country. The exodus, born of desperation, was the result of a steady migration and years of careful planning and preparation. The blacks eagerly sought to live where they would be granted political recognition, free of economic exploitation and the dreaded activities of the Ku Klux Klan. An aged eccentric, Benjamin "Pap" Singleton, who called himself "The Moses of the Colored Exodus," reportedly started the migration and led some 300 blacks to Cherokee County, Kansas, to found "Singleton's Colony."[12]

Edwin P. McCabe, who edited the newspaper, *The Herald*, led a movement to make Oklahoma a state to be governed entirely by blacks. He devoted his newspaper to this cause, encouraged blacks to organize land purchasing societies, and 25 self-governing all black communities were established there.[13] Although Oklahoma did not become a black state, the movement symbolized the budding consciousness of a black nationalism intimately related to the possession of land. Without land, McCabe felt, the condition of blacks in the United States would never be elevated.

The history of the Jewish people may have inspired the land-oriented approach to black liberation. Faith alone might not have sustained the Jewish people during the 1900 years of exile, while faith combined with the hope of returning to their own land did preserve their unity. The establishment of the State of Israel has not only liberated persecuted Jews from Europe and from Arab lands, it has also restored pride wherever Jews felt themselves an alien and powerless minority. But unlike the Jews, for whom Israel was the ancestral homeland, the Pan-African leaders faced a choice: which one of the many possible homelands should they adopt? Carmichael favored Ghana as the site for rebuilding the black nation.

In the 1890's Bishop Henry M. Turner of the African Methodist Episcopal Church promoted Liberia as the country where blacks could realize their manhood in total freedom. This was where "each black feels like a lord and walks the same way." A leading proponent of the back-to-Africa idea, Turner could see no future for blacks in the United States. So vehement were his feelings against America that he longed to see it in ruins and its memory erased. "A man who loves a country that hates him is a human dog and not a man,"[14] he exclaimed. He also made derogatory remarks about the American flag and the Constitution. Black Americans, he argued, could help redeem Africa culturally and religiously and make Africa prosper. It was for this purpose, he maintained, that God brought the African blacks to America.

Turner was joined in this chorus by Chief Alfred C. Sam in Oklahoma, who claimed to be an African tribal chief, and Edward Wilmot Blyden, who lived in Africa. So anxious were Turner and Sam for blacks to return to Africa that they jointly sponsored an exodus in 1878, when 206 blacks left Charleston, South Carolina, for Liberia.[15]

Blyden, who served as Liberian Ambassador to the Court of St. James and as president of Liberia College, maintained that only by returning to Africa could the blacks be rescued from oppression and elevated to respectability. So firm was he in this conviction that when Martin R. Delany, a recognized black leader, advocated the establishment of a black colony in the Caribbean, Blyden attacked the scheme.[16] He argued that racial separation was the will of God. Maintaining that each race has its own strength and is in this sense a chosen people, he felt it would be blasphemous for blacks to surrender their personality and to give up the "special work to which they were called." To do so "would mean to give up God which is the worst suicide." He did not, however, encourage a mass exodus of blacks to Liberia. Rather, he recommended that only educated and talented blacks, not mulattoes, do so.[17] His Pan-Negro ideology is regarded as the most important historical progenitor of Pan-Africanism, the term that gained great currency during this first Pan-African Conference held in London in 1900. Blyden himself, however, did not attend this gathering.[18]

In the early 1900s, W. E. B. DuBois and Marcus Garvey in the United States and H. Sylvester Williams, a West Indian lawyer in London, proposed the establishment of a strong central Negro state in Africa.

DuBois, who held a Doctor of Philosophy degree from Harvard University, was one of the founders of the National Association for the Advancement of Colored People. He established the Niagara Movement that spearheaded protests against the cruelties inflicted upon American blacks, and was second only to Booker T. Washington as the most prominent black American during the early years of this century. Praising the African continent as the "greater fatherland" of the blacks, he at first favored the Congo Free State as the site for the establishment of "a great central Negro State of the world,"[19] and then added Uganda, Angola, French Equatorial Africa, German Southwest Africa and Mozambique to his proposed black nation. Washington, however, disagreed. He was frank to admit he could "see no way out of the Negro's present condition in the South by returning to Africa" and that there was "no place in Africa for him to go where his condition would be improved."[20]

Academic in manner, DuBois disparaged Marcus Garvey, the short, rotund founder of the Universal Negro Improvement Association, calling him "ugly, but with intelligent eyes and a big head." Garvey's slogan was "Ethiopia, Thou Land of Our Fathers." To him, Ethiopia was representative of the whole African continent. Despite DuBois' prestige, Garvey gained greater mass support because American blacks were ready to follow any vigorous spokesman who would provide them with any measure of dignity and self-respect. His many faceted Universal Negro Improvement Association aimed "to work for the general uplift of the Negro peoples of the world,"[21] and fostered a strong sense of black racial pride. The

U.N.I.A. was the first significant black nationalist movement that responded to the needs of the blacks in the economic, political, religious, social, cultural and recreational areas. In Garvey's theology, blacks were the chosen people of God.

Another back-to-Africa leader was tall, deep-voiced Bishop George Alexander McGuire who was invited by Garvey in 1920 to become Chaplain-General of the U.N.I.A. In response to discrimination in the Episcopal Church and to the refusal of ecclesiastical authorities to legitimatize his newly founded Independent Episcopal Church, McGuire established the African Orthodox Church in 1921. He was consecrated its Bishop by the Most Reverend Joseph René Vilatte, Exarch and Metropolitan of the American Catholic Church.[22] Perhaps as a result of his high praise of Garvey, comparing him to Moses, Paul and John the Baptist, McGuire's church came to be regarded as an official U.N.I.A. denomination. "We are somewhat like the Hebrews," he said. "Like them we have left our native land and have no place to go." The Jews have Palestine; "why not the Negroes another Palestine in Africa?" was his comment at the 1922 Universal Negro Improvement Association Convention.[23]

Garveyism so resembled Zionism that Garvey actually called his followers "Zionists."[24] Harriet Tubman, the "Joan of Arc of her people," who helped many slaves escape from the South by conducting an underground railroad, also used the same terminology. When she wrote to her fellow conspirators, she alluded to the Biblical homeland, saying, "tell my brothers . . . when the good old ship of Zion comes along, to be ready to step aboard."[25]

Marcus Garvey and Theodore Herzl, the father of modern political Zionism, had many similarities. They both advocated that the solution to prejudice was to leave home and settle in a country free of bigotry and discrimination. In their younger years, neither Garvey nor Herzl had been exposed to strong anti-minority feelings. When they were, they did not attempt to deal with the situation, but advocated escape. Perhaps they realized the futility of such an endeavor. Each adopted a nationalistic approach that was both chauvinistic and religious, and each was fervent in his determination to help his people.

Both of them secured public support of those most adamantly prejudiced against their people. Garvey viewed every white man as a potential Klansman; Herzl regarded every non-Jew as a potential anti-Semite. Zionism succeeded, however, while Garveyism faded away. Zionism had the support of Jews throughout the world; it was a people's movement. Garveyism's only strength was Garvey. His movement was the personal crusade of a single leader who was autocratic in his methods and slipshod in his financial practices—factors that alienated his supporters.

It is ironic that despite the similarities between their respective groups, Garvey was prejudiced against the Jewish people, echoing the anti-Semite Houston Stewart Chamberlain in denying that Jesus was of Jewish ancestry.[26] At first his anti-Semitic sentiments were covert, but as time moved on he became embroiled in a running battle with American Jews. When he was tried for mail fraud in 1923, he made many unfavorable remarks about Jewish people. The fact that the judge and prosecutor were Jewish only aggravated his position. When the jury brought in a guilty verdict, he shouted "the dirty Jews," although the panel included only two.[27] Sentenced to five years in the Atlanta federal penitentiary, he was pardoned by President Calvin Coolidge after serving half his sentence and was deported to Jamaica.

Despite Garvey's anti-Jewish utterances, a sizable group of his New York zealots were black Jews. More intensely black than Jewish, they well knew that their future was bound to the future of black people.[28]

Among his Jewish followers was an unordained rabbi, Arnold Josiah Ford, whose early religious training was in his father's Christian evangelical sect in Barbados. Possibly his home environment or other factors turned him against the faith of his father. Rejecting Christianity as the religion of the white man, Ford taught that Judaism was the true religion of the blacks. Africans, he said, have never been Christians but blood Hebrews. However, their native African Hebrew traditions, which can only be taught orally because of their "kabbalistic" nature, were unsettled by slavery and influences of the Christian New World. He viewed the exile of the blacks from Africa as a duplication of the earlier exile of the Jewish people from Palestine. Calling the black a "man of sorrows" who had been refined in the fire of slavery, he contended it was the responsibility of every black person to help in the reawakening of the African continent. Ford organized the *Beth B'nai* Abraham Congregation and brought most of his congregants into the U.N.I.A. He fervently hoped that Judaism would be adopted as the official religion of the Association and was deeply disappointed that it was not.

As musical director of the U.N.I.A., Ford and his band performed at conventions and at fund-raising events around the country. For a while, his influence and prestige within the movement was second only to Garvey's. But due to personal clashes with Garvey, he was expelled from the organization. Unhappy at having fallen from grace, he reportedly took his family to Ethiopia in 1926 to practice Judaism among the Falashas,[29] a tribe of black Jews who claim descent from Abraham, Isaac and Jacob. A later version tells that he left for Ethiopia in 1930 after meeting a Falasha who had toured the United States a year or two earlier. Ostensibly, his congregation sent him there to represent them at the coronation of Emperor Haile Selassie and to help found a settlement there.[30] *Beth B'nai* Abraham ceased to function as a congregation in 1930.

Still another and perhaps more plausible account traces Ford's interest in the Falashas to the accidental discovery that they were experiencing poverty and persecution in Ethiopia. Jews in Great Britain and the United States organized the Pro-Falasha Committee to aid these stricken people. Dr. Jacques Faitlovitch, a French Jew and leader of the Committee, visited the Falashas in 1904-5 under the sponsorship of Edmund Rothschild and, interestingly enough, was not permitted to enter their synagogue until he first prayed for seven days and underwent ritual immersion.[31] He returned again in 1908 and in 1913 under the sponsorship of The American Pro-Falasha Committee. Upon learning of the existence of a black Jewish congregation in New York City, Dr. Faitlovitch called on Arnold Ford in the latter part of the 1920s to inquire whether the membership consisted of Falashas. Until then

Ford had not heard of the Falashas. From then on, he and "Rabbi" Wentworth Matthews whom he ordained, and who became the best known of all black Jewish leaders, seized upon this new information to bolster their identity as Ethiopian Hebrews. It certified to them not only that blacks had been Jews, but that they are the original Jews.

Howard Brotz writes that when Garvey refused to adopt Judaism as the religion of his Pan-African movement, it was said that Ford, who was already tiring of Judaism, may have emigrated to Africa in the early 1930s and possibly became a Muslim.[32] Brotz, however, discounts this as a possibility because America was then in the throes of its worst economic depression and Ford would have been hard put to finance such a venture. He speculates instead that Ford went to Detroit and founded an Islamic cult under the name of Fard or Ford or Farrad.[33] While this conjecture is intriguing since The Nation of Islam (commonly known as Black Muslims) did originate in Detroit in 1930, it is without merit on two counts. One: Elijah Poole, better known as the Honorable Elijah Muhammad,[34] spiritual leader of The Nation of Islam, tells that he was taught his beliefs by Wallace D. Fard, called Master Wali Fard Muhammad.[35] Two: Howard Waitzkin[36] and Carleton Coon[37] both confirm that Ford did arrive in Ethiopia from the United States in the early 1930s and distinguished himself in Addis Ababa by means of his musical abilities. Coon elaborates that Ford was a main attraction at the Tambourine Club until the government closed it down for discriminating against local Ethiopian patrons.[38] He remained in Ethiopia until his death during the Italo-Ethiopian War in 1935-36. His widow, Mignon Ford, together with two other West Indian women, founded the Princess Zännäbä Wärq school in Addis Ababa in 1940.[39] Recently, writes Waitzkin,[40] Ford's son, Joseph, returned to America to raise money to promote literacy in Ethiopia.

It should be noted that the Black Muslim movement arose out of motivations similar to those that prompted the Black Hebrews. Dr. Martin Weitz, while Director of Interfaith Studies at Lincoln University (1967-1974), invited Rabbi Wenthworth Matthews to visit the campus. From a companion who traveled with Rabbi Matthews, Weitz learned that Elijah Poole was at one time associated with Matthews. He also stated that Poole urged Matthews to start a different type of black religious movement because "we will not be recognized as Jews and we will never be accepted." Matthews demurred, saying he had too much invested in meat and dairy dishes, silverware and utensils to give up the dietary laws. He declared, "I will remain what I am." Elijah Poole then left Matthews and joined The Nation of Islam. The same anecdote was related by Robert Coleman, formerly of the Social Justice Committee of the Synagogue Council of America, to several of Dr. Weitz's classes at Lincoln University during 1971-72.

Unlike Ford's earlier construction of a historic Jewish tie, Carter tended toward Garvey's fervency and focused on his followers' blackness. "Only in Africa can we be truly free people," he insisted. Although his enthusiasm fired his listeners, Carter lacked the dynamism and flamboyant style that made Garvey's proposal the subject of popular discussion among blacks and whites. Devoid of Garvey's vision, Carter did not advocate the founding of a black nation in Africa— merely that they locate themselves somewhere in Africa as a religious act based on faith. His group was not part of the Harlem Renaissance, black intellectuals who abandoned the religious mysticism that had dominated nineteenth century black nationalism and who believed they were bringing about the rebirth of their people. Nor did Carter claim that leaving the United States would in any way benefit his followers specifically as Hebrews.

Yet, while almost every black leader spoke of "land hunger," of black identification with their ancestral home on the African continent, every one of their attempts to establish a haven there has failed.

A possible explanation for this continued lack of success was proposed by Leroy Eldridge Cleaver, the former Black Panther leader.[41] Comparing the black Americans' aspirations for land to that of the Jewish people's eagerness to return to the Holy Land, he noted a marked difference between them.

Psychologically, the various back-to-Africa movements

adopted the same outlook as had the Jewish people that the only solution to their low estate was to reestablish themselves on a piece of land. They lacked, however, one important ingredient which spelled the difference between success and failure. As with the Jewish people, a national consciousness was awakened among the blacks. But the reason the Jews succeeded in securing a national home and not the blacks, Cleaver explains, is that the Jews founded a government-in-exile in the form of the Zionist Congress, which was already functioning when the United Nations returned Palestine to the Jewish people. All the Jewish people had to do was to place the government and the people on the land. Black Americans, however, were delinquent in this respect. If they are to realize their aspirations, Cleaver insists, they must do the some thing as had the Jewish people. It worked for them; it will also work for the blacks.

Returning to the United States in 1975 after spending six years abroad in a self-imposed exile, Cleaver produced an interesting document in his cell in the Alameda County Jail in Oakland, California. Imprisoned soon after arriving in this country, he remained confined until he was released on bail in August 1976. Expressing admiration for the State of Israel and Zionism, he altered his view and opposed blacks establishing a national home in Africa. He admonished people who reside in countries where they are "enjoying democratic liberties and traditions of freedom," to oppose "Communist (and) theocratic Arab dictatorships, and economically dependent Black African dictatorships," because they are stifling "democratic forces inside their own borders." They are an unholy "combination" undeserving of respect and "must be struggled against."[42]

Like Cleaver, some American blacks in Africa are discovering virtues in American identity they never suspected existed. One such man is quoted as saying, "Please don't misunderstand but I find myself thinking: Thank God for slavery! It got me out of this and made me what I am instead."[43] He is representative of others who no longer see returning to Africa as the ultimate option, because they have not surrendered the hope that blacks might yet live as free men in the United States.

Other groups shared with Congregation *B'nai Zakin Sar Shalom* the belief that American blacks are descendants of the Biblical Hebrew patriarchs. In 1967, when there was great impatience to return to Africa, a number of them merged and they met at A-Beta.

A faction called "One," organized in 1963 by Louis A. Bryant (who now resides in the State of Israel), was one of them. Registered as "An Association in Illinois, U.S.A.," Shaleak Ben Yehudah of Indianapolis, Indiana, headed the organization and Earl Carter of Chicago served as vice-president. Bryant claimed he labored for ten years to draw up a platform dedicated to the following goals: to lecture and teach Hebrew prophecy; to enlighten black people of the Hebrew culture and heritage they had lost; to bring together those who seek their proper identity through language, place of birth, etc.; to provide the necessities of food, shelter and medicine for the survival of an exiled and scattered people until they can establish their nation. "One" services were held in Bryant's print shop, located on the ground floor of an old, four-story building at 4340 South Cottage Grove Avenue in Chicago and in homes. It circulated its program in churches, schools and universities, and established many branches.

One of its alleged offshoots was located in the basement of 6326 South Stony Island Avenue in Chicago, and had over its door the sign *B'nai Zacken* in bright red, orange and green. One day the police raided the basement "temple" and found there a cache of weapons, ammunition and machetes. Fredrick Walters, who headed the branch and who called himself Prince Amazait, was arrested while delivering a sermon to more than thirty followers. Walters, garbed in red robe and turban, explained he had purchased the weapons a year earlier for a trip to Africa that did not materialize.[44]

The committe of three met on the Saturday night after Carter's announcement, as planned. They had a grave responsibility, Carter began, and he prayed they would be equal to it. He then asked, "Have you given the matter any thought?"

Brother Greer admitted that he had worried about it all day. "But I don't know," he said with a shrug. "Any place is okay with me."

"I feel the same way," Brother Blackwell added. "What do you think?" he asked Carter.

"Ethiopia," Carter announced without hesitation, as Garvey had done years before. "Ethiopia is the most suitable place for us," he explained, "because its King is a descendant of King Solomon and the Queen of Sheba, and the Falashas live there. Since the Falashas and we are all descendants of the same Hebrews who left Judea and settled in Ethiopia after the destruction of the Temple, Ethiopia would be the place for us to start over.

"We would be like the Israelites in the Bible. They crossed the Red Sea when they fled from Egypt. We'll be escaping from slavery too. We should cross the Atlantic Ocean by ship."

Unable to offer any suggestions of their own, Blackwell and Greer accepted uncritically Carter's proposal.

Carter volunteered to check ship schedules, prices and anything else he could learn that would help facilitate the move. Two days later he reported with regret that "no ships go directly from the United States to Ethiopia." Embarrassed, he explained the impracticality of his suggestion. It would be too complicated and too expensive to transfer from one ship to another. Besides, it would take too long. While his choice of country and mode of travel proved disappointing, at least it was a start. Perhaps there was a better alternative than Ethiopia. "Tomorrow I'll go to the library and see what I can find," he volunteered again. "We'll meet here again tomorrow night."

Blackwell and Greer were annoyed with so many meetings. It would be the third in four days, and they knew no more than when they started. Noting their frustration, Carter emphasized their responsibility. "We must not let our brothers and sisters down," he insisted. "We accepted the job, so let's do it right."

Poring over books in the Chicago Public Library, Ben

Ammi Carter discovered Liberia. The oldest black republic and the only independent one on the African continent until 1957, Liberia was founded by former black American slaves who chose to return to Africa. Here was something his followers could grasp and identify with. Intrigued, Carter spent the remainder of the week familiarizing himself with the annals of Liberia. He was fascinated by its history.

Long before the Civil War erupted, perhaps as many as several hundred thousand free blacks had resided in the United States. Some had been voluntarily set free by their owners; others had been released from captured slave ships; and thousands had fled their owners and found sanctuary in non-slave territory. Their freedom, however, was not without its problems. The freedmen scorned the slaves, and were in turn despised by those still in captivity. Worse was society's refusal to accept the manumitted blacks or to grant them equal rights of citizenship. Their freedom was meaningless.

Disheartened by the prevailing situation and bearing in mind the desire of some blacks to return home, Thomas Jefferson and other liberals proposed the establishment of African colonies of liberated slaves. Believing the blacks capable of self-government in an all-black society, Jefferson advocated "that they be freed and sent off to Africa or the West Indies or beyond the Mississippi with all the tools and capital necessary to start a new state."[45] He later felt that the two races might even be able to live together, saying, "nor is it less certain that the two races, equally free, cannot live in the same government." This is the omitted second half of a statement that appears on Jefferson's memorial in Washington.[46]

Laudable as was the intention of these liberals, their idea remained dormant. Not until December 28, 1816, was the American Colonization Society organized "to promote and execute a plan for colonizing in Africa, with their own consent, the free people of color residing in the United States." Bushrod Washington, an Associate Justice of the United States Supreme Court and nephew of George Washington, was elected president.

Different groups supported the Society out of diverse motives. Some felt colonization would afford the free slaves an asylum from oppression and would extend the blessings of Christianity and civilization to the peoples of Africa. Others argued colonization would accelerate the abolition of slavery, or that the removal of free blacks from the United States would enhance the value of slave property and would promote the security of possession. Still others rationalized that colonization would rid the country of "a bad population without the trouble or expense of improving it."[47]

The Society was established through the efforts of the Reverend Robert Finley, pastor of the Basking Ridge Presbyterian Church in New Jersey, with the encouragement of President James Madison, Henry Clay, Daniel Webster, Francis Scott Key, missionary groups, and other influential leaders. Their motives stemmed partly from religious convictions violated by the institution of slavery, and partly from the alarming increase of a Negro population without normal political and social status. Nor was the anxiety that the freed blacks aroused in many white people to be overlooked. Also, their presence fomented great dissatisfaction among blacks still in bondage, while they themselves shuddered at the thought of sharing the same status with "lowly" blacks. Although the Society was privately chartered, Congress two years later appropriated $100,000 toward "the keep and deportation of the liberated Negroes."

In 1819 the American Colonization Society purchased land on the western coast of Africa, called the "Grain Pepper Coast" or the "Pepper Coast," to serve as a home for the "dispersed and oppressed children of Africa." In 1820, the first settlers of 88 men, women and children came to Sherbro Island, a headland of the Liberian coast near Freetown, Sierra Leone. Compelled by poor health conditions to move, they wandered south to the site that later became the capital of the newly established country. Survival was a struggle and, to their chagrin, skin color proved to be no sympathetic bond with their black neighbors; it did not open the door of acceptance into African society.

The foundations were laid in 1828 and the country and its capital were named. Robert Monroe Harper[48] of Baltimore suggested Liberia, adapted from "liberty," and Monrovia to honor James Monroe, President of the American Colonization Society, who was less than three years out of office as President of the United States.

The settlers were given limited political power with the understanding that when they acquired the skills to conduct the affairs of government, or if they decided to claim it, the Society would relinquish its delegated power. Gradually, the Society withdrew from active administration of the colony, but retained the power to appoint the governor, who was to be a colonist, and initially white.

All political connections were finally dissolved in January of 1846 and the people were left to govern themselves. A year and a half later, on July 26, 1847, Joseph Jenkins Roberts, the first non-white governor of the country, proclaimed Liberia an independent republic. A Declaration of Independence and a Constitution modeled after that of the United States were adopted, and Roberts was elected the first president. Most powers recognized Liberia's independence in 1848 and 1849, but the United States withheld formal recognition until June 3, 1862, when Abraham Lincoln won approval for it.

The Liberian Constitution provides that "all men have a natural and inalienable right to worship God according to the dictates of their consciences, without obstruction or molestation from others."[49] It declares that all religions are to be tolerated alike "and no religious test whatsoever shall be required as a qualification for civil office, or the exercise of any civil right." Citizenship, however, was restricted to "Negroes or persons of Negro descent."[50]

Liberia's Constitution and its motto, "The Love Of Liberty Brought Us Here," convinced Ben Ammi Carter that he should propose settling in Liberia. An additional consideration was the fact that English was the official language of the country (although only about 20% of the people could speak it). With the ready agreement of Greer and Blackwell, he presented the committee's findings to the members of Congregation *B'nai Zakin Sar Shalom* on Friday evening as he had promised. He described Liberia's history to them and convincingly laid before them the reasons for the committee's recommendation.

Like DuBois, he overlooked Liberia's earlier practice of slavery and its indenture system, under which "Liberian labor" was sold to France and Spain. He also neglected to mention that Garvey openly broke with the Monrovia government and exposed it as being traitorous to the Negro race. What he probably did not know and therefore could not have told his followers was the treatment accorded present-day native Liberian workers. As recently as 1972, the Firestone Rubber Company provided the Liberian laborer with housing, some medical care, and a modicum of education for children, plus approximately $1.00 or $1.50 as wages for an eight-hour day.[51]

Relying on what Carter told them, the congregants voted unanimously to make Liberia their home. Confident that their future lay there, that Liberia would provide a life unhampered by discrimination, intolerance and bigotry, they foresaw no obstacles to becoming part of Liberian society.

Carter praised the group for its forthright action. When the American Colonization Society was founded, he told them, other black people had felt as they did. Even some who at first opposed colonization later favored relocation. Three such leaders were Reverend Henry McNeal Turner, the first black to be commissioned a Chaplain in the United States Army, Dr. Martin Robinson Delany, a black physician who graduated from Harvard and authored novels and essays, and John B. Russwurm, coeditor of the first black American Newspaper, *Freedom's Journal*. Turner felt that moving to Africa would serve a great spiritual purpose.[52] Delany had fervently declared, "Here were we born, here raised and educated; here are the scenes of childhood . . . from here will we not be driven by any policy that may be schemed against us . . ." However, despairing that blacks would ever achieve full citizenship in the United States, he became a migrationist by 1852 and devoted himself to a number of unsuccessful migration schemes.[53] Oscillating between Africa and Central America as the better place for colonization, Delany concluded after a visit that Africa would serve their purposes better. In 1859 he explored the Niger River in West Africa and signed a treaty with the Yoruba granting him a tract of land on which black Americans could settle. Russwurm became an ardent migrationist in 1829 and eventually settled in Liberia himself.

Either because he did not know about it or he wanted to conceal it, Carter did not share with his congregants the changing attitudes concerning relocation that had prevailed among black leaders.

Initially, blacks had favored colonization because they were disillusioned by the American Revolution's failure to end slavery. Paul Cuffee or Cuffe, a wealthy black Quaker shipowner of Westport, Massachusetts, personally financed and led the first black nationalist movement in America that relocated blacks to Africa.[54] All such attempts prior to this one had been sponsored by white men and had met with little success. On December 10, 1815, he transported 38 Negro settlers, 18 adults and 20 children, to Sierra Leone in Africa. They were prepared to abandon the United States for an uncertain but unbowed existence in Africa. Cuffee also influenced black leaders to unite in the African Institution, an organization that aimed to move American blacks to Africa.[55] He endorsed the work of the Society, as did Daniel Coker, a respected minister who accompanied the first expedition sponsored by the American Colonization Society. Still others, such as clergymen Newport Gardner and Lott Cary, departed for Africa on their own. All viewed returning to Africa as an opportunity to tread the soil of the "mother country" and to preach the gospel to the "poor Africans" and thus lead "Africa's sons out of the devil's bush."[56]

Yet when the American Colonization Society was founded to further the same objective, many blacks turned against resettlement. They had come to realize that the purpose of the colonization program was not to rid the country of slavery, but to strengthen the institution. By removing the most vigorous and outspoken opponents of slavery—the free blacks—the Society tightened the vise of oppression. Henry Clay and John Randolph made it clear that the Society had no intention of upsetting the status quo in the South, and William Lloyd Garrison, the well-known pre-Civil War abolitionist, showed it to be anti-Negro.[57] Mistrusting the Society, blacks rejected and resisted its efforts, and dismissed escape as a solution to slavery. "Why should we leave this land," they asked, "so dearly bought by the blood, groans, and tears of our fathers?"

James Forten of Philadelphia, who had exclaimed in 1817 that "blacks will never be real people until they separate themselves from the white people," was one of the men who reversed himself. He opposed colonization because he felt it diverted American Negroes from the struggle for a better life in America, and relieved whites of their responsibilities to all citizens regardless of race or color.[58]

Frederick Douglass, a fugitive slave and an outstanding black leader, was convinced that the destiny of black Americans was tied to the United States. "This is our country," he said. He warned blacks not to withdraw from white churches and form congregations of their own. "The race church," he said, "benefited the Negro-haters by compounding misunderstandings between blacks and whites and therefore making social equality harder to attain.[59]

He exhorted his readers to combat church discrimination by conducting a "stand in." "Stand in the aisles, and rather worship God upon your feet, than become a party to your degradation. You must shame your oppressors and wear out prejudice by this holy policy."[60] Apparently Frederick Douglass' admonition was the antecedent for Harry Golden's "Golden Vertical Negro Plan"[61] to end segregation by removing all seats from schools and eating places so blacks and whites would not sit with each other.

Nevertheless, although he was so forcefully outspoken that the future of the blacks lay in their remaining in the United States, Douglass was not immune to ambivalence. Frustrated by President Abraham Lincoln's temporizing with the white South and the moderate stand the Republican Party took on slavery in the election of 1860, Douglass veered toward colonization. While he had no intention of emigrating himself, he made plans to visit Haiti to investigate the possibilities for settlement there by blacks who wished to flee the United States. He never got there, however, because the Civil War broke out.

Even Dr. Martin Delany, who advocated that blacks move to Africa, denounced the American Colonization Society as "anti-Christian" and "misanthropic in its pretended sympathies."[62] He branded its leaders "arrant hypocrites seeking every opportunity to deceive" free blacks. At one time he wrote William Lloyd Garrison, "Heathenism and Liberty before Christianity and Slavery."

On September 1, 1831, blacks in Pittsburgh expressed the same view at a meeting called to determine their attitude concerning the American Colonization Society. One of the unanimously adopted resolutions stated: "Here we were born—here bred—here are our earliest and most pleasant associations—here is all that binds man to earth, and makes life valuable. And we do consider every colored man who allows himself to be colonized in Africa, or elsewhere, a traitor to our cause."[63]

The degree of the rejection of colonization by blacks is demonstrated by the small number who actually left for Africa. The estimates vary. From 1816 to 1867, despite the support of government and private resources, the American Colonization Society moved only about 6,000 blacks to Africa.[64] Miles M. Fisher, on the other hand, quoting the Library of Congress Ms. Register of Emigrants, 1835-1853, says that 8,204 blacks sailed for Liberia from 1820 to 1853, plus an additional thousand sponsored by the Maryland Society. Also, that up to 1853, 4,549 blacks had been manumitted for the purpose of emigrating for African colonization.[65] Whatever the actual numbers, recolonization was low.

The antipathy of blacks to resettlement is further documented by the fact that some of them assiduously excluded the words "African," "Negro" and "colored" from the names of churches, schools, organizations and other institutions lest it be interpreted that they were in favor of leaving America. Blacks who were interested in promoting a broad humanitarianism organized the American Moral Reform Society for Improving the Condition of Mankind in 1834 and held annual conferences until 1841. Accused by blacks of lacking racial pride and unable to attract white members, this unrealistic group made little impact.[66]

In their desire to assert themselves, blacks came in conflict with William Lloyd Garrison, the founder of the celebrated abolitionist newspaper, *Liberator*, and with other leaders of the white community. Although Garrison portrayed himself as unselfishly seeking to encourage blacks to become independent, self-assertive citizens, he attempted to restrain them. While he encouraged the founding of a Negro press to vindicate the rights of the race, he discouraged blacks from making editorial comment.[67]

In 1837 he counselled Samuel Cornish not to launch the projected newspaper, *Colored American*. When he did it anyway, Garrison criticized his policies and acted at times as though the newspaper did not exist. When the editors of *Colored American* blasted white abolitionists who "outwardly treat us as men, while in their hearts they still hold us as slaves," they were pointing the finger at Garrison. Years later, when Cornish died, the *Liberator* carried no obituary of him.

Douglass ran into a similar situation with Garrison, his sponsor. The Massachusetts Anti-Slavery Society hired Douglass to lecture on his experiences as a slave. The job enabled him to grow intellectually and he was motivated to share ideas with his audiences rather than to merely display himself as a fugitive slave. But instead of portraying him as an exemplary model of Negro potentiality, the officials of the Society sought to stifle his intellectual progress and his striving toward manhood and independence. "We will take care of the philosophy," he was told. "You give us the facts." To be effective, he was advised, his presentation should include a bit of "the plantation manner of speech," otherwise his audience would doubt he ever was a slave.

Douglass' ambition prompted him to go his own way and to found a newspaper, *North Star*, in Rochester, New York, also over Garrison's objections. Later, Garrison denounced him as "destitute of every principle of honor, ungrateful to the last degree and malevolent in spirit."

Garrison's behavior might corroborate the theory that in reality a reformer is a racist of sorts. Basically, he regards blacks as inferior to whites, but attributes it to environmental influences. He is willing to support the extension of basic rights to blacks—the right to vote, economic opportunity, and the like—but only if white supremacy and control are maintained.[68]

Soon after the members of Congregation *B'nai Zakin Sar Shalom* agreed to settle in Liberia, the three committee members, Ben Ammi Carter, James T. Greer and Charles Blackwell, embarked on a mission to Liberia to probe the land and to lay the groundwork for their move. Upon their return to Chicago after a month's stay, they presented their investigative findings at a special meeting at A-Beta. Whereas 10 of the 12 spies Moses had sent to explore the Land of Canaan returned with an unfavorable report, these three were unanimously enthusiastic about Liberia.

"Liberia has tremendous possibilities," Carter reported. "Some of the government officials told us they were pleased that we are planning to settle in their country. They feel we will promote growth and development in Liberia."

The congregants were elated. What had hitherto been fantasy was now about to become reality. Enthusiasm ran so high that one man shouted, "Brothers and sisters, let us praise the Lord for blessing us with such fine leaders."

Carter continued. "We can establish an agricultural community there. We saw some land we will want to buy when we arrive. The soil is black and rich and good for farming, but it is heavily overgrown. That's why we will be able to get it cheaply—300 acres at 50 cents an acre, $150.[69] We will also have to give the elders of nearby settlements an equal amount of money as a gift. That's the custom, we were told. The land will cost us $300."

The thought of owning land had a sobering effect. Not a person stirred. A tear or two rolled down the cheeks of both men and women.

"My brothers and sisters," Carter said with a tremor in his voice, "we have made a far-reaching decision that affects not only us, but future generations. It will give heart to those who hesitate to join us because some misguided leaders discourage them. We will go down in history as the people who dared to take action to save themselves."

The mood changed; near pandemonium broke out. "Down with Rabbi Devine," was heard above the din. (They referred to black Rabbi Robert Devine of the House of Israel Hebrew Cultural Center, an outspoken opponent of black exodus from the United States at this time. They felt that Devine was caught up in white Jewry and was not really interested in cooperating with and supporting ventures by black Jews.) "Rabbi Devine refuses to join our great adventure. He is a child of Satan." Enlivened by the shift from dreaming to planning for their new homeland, they laughed and cried at the same time, and their excitement did not soon subside.

Carter sat down and waited until the outburst had dispelled their tensions. Finally, he stood, raised his hands high above his head, and spoke in a solemn but firm voice. "My brothers and sisters! Listen to me!" They became quiet, expectant. "The land is undeveloped and will require a lot of hard work."

"Don't worry about that, *Abba*," one of the men assured him. "We'll be like the pioneers who settled the West."

"We will be a distance from the nearest city," Carter persisted. "We'll have to depend upon our own resources and upon each other." To strengthen the group, he was demanding sacrifice on their part for a great cause. Once made, the people would have too great a stake in the future of the group to break away from it.

"We'll manage," a voice echoed.

Carter's tone brightened, "Your courage makes the committee very happy. We are pleased you support our judgment." Carter then added, "But there will be a problem when we want to buy the land."

"What problem?" one of the men asked with concern.

"According to the Liberian Constitution," Carter explained, "only citizens of Liberia may own real estate."[70]

"But we can become citizens."

"That's true. And what's more, you remember that only black people can be citizens of Liberia. We certainly qualify on that score. But we do not become citizens of Liberia immediately, so we will not be allowed to buy land. We will not be eligible. I am telling you this now so you will not be discouraged when we get there."

"Then how will we get the land?" a woman asked.

"Let me explain, sister." Carter hesitated momentarily and then continued. "We met a man there, James W. Flemister. He moved to Liberia from Cincinnati in 1951 with his wife and eight children. He's in his early sixties and lives in Gbatala, where the land we want to buy is located. It's about 100 miles from Monrovia. He will buy the land for us in his name. When we become Liberian citizens, he will transfer the land to us."

"Is he honest?" a male voice questioned.

"We have confidence in him. Brother Blackwell, Brother Greer and I stayed with him while we were in Liberia and we are convinced he will not cheat us. Really, we should be grateful to him for agreeing to help us out this way. When we move to Liberia, we will have to show our appreciation to him."

"If you say he is honest, *Abba*, that's enough for us."

"Mr. Flemister will keep in touch with us through Dr. William H. Jones, the Liberian Consul, here in Chicago. Dr. Jones has agreed to work closely with us. We can start getting ready for the Great Exodus to Liberia."

Chapter II

TROUBLES IN LIBERIA

Having chosen Liberia, the members of the Congregation *B'nai Zakin Sar Shalom* began to ready themselves for the move that would rid them of the racism and deprivations of American living. One problem loomed above all others before they could leave the United States—how to finance their departure and the new colony.

Those who were employed pledged to set aside part of their incomes toward this end. On a regular salary from a government or school system or industrial job, it was possible to live and still save a little something. Day laborers on a hand-to-mouth existence could hardly accumulate anything. All agreed to sell their homes and furniture and those personal effects that could not be transported and had no foreseeable use in Liberia. The rest they would pawn for whatever cash they could get, giving the tickets to relatives and friends who might want to redeem the articles. With their own financial resources inadequate, they would need to turn to the black community.

Portraying their project as a "Back-to-Africa" movement, Carter and other members of the group solicited contributions from anyone who would give them a hearing. Associating their project with the lingering memory of Marcus Garvey's passionate oratory and racial pride cast a prophetic glow over the fund-raising effort. It strengthened their appeal as did the explanation that Liberia had been officially set aside for repatriation; now the followers of Ben Ammi Carter were ready to avail themselves of it. They neglected to mention, however, that Liberian repatriation had been formally terminated in 1912 when the American Colonization Society dissolved, and before then, since 1865, the Society had merely served as caretaker of the colony.

To their amazement, this effort won Carter's congregants many sympathizers and raised more money for them than they had imagined possible. Some contributors aided them because they viewed them as heroic people—courageous and daring. Those who lacked the vision and fortitude to join the movement helped finance the undertaking to assuage their guilt for remaining behind and to mitigate their feelings of inferiority to these super-blacks.

In this fashion Carter and his followers accumulated sufficient funds to purchase airline tickets for themselves and their families. Some also had sizable sums which they hoped would last until they had an income from their labors in Liberia.

In July 1967, the exodus from the United States began. Joseph T. Greer, who had adopted the Hebrew name, Ben Yaakov, was the settlement leader of the first contingent. Men, women and children from Chicago, joined by non-member blacks from other parts of Illinois, Arkansas, Louisiana, Georgia, Missouri and New York City, embarked on the flight to Liberia via Pan Am Airlines and Air France.[1] Others, as they became ready, followed in groups of 10 and 12. By November 1967, 160 people had landed at Roberts Field, the international airport approximately 10 miles outside Monrovia. The Liberian government was wholly unaware of their arrival and presence in the country. No government official had been advised that they had finally decided to settle there or that they had, in fact, moved in.

Because of almost unbelievable lack of planning, they arrived in Liberia during the rainy season, the most unsuitable time of year. No type of shelter had been erected in advance. They had no place to go from the airport, except Mr. Flemister's farm. He provided rudimentary accommodations which they were able to endure only because they had no alternative.

The land purchased from the Guryea Clan in Flemister's name was about 15 miles away, in Bong County. On the cleared area, called simply "The Camp," they erected 50 blue and green tents they brought from America. Raised on a log platform and covered with a thatched roof, each tent housed a family unit. They also began construction of a log frame structure to serve as a community hall and synagogue. Food was available at a store about a mile away and from local hunters who sold them meat. Gbatala, where they could do more general shopping, was 11 miles away. At first they cooked in pots over a wood fire; later they acquired kerosene stoves.

Once the tents were up, land was cleared for growing beans, corn, peppers, sweet potatoes, mustard greens and for cultivating rice. With the aid of Liberians they began to erect "mud gob" houses of sticks or bamboo and mud with tin roofs and cement floors, to replace the tents. Each dwelling had a zinc tub, but no running water. At first a single well furnished just enough water for cooking and drinking. Two additional wells soon provided them with the luxury of bathing and washing clothes. A lone generator furnished the electricity.

Despite their primitive life, the settlers' morale remained high during the early weeks and months in Liberia. The lack of indoor plumbing was no incidental modification in their lifestyle, not to mention the invasions of ants and other discomforts in their quarters. "This is the kind of life we anticipated," Carter said, and his devotees concurred. They were convinced that if they endured the present, their future held the promise of contentment and hope in Liberia.

Powerful emotions animated the settlers. Likening themselves to the early American pioneers who moved to a wilderness to find freedom for themselves and their descendants, they were convinced that their decision to move to Liberia was vindicated. They felt snug in homes they helped construct—no matter how frail. They were proud when the soil cracked and yielded food planted by their own hands. "We'd rather live in the jungle in Africa than in a house in Cicero (a subdivision of Chicago)," said Ben Ammi Carter. "In America we were an oppressed class." Africa was their Land of Promise; Liberia was the home they lost, and found.

Three months after the first group arrived, *The Liberian Star* of September 18, 1967, reported the presence of the American immigrants, stating, "Twenty-seven United States Negro immigrants between the ages of 88 and one have arrived here to begin settlement. All are qualified and among them are Black Muslim Priests." Apparently they were not interviewed in depth, if at all, and it was undoubtedly assumed that the head coverings worn by the men were Moslem turbans. It was impossible to determine what was meant by "all are qualified" since the writer of the article was no longer with the newspaper.

On December 5, 1967, *The Liberian Age* published an extensive report on the new arrivals. It dealt with their reason for emigrating from the United States, their hopes for the future in Liberia, and the government's first efforts to deal with them.

It quoted Moses Buie,[2] the "deputy leader" of the group, at length. The reason they fled the United States, Buie said, was that they were "debarred by law of all rights and privileges of man" because "America is getting violent . . . things are getting worse and worse against our people . . . tanks are being used on us." Despairing of ever achieving real freedom in the United States, he said, they decided to renounce their American citizenship (they never did) and "return to Africa and to our people" where they could "live in freedom." They did not come as politicians or revolutionaries, he said, but "to do what we can to help this land so long as we are in a free society. We want to be Liberians, we don't want to be Americans. We are in Africa to stay and there is no turning back." Ninety-eight percent were reported to have said that if the government would waive the three year waiting period (it is really two), they would take up naturalization at once. While the article read optimistically, it hinted all was not well.

A 31-year-old former United States Army paratrooper, Ellis Kannan, better known as El Kannan, said, "I left the United States with my wife and daughter to escape economic slavery, hatred and murder." He had a good job in Chicago, he said, owed no money on his car, and was about to purchase a $45,000 home, but the call to Liberia was compelling. So he retraced his steps to Africa with the others, from where "we were kidnapped." Asked why they had assumed Hebrew names, he replied that the names their parents gave them are remnants of slavery. "American names were given to slaves by their masters. I am no longer a slave, and my only Master is the God of Israel."[3] (Tragically, his daughter later accidentally drowned in a well in Liberia.)

Statements of this nature by Carter, Buie, Kannan and others contradict Era Bell Thompson's assertion that their going to Liberia "was more religious than racial."[4] A Liberian official observed that at no time did the American blacks mention religion as a factor in their decision to leave the country, nor as a matter of fact did religion surface in their deliberations while still in the United States. They were firm in their conviction, however, that "blacks have no future in the United States."

The same Liberian official noted that he inquired why children greatly outnumbered adults among the new arrivals. He was told that black American parents are convinced that their children cannot acquire appropriate self-concepts in America. He cited the example of a black Jewish mother who left her light-skinned daughter in America, but brought her darker skinned son to Liberia. He would be able to "establish his manhood" in Liberia, she said, would live a better life there and be more successful. While the standard of living might be higher in the United States, she felt it was a meaningless norm since he would be unable to achieve it. In Liberia, she felt he had a future.

She echoed the thinking of nineteenth century Bishop Henry McNeal Turner who declared, "There is no manhood or future in the United States for the Negro. He may eke out an existence for generations to come, but he will never be a man—full, symmetrical and undwarfed."[5]

The immigrants found Liberians friendly, the news report continued, including members of the Kpelle tribe near whom they settled. They wanted to acquire a taste for native foods and learn to speak Kpelle, one of the 28 dialects spoken, in order to be like the people around them. Also, they hoped to build a trade school and "to study Hebrew thoroughly and deeply." At the time the article appeared, 80 children were receiving only a smattering of kindergarten and elementary education.

Initially, the challenge of the undertaking sustained a pioneering spirit among the immigrants, but time chipped away at morale. Once The Camp was built, it became painfully apparent to them that they would be unable to improve their crude standard of living. Life in an isolated area served only by a farm-to-market road (financed, incidentally, by American aid) proved too difficult, if not impossible. The outland Liberians did not speak English, so they were denied communication with anyone outside their own group. Their farming yielded too little to feed them, and as their money dwindled, so did their optimism. The memory of cars, electric washing machines and driers, television and all sorts of conveniences stubbornly persisted, while the two-mile walk to the country store for daily necessities, and the 11 mile trek to Gbatala where they obtained most of their food and supplies, became a burdensome chore. Some, recalling that they had once earned $100 to $150 a week—a salary beyond the dreams of even an educated African—and had once possessed more than many Africans will ever see, wondered about their initial resolve and the clarity of their vision. They were dispirited, not only by the austerity of their life and the lack of recreation, but also because they had neither the taste nor the talent for farming. Although tutored for just such an eventuality in Chicago, they were incapable of coping with the problems of primitive living. By the time the last of the group arrived from the United States in November, the esprit de corps of the early arrivals had slumped markedly.

The Liberian Age account of December 5 mentioned that Allen H. Williams, Under Secretary of Internal Affairs, had visited The Camp. Word had reached the government that a group of American immigrants living in Gbatala were in critical circumstances. Some had been treated for malaria at a local health station and an epidemic was feared unless assistance was rendered them immediately.

President William V. S. Tubman was sympathetic. A descendant of relocated former American slaves, he had held Liberia's highest office since 1944. He keenly hoped to effect "the harmonious assimilation of the immigrants into the Liberian community." Under the auspices of the Immigrant Adjustment Board, he appointed a commission of 5 men to investigate the needs of the settlers. With Allen H. Williams as Chairman, and J. Newton Garnett as Secretary, the commission made a visit to the colony in Gbatala the first order of business.

Residents who saw the visitors arrive eyed them suspiciously and refrained from approaching the automobile, even though the men had alighted and stood waiting to be received. The pioneers were reluctant to speak to strangers, whether black or white. Announcements and statements of policy were left to their leaders. As James W. Flemister explained, newcomers to Liberia are wary and suspicious of everybody. "You think everyone's against you, American and Liberian."

Secretary Williams, a forceful man, walked over to the nearest person and asked who was in charge. He was shown Carter's hut and learned Carter's name only when he demanded it.

Carter appeared startled by the strange voice and sharp knock that brought him to the entrance of his hut. A scarlet skullcap topped his matted ringlets and his beard was untrimmed. He smiled tentatively, studying the 5 men through narrowed eyes.

"Are you Mr. Carter?" Secretary Williams asked.

Carter nodded slowly. "What do you want?"

Williams identified himself and the other members of the Commission. He stated the official purpose of their mission, then clarified it, saying simply, "We would like to help you."

Carter paused, as if vacillating between two attitudes, then said with contempt, "It's about time. We could have rotted to hell for all the government cared. No one welcomed us when we arrived. No one came here 'til now; in 6 months, you are the first. If this is how black men treat their brothers in Liberia, I have no use for any of you." Relieved of his accumulated frustrations, Carter's tenseness eased.

By now the residents of the camp, alarmed by the crescendo of Carter's voice, encircled the commissioners. They were wide-eyed, perplexed, then shocked to hear Williams shout, "You have your damned nerve. Who do you think you are? We came here to help, and you attack us. And who do you think you are talking to? I met you and your two friends when you came here last year."

Carter had not recognized Secretary Williams. He knew at once he had chosen the wrong attitude toward the visitors. Now his apology could only diminish him in the eyes of his followers and it could not stop Williams from telling the government's side of the story. He kept silent.

"You are an ungrateful . . ." The Secretary caught himself. "When you came with your friends, you told us you wanted to operate a large, modern farm. You told us the immigrants would include qualified builders, farmers, teachers and businessmen. You wanted to live in a black country where you could get education and employment without discrimination. And look at you." The Secretary's hand drew everyone's eyes in an arc that took in the whole dismal scene of makeshift shelter, improvised sanitation, and men, women and children in varying degrees of neglected health and hygiene.

Carter still kept silent. Williams had recapitulated in detail the plan he, Greer and Blackwell had presented in 1966.

Williams sensed Carter's feeling of failure. His bitter attack on the Liberian government indicated how frustrated Carter must have felt; how incapable of achieving the stated goal. Softening his tone, Williams admitted his own miscalculation. "We were pleased with your plan. Liberia needs skilled people. We can't grow without them. We need businessmen to boost our economy. And modern farmers—the methods used here don't even produce enough rice to meet our needs. We have to import our staple food." Williams conceded that he and other government officials had too readily believed Carter's claims, perhaps through wishful thinking. "But," he added, "you and your friends, Mr. Carter, are frauds. You gave us to understand that you were sponsored by a large well-to-do organization in the United States and that you would have no financial problems."

Carter had more than met his match in Secretary Williams. His followers were hearing for the first time what had actually transpired when he and his committee visited Liberia. Williams was exposing him and he was in no position to command their confidence as God's appointed leader. Nor could he respond to Williams' charge, which was obviously true. Carter, who could always convince his submissive and deferential followers, was unable to find words to defend himself in this confrontation.

"Why did you conceal your arrival?" Williams demanded. "You had tourist visas. How were we to know you intended to remain in the country? You did not notify us, and yet you expect the Liberian government to extend a helping hand." In a more conciliatory tone, he added, "We learned of your situation accidentally. Otherwise we'd still be in the dark about you."

Taking advantage of the pause, Carter said, "Let me show you around the camp."

He suggested that his followers return to their own huts. If he proclaimed now to his devotees, "I am the only one that the Lord High God will deal with, and I will live forever," would they accept it as they had before? He wondered. That they heeded his request was a small measure of reassurance.

The five commission members who had made the tiresome trip to Gbatala now followed Carter from one hut to another. They were appalled by what they saw. Field mice were plainly visible among the litter strewn about the camp. They found the interior of the huts deplorable, lacking in the most rudimentary comforts of civilization. Hardly any food was seen. Some of the people were visibly ill, and many, under the scrutiny of the strangers, seemed acutely embarrassed by their circumstances. The men shifted their postures and the women made futile gestures aimed to improve their appearance, or that of their children or their dwellings.

Concerned about their health, Secretary Williams recalled, "You told us a doctor would be in the group, and that he would bring equipment for a small clinic. Where is he?"

"He changed his mind." Carter was too embarrassed to tell Williams, the only medical attention available to the group members was through his assistant, El Kannan Ben Israel, who had received first-aid training in the United States Army.

The commission returned to Monrovia and reported their findings to the Cabinet. The American immigrants were in desperate straits, the commission noted, and were receiving no significant financial assistance from the United States. They were in woeful need of food and medical attention, and they owed money. In these and other areas, they could use help.

The cabinet members listened attentively. They voted to liquidate all the debts the immigrants had incurred up to the time the commission was established. They also agreed to grant them the immigrant land allotment of 25 acres per family, machinery with which to clear the land, and the services of Bong County specialists to assist them in making the land arable. It was understood, however, that the land was not an outright gift; they were merely privileged to cultivate the land with an option to purchase it when they became citizens of Liberia. According to law, an immigrant of Negro descent may voluntarily file a declaration of intention to become a Liberian citizen after residence of two years. However, the president may waive the waiting period and grant immediate citizenship to deserving immigrants who request it, giving them the right to buy land immediately. The Americans never did settle on the land; it was not adjacent to the acreage they purchased in Gbatala.

One Cabinet member further recommended that the government give a grant of money to each of the American families in Gbatala. "It would be the Christian thing to do for our black brothers," he argued. Although prompted by humane considerations, he provoked fierce disagreement.

"Why should we give them any money at all?" he was questioned. "We didn't invite them to Liberia."

"Besides," said another, "there are many native Liberians as poor as they, maybe even worse off. Why should we give them money and not our own citizens?"

"We do not give this kind of assistance to any other immigrants," said a third Cabinet member. "Why should they be given preferential treatment?"

Finally, a compromise was effected. Each American immigrant family was granted a $50 monthly stipend for three months. Seventy-eight families received the allotment, which they acknowledged by signing a roster upon obtaining the funds.[6]

Notwithstanding the benevolent and salubrious treatment accorded them and contrary to their earlier declaration, the American immigrants did not request immediate Liberian citizenship.

Concerning the Commission's recommendation to disperse them throughout the country and to find jobs for them "according to their individual skills," Buie affirmed that they did not mind being separated, but insisted that Gbatala would remain their headquarters, "even if we all branch out."

Employment was found for some at Lamco (Liberian-American Mining Company), a mineral developing consortium of Swedish companies, a Bethlehem Steel Company subsidiary, and the Liberian government. One woman received assistance to open Hana's Afro-Diner in Gbatala where she specialized in home-cooking, another took a job as a secretary, and a couple of men were hired by a Dr. Baker to work on his farm. James Greer and his wife, Rachel, manufactured coat hangers and chairs, and operated a vocational and industrial school on a rented farm. One immigrant, Carl Parker, broke away from the group, forsook his Hebrew name and prohibition to work on the Sabbath, and went to work for James Phillips, Liberia's only pineapple exporter.

Two men went to the United States early in 1968 and, with loans from a Liberian bank, brought back Tasty Freeze ice cream machines for three shops they opened in Monrovia and Bong County.[7] They called the ice cream "Soul on Ice." Also in Monrovia, Carter operated a snack bar, "Mr. C's *Misadah Tovah* (Hebrew for "Good Restaurant"). He served "soul chicken" (southern fried), the "best hamburgers in Monrovia" and slushade, a colored soft ice advertised as "first time sold in Africa."

Charles Blackwell organized a five-man band, "The Soul Messengers," that played rock and roll at nightspots in Monrovia. He complained, however, that the Lebanese businessmen who owned the bars underpaid them. After they dismissed a Liberian manager whom they accused of fleecing them, Carter took over the group's management.

For the Sabbath, Carter would return to The Camp where a *shofar* (ram's horn) was blown at sundown on Friday to mark the beginning of the holy day. He would conduct services for those who were there by reading psalms and singing songs to the accompaniment of a harmonica.

One year later, Carter boasted to John Barnes of *Newsweek* that The Soul Messengers, commanding $100 a night, had earned about $40,000 that year which supposedly went into a community bank account. Curiously, none of the money was spent on farm machinery or housing improvements needed at The Camp. Questioned about it, Carter changed the subject, asserting that he preferred to talk about his mission, not money. He told Barnes, "I tell all Afro-Americans that unless they return to Africa and respect the Lord High God, they will perish. . . . We have the only solution to the racial problem of the United States."[8]

Those for whom no jobs could be found, but who refused to remain in Gbatala, moved into the Chief's Compound on Camp Johnson Road, where tribal chiefs of the interior were housed when they visited the capital. When they did find jobs, some of them moved away while others stayed on.

Gradually, some of the immigrants adapted themselves to Liberian life and one man and one woman married Liberian nationals. This, Carter later said, was their aim—to integrate the immigrants into the Liberian way of life, not to set up a separate community. Some who returned to the United States to visit with their families were eager to return to Liberia. Asked whether he would like to live in the United States again, King Craig shook his head violently. "No! No!" he exclaimed. When he visited the United States in May 1972, he was shocked by the high rate of crime, exceedingly higher than that of Liberia. "Slowly but surely," he said, "the United States is falling. It will tumble." One man who returned to Chicago from Liberia told Craig that he would fly back to Liberia on a moment's notice if he had the money, because conditions have worsened in the United States. Those who have returned to America, he said, have organized small groups of people who are planning to emigrate to Liberia.

Although their conditions had improved somewhat, the immigrants' resources still were limited. To conserve the little money they had, they applied to the Non-Government Department of Education for a permit to purchase school supplies duty-free. The request was denied because this privilege is granted by the Ministry of Foreign Affairs only to accredited missionaries and they were not registered as a missionary movement. When some members of the group suggested that they claim to be evangelists, it was pointed out that *The Liberian Age* had quoted Buie to the effect that they did not come to Liberia "to change anybody's religion nor are we here to convert people to our religious philosophy." Since they were only a religious communion, they were not eligible for tax-free status.

Despite assistance from the government, some of the American blacks were unable to adjust to Liberian life. They wanted to succeed, but could not. Their livelihood depended on "friends, relatives and well-wishers" who supported them with driblets of cash from the United States. Greater freedom was useless without the amenities of their former standard of living. Disillusioned, 49 of the original 160 immigrants returned to the United States, leaving the 300 acres of land they had purchased in Gbatala to the 111 members of the group who remained. Racism and intolerance had become more acceptable than deprivation. Their heightened idealism withered under the impact of reality.

Many of the blacks roamed the country. Others who had come with some money, lived on it until it was gone. Some devoted themselves to music—The Soul Messengers, presumably—but "music is not land development," an official protested; it is a cultural aspect of life to which they could have applied themselves after they had developed the land and made it productive. Liberia, he continued, is a country with many opportunities for industrious people to make worthwhile lives for themselves, but the Americans did not take advantage of them.

Following the Commission's visit to The Camp, their relations with the government were essentially good. Only a few minor incidents brought them to the attention of the authorities.

The Soul Messengers protested to the police when they became convinced that their Liberian manager was cheating them of their earnings.

At another time, the men petitioned the government for the right to take more than one wife. Although Liberian law does not prohibit polygamy and many non-Christians practice it, the government nevertheless discourages it. The colonists asserted that their religion, emanating from the Five Books of Moses, sanctions multiple marriages. Under the doctrine of religious freedom, they claimed the right to practice polygamy. The government denied their request. Some then claimed that the women in question were already their wives in the United States. Then why marry them again? they were asked. Why are they not listed on your passports and visas? Why are their surnames different? Unable to respond to these direct questions, they lost their case.

A third incident concerned a Black Hebrew who was involved in a traffic accident, and a fourth related to working conditions at Lamco. Lamco, a highly respectable and responsible enterprise which has the highest wage scale in the country, expected its employees to work 6 days a week, including Saturday. The Black Hebrew workers advised the company that since they adhere to Hebrew Scriptural law, they are forbidden to labor on the Sabbath, the seventh day of the week. They requested a change in schedule. The company took their petition under advisement, but before the question could be resolved, the Black Hebrews quit.

"Except for these incidents," said Winston Tubman, Deputy Minister for Foreign Affairs and Councilor for the Department of State, "the Black Hebrews gave the government no trouble." No member of the group had a police record, and no difficulties with the local population were reported.

Chapter III

LIBERIA RECONSIDERED

Before the year 1967 ended, Carter was compelled to re-assess the decision to settle in Liberia. Less than 20 members of the group had found meaningful employment, while more than 90 of them were languishing at The Camp with no prospect of productivity. Their wretched condition troubled Carter, and he was disturbed about himself.

Evaluating what had transpired, Carter realized that the weakness in his leadership was not a failure to inspire and lead —his people would have followed him anywhere—it was a failure in planning. He didn't know enough about Liberia. The scouting expedition with Blackwell and Greer was intended more to sell themselves to the Liberians than to assess the country's potential for settlement. Furthermore, he did not know how to organize the group's resources to meet its needs. Their effort as a colony was apparently doomed, and he pondered what could be done to save the project.

Carter finally decided that the answer to the problem was to bring additional settlers. They would infuse the older group with an enthusiasm and energy which would revitalize the colony and secure its future. So, in January 1968 he returned to the United States to recruit new pioneers to move to Liberia. He was successful. Twenty-six additional immigrants came. This raised the total number of immigrants from the United States to 186. Subtracting the 49 who had returned to America, the number of Black Hebrews in Liberia stood at 137. If the presence of newcomers could not prevent the demise of the Liberian venture, at least it would show that Carter had tried. Regrettably, the new arrivals did not turn the tide, and the prospect of imminent failure depressed him.

At a meeting with Charles Blackwell concerning the schedule of The Soul Messengers, Carter was unable to conceal his gloom. "Things are not going well," he admitted, studying his friend's face.

"Why do you feel this way?" Blackwell asked attempting to allay Carter's obvious agitation. "The band's going great," he assured him. It was true that young Liberians flocked to hear their American rock music, but not many could pay. Blackwell avoided Carter's eyes. He had never criticized Ben Ammi Carter and was reluctant to do so now. Still, he shared Carter's pessimism.

"That isn't what I mean, Brother Charles, and you know it. What do you think our next step should be?"

Blackwell's silence indicated that he concurred with Carter's appraisal. After a long pause, Blackwell shrugged, "You're the leader."

"What should we do next?" Carter persisted.

"Here? In Liberia?"

The two men tried to read each other's thoughts. They both knew too well it was impossible to keep the group intact for long and that they could not live off the land. They were aware that the government subsidy would soon end and that the few brothers and sisters who were working could not support the many who were idle. They also realized that their Sabbath falling on a regular work day would require special arrangements—something they could not expect in unskilled jobs for which there were plenty of Liberian workers. In America they were disadvantaged because they were black, in Liberia because they were Hebrews.

"Is there a future for us here?" Carter demanded.

Blackwell was slow to respond. Finally he admitted his position. "Frankly, Brother Ben, Liberia was a bad choice. We goofed. We'll never make it here."

"I know that," Carter snapped. "The question is what do we do next? We've got to think ahead."

"We'll have to leave Liberia," Blackwell ventured. Carter nodded agreement, but did not speak. "But where?" Blackwell asked. "If not back to the States, then where?"

"You tell me, this time," Carter said. Without waiting for Blackwell to reply, he asked, "What is the one place in the world where Black Hebrews belong?" The glint in his eyes and the smile that flickered on his face told Blackwell the question was rhetorical. Carter had already selected the next destination for his followers. Shrewd Ben Carter, he thought —gathering support before he proposed a move to the brothers and sisters.

More than once Charles Blackwell had thought about the State of Israel. In June 1967, the same month the Black Hebrews began their migration to Liberia, that small democracy defeated several Arab countries in only six days of fighting. With that victory, Israel once again burst upon the awareness of the world. Jews who escaped persecution in Russia, in Europe and in the squalid ghettoes of Moslem countries flourished in their ancestral homeland. Light-skinned and dark, they became one people, modern, advanced in education and technology. To Charles Blackwell it seemed that anything was possible in Israel. He was certain that these were Carter's thoughts, too. "You're thinking of Israel," he said.

"Of course!" Carter slapped his hands together. "We're Jews and Israel is our ancient homeland!" Suddenly his tension and gloom were gone. "I've been thinking about this for weeks. Last time I was in the States I talked to some people about it. There's plenty of basis in the Bible for us to go to Israel. We'll be returning to the land of our fathers, Abraham, Isaac and Jacob—to the Promised Land. It's like we've been slaves, and now we're in the wilderness as in Moses' time, and soon we're going to cross over into the Holy Land. Liberia was a stopover to rid ourselves of our negrotism (sic), our slave thoughts, so we could start a new life as our ancestors did when Joshua led them across the Jordan River." He paused to study Blackwell's reaction. "Do you think the brothers and sisters will accept it, after I've told them again and again that Africa is our home?"

"You know they will, Brother Ben," Blackwell reassured him. "They will believe you if you tell them the moon is made of white hominy. Besides, what have they got to lose?"

"Well, confidence in me, for one thing," Carter laughed. "Seriously, though, I really thought Africa was the answer for our black people. DuBois, Garvey, (Roi) Ottley and many others kept talking about returning to Africa. But that's not the answer—not after living in the United States. "We've got our freedom here, but that's all we've got."

Blackwell nodded in agreement.

"I wouldn't want the Liberian government to find out we are leaving," Carter warned. "After giving each of us $50 a month, they won't like it when we take their money and run."

"We will have to be careful," Blackwell agreed. "And this time it must be different."

Carter waited for an explanation.

"We will have to be absolutely sure, 100% sure, we are doing the right thing. Look, Brother Ben, I'd like to spend enough time in Israel to know something about the country, what kind of work we can do, where we can live. We need to know what attitude the people will take toward us. Someone will have to speak Hebrew, not just a few words but really speak it."

"That would take months," Carter protested.

"We don't even know if the government will let us in," Blackwell said. "Let's go together and look it over. You can come back; they are really going to need you here. I will keep you informed and, if things go right, you can get them ready for the move."

"And Greer? Shall we take him along too?" Carter asked.

"He's no help." Blackwell was no longer willing to follow blindly. His ideas and opinions suddenly had worth to himself and to Ben Ammi Carter. Confident in their new relationship, the two worked out a plan to save their group from failure. The first step called for Blackwell to visit the Israel Embassy in Monrovia to borrow material to learn all he could about Israel and its laws.

Until now the Black Hebrews' knowledge of Judaism was limited to Scripture, and particularly to those Biblical passages that appeared to link contemporary black people to the Hebrew patriarchs. The books and pamphlets Blackwell borrowed disclosed to him the long history of the Jewish people. He was especially fascinated by the exile that began in 70 C.E.[1] and ended with the reestablishment of the Jewish nation as the State of Israel in 1948. If the Black Hebrews hoped to settle in Israel, a knowledge of this history would be indispensable.

From the time when Rome destroyed the Jewish State in 70 C.E., the hope of restoring their homeland never died among the Jews. Wherever they lived, they periodically suffered from anti-Semitism because of their religious and cultural differences, and because political reasons made a homeless and powerless people a convenient victim. The resurgence of hatred for Jews in Russia toward the end of the nineteenth century, and later in France, Germany and Austria gave powerful impetus to this yearning to return to Palestine.

A society called "Lovers of Zion" was founded in Russia in response to these persecutions by Rabbi Samuel Mohilever, who died in 1898. A political action group with branches throughout Russia and in other countries, its aim was to purchase land in Palestine and encourage Jews to settle there. One of its most able leaders was Judah Pinsker, a former officer in the Russian Army Medical Corps, who, like many Jews, originally advocated that Jews should integrate themselves among the Russians, or the people in whose country they happened to live. But when Judah Pinsker saw Jews massacred in Odessa, he reversed himself and denounced accommodation. As long as Jews were a stateless minority, he concluded, they were subject to violent anti-Semitism. Thereafter, he urged Jews to seek territorial independence and to return to a Jewish national consciousness.

Another group advocating return to Palestine was called *Bilu*, an acronym of a Hebrew line from Isaiah (2:5), "House of Jacob, come ye, and let us walk In the light of the Lord." Young Jews, to protest the carnage of pogroms, participated in a general fast that was observed in Russian Jewish communities on January 21, 1882. From this hunger strike, *Bilu* was born. Their ideology, expressed in various and even contradictory ways, was stated by Zeev Dubnow, who wrote that *Bilu* aimed "to conquer Palestine and return to Jews the political independence stolen from them two thousand years ago."

Those who emigrated to Palestine struggled desperately to survive. Neglected for centuries, the barren land yielded little for their efforts. Malaria, trachoma and cholera were rampant, and the Turkish government presented them with many difficulties. Nevertheless, they were able to establish the village named Gedara.

Then came Theodore Herzl, described by Israel Zangwill as "a majestic Oriental figure," who founded modern political Zionism. Herzl's father, Jacob, and grandfather, Simon Loeb, imbued in him a love of Zion from early childhood and instilled within him an attachment to the Jewish community.[2] At age eight his father enrolled him as a member of the Budapest *Chevra Kaddisha*, a burial society that also fostered Jewish brotherhood. Because it was unusual for a lad that young to become affiliated with the *Chevra*, the society arranged an impressive ceremony to initiate him into the organization. Young Herzl must have been quite impressed with the proceedings when the entire assembly, formally attired, accepted him into the body with the concluding words *achinu ata* (you are our brother). At age 13 he became a *Bar Mitzvah* in the traditional manner.

Later in life his link with Judaism weakened to such a degree that only pride and tremendous respect for his parents stood between him and baptism. Regarding his "Semitism" as a handicap, he became an escapist Jew and advocated that all Jewish children in Austria be converted en masse to Catholicism as a solution to the Jewish problem.[3] But when, as a correspondent for a Viennese newspaper, he witnessed the infamous Dreyfus Trial in Paris in 1894, the incident reawakened within him the Zionism of his youth and he began a new era in Jewish history.

Captain Alfred Dreyfus, the only Jewish officer of the French Army General Staff, was accused of passing secret military information to the German Military Attaché in Paris.

Although the French military knew the real culprit, and that Dreyfus was innocent, he was chosen as a scapegoat because he was a Jew, although a nominal one. Fully aware of this, he remarked to his guard before the trial began, "I am being persecuted because I am a Jew."⁴ Predictably, a ground swell of anti-Semitism arose, sweeping French mobs into the streets crying "Death to the Jews!" Later, Edouard Drummond's anti-Semitic weekly, *La Libre Parole*, demanded "Out with the Jews from France! France for the French!"

Judged guilty, Dreyfus was sentenced to life imprisonment on Devil's Island in French Guinea. When in 1898 Colonel Hubert Henry admitted having forged the only material evidence that convicted Dreyfus, it only resulted in a reduction of Dreyfus' sentence to ten years' imprisonment. Later Dreyfus was pardoned due to "extenuating circumstances." Dreyfus' final rehabilitation by the French Supreme Court and reinstatement as a Major in the French Army did not come until July 1906, and then only after a long legal struggle abetted by Lieutenant Colonel Georges Picquart, chief of the espionage department of the French General Staff, the famous statesman Georges Clemenceau, the novelist and critic Emile Zola, the writer and poet Bernard Lazare, the leader of the French Socialist Party Jean Jaures, the vice-president of the French Senate Scheurer-Kestner, and others.

At first, Herzl, like Zola and many other Frenchmen, believed Dreyfus to be guilty, but soon became fully convinced of his innocence. For the first time he realized, as he wrote in 1899, that anti-Semitism stemmed from the social structure, that "the Dreyfus Case embodies more than a judicial error; it embodies the desire of the vast majority of the French to condemn a Jew, and to condemn all Jews in this one Jew."⁵ Herzl, who had harbored the thought of leaving his faith to escape anti-Semitism, now turned his mind to the problem of Jewish survival. He concluded that the only way to curb anti-Semitism is for the Jewish people to return to Palestine.

Herzl summoned the first Zionist Congress in Basle, Switzerland, on August 29, 1897, where the aims of Zionism were stated: "The object of Zionism is to establish for the Jewish people a publicly and legally assured home in Palestine," and the movement undertook to create such a homeland "secured by public law." Prophetically, Herzl declared that the dream of a Jewish State would be realized in 50 years. It was established by the United Nations in 1947, and came into existence the following year.

Charles Blackwell's introduction to Jewish history struck a deeply responsive chord. He could identify with a people who had been subjected to massacres, looting, rape and exile. He understood their helplessness under governments that sanctioned, even encouraged, violence against them. Jews and blacks shared many sorrows.

The literature from the Israeli Embassy acquainted Blackwell with the various types of settlements the colonizing Jews had built, and continued to build in Israel. Reading about the *kibbutz* (group settlement), the *moshavah* (privately-owned village), and the *k'vutzah*, where socialism is the motivating force, he realized that no such plan of organization existed in the settlement at Gbatala. Perhaps that explained their failure. He became increasingly convinced that he must go to Israel to see how these systems worked.

When Blackwell read about the Israeli Law of Return, he was unable to believe his eyes. He read it a second and third time. The Law of Return gives "every Jew . . . the right" to move to Israel and take up residence there as a permanent immigrant, and the government undertakes the responsibility of providing housing, jobs or training, medical care and many other benefits for those Jews who actually settle there. Like Archimedes who ran through the streets in the nude shouting "Eureka" when he suddenly came upon the solution to the problem of the gold crown, Blackwell rushed to tell Carter what he had found.

Ben Ammi Carter was astonished at Blackwell's enthusiasm. In a few days his friend had broken out of his accustomed role as a respectful and self-effacing follower. "I found it! I found it!" Blackwell shouted. "I found our ticket into the country." He then explained to Carter the details of the Law of Return.

"Not so fast, Brother Charles." Carter soberly tried to calm

Blackwell's fervor. "Let's read it again." Carter felt compelled to scrutinize the suggestion either out of genuine caution, or to avoid relinquishing his leadership.

After a lengthy discussion, they agreed on two points: that the Law of Return could be interpreted as an invitation, and that as immigrants they would require governmental assistance. They decided to test whether the State of Israel would accept the Black Hebrews as Jews under the Law of Return and grant them immigrant rights. If it did, then all well and good. If, however, Israel would not regard them as Jews and they still wanted to settle in Israel under the Law of Return, then they would need to embrace Judaism by conversion. Together they tried to anticipate obstacles.

"We'll have a hard time getting recognition there as Jews," Carter warned. "It's tough in the United States. Israel will be even tougher."

"First we need to know all we can about the country," Blackwell insisted. "I will visit various settlements and see how they function. I would like to find out how they treat black people and what they actually do for immigrants. Is it as the pamphlets state or is that propaganda? We can't take any chances this time."

"Do you think the brothers and sisters will go?"

Blackwell sensed Carter's waning confidence. He had glimpsed a great new opportunity and was determined not to allow it to slip away. "Come now, Brother Ben. Don't back out now. We planned to go to Israel. Announce it to the brothers and sisters this week to give them hope."

"They might think we're running out on them," Carter smiled wryly.

"No, Brother Ben, they believe in you," Blackwell emphasized. "If you go with me and come back with a good report and a well thought-out plan, they'll continue to follow you."

"It shouldn't be hard to convince them," Carter agreed. "They have nothing to lose."

A meeting reminiscent of the one held at the Alpha Beta Israel Hebrew Center in Chicago was called in Gbatala.

Ben Ammi Carter addressed his followers in a solemn voice. He recalled their ancestors' slavery in the United States and their own suffering in an inhospitable land where opportunity was denied them. He recalled the sacrifices they had made to come to Africa to regain their freedom and their dignity, and he likened their hardships in Liberia to those of the ancient Hebrews in the wilderness after their escape from Egypt. Finally, he told them that his ultimate duty was to lead them into the Promised Land, where they could live in peace and righteousness and worship the God of Abraham, Isaac and Jacob. The time was not yet ripe, but it was drawing closer. For now, they must be content to send scouts to look over the land and prepare the way. As they had been sent to Liberia, Brothers Carter and Blackwell were dispatched to the Holy Land without dissent.[6]

Chapter IV

THE ADVANCE PARTY

Blackwell and Carter entered Israel early in 1968 as bearded tourists. They did not identify themselves as immigrants, nor did they reveal to any official that their purpose in coming was to study the prospects of permanent settlement for themselves and their families and friends in Liberia.

Once they entered Israel, nothing further is heard of Carter. It is not known what he did in Israel, when he left the country, or when he returned to Liberia. Blackwell, Hebraizing his first name to Hezekiah, found his way to *Kibbutz Ayn Tzurim*, a religious community where Orthodox Judaism is meticulously observed. Here, as with other transients, he was offered a taste of life in Israel.

Adolescents and young adults from abroad come to this settlement and to many others like it, to remain for weeks or months at a time. Donating their labor, they work in the groves picking apples, oranges or pears; they care for chickens, milk cows or do whatever is needed to support the *kibbutz*. As compensation, they are given bed and board and a little spending money.

Blackwell remained at *Ayn Tzurim* for only a short time, however, because he felt "the spirit of God was missing among the people." They observed the rituals, but lacked the spirituality he expected. He left with a letter of gratitude and commendation from the *kibbutzniks* for the valuable services he rendered the community.

On moving to a secular *kibbutz*, Blackwell found more amiable associations. The change suited his taste better and the *kibbutz* members developed a fondness for him. The earring bearing the Lord's name which he wore in his right ear did not offend them, as it had his previous hosts. Here he worked as a carpenter and supervised the volunteer workers.

Blackwell encountered no racial barriers or unwholesome attitudes at either *kibbutz*, and admitted he was never shunned or ostracized. Of these benign experiences he exclaimed, "I learned in these *kibbutzim* more than I learned in my entire life." When he left there after about a year to live in the city, an open invitation was extended to him to visit and take meals with them whenever he chose.

Although Blackwell did not identify himself as a Jew or as a Hebrew, the members of the *kibbutzim* were titillated by his observance of Judaism. His practices differed from their customs and rituals, but no one disparaged him. He experienced a spiritual uplift in the Holy Land; he did a creditable job; he studied Hebrew at the *Ulpan* (school for adults). There was no reason for anyone to question him about the future. He was not merely tolerated in Israel, Blackwell readily acknowledged; he was accepted without question or reservation and was given responsibility on a par with other members of the community.

Enthusiastic reports stirred his brothers in Liberia. Blackwell wrote that he found Israel a truly democratic country, free of any racist taint. Unblemished by prejudice, the Israelis judged a person according to his competence, trusted him, and assigned responsibility to him without investigating his background or his intentions. He sensed he was easily integrated into *kibbutz* life.

The American immigrants in Liberia read his letters avidly and with a touch of jealousy. Charles Blackwell was finding fulfillment in the Holy Land while they were mired in Liberia. Their interest in Israel mounted, but they would have to bide their time in Liberia until *Abba* Carter gave them word to depart. And as they waited, one question surfaced regularly. Would not leaving Liberia contradict their purpose in coming to Africa? Ambivalent, they were assailed by doubt. While they were strongly persuaded to go to Israel, perhaps their salvation lay just where they were—in the black nation of Liberia.

The dilemma remained theoretical for about a year. Blackwell then decided it was time to test the Law of Return. In a letter to Carter, who had returned to Liberia in the interim, he advised that the group request visas of the Israel Embassy in Monrovia to immigrate into Israel under the Law of Return and for financial assistance to enable them to make the trip. Should governmental aid be secured, it would be lavish and would signify their acceptance by the State of Israel.

In the spring of 1969, Carter approached the Israeli Ambassador as instructed and was told that the Law of Return did not apply to the members of his group. Thus, grants would not be available to them. Since he was powerless to help them, the Black Hebrews claim the Ambassador suggested they send a delegation to Israel, where hopefully The Jewish Agency might assist them. After traipsing from office to office in Jerusalem without success, the representatives returned to Liberia, except for one man who allegedly remained to seek permission to send their children to Israel for an education. He, too, the blacks claim, failed to get an affirmative reply.[1]

Undeterred, Blackwell instructed Carter to send a half dozen brothers and sisters to Israel. Upon arrival, they should declare themselves Jews and demand all immigrants' rights in accordance with the Law of Return. Israel's reaction, he said, would be a fair guide to what their next move should be.

Soon thereafter, five Black Hebrews arrived in Israel from Liberia—a family of three, Gabriel, Techiyah and their child; and, Tziona Israel, a tall, beautiful woman with her four-year-old son, David. It was not explained why Blackwell's wife and four children were not chosen to make the trip. Blackwell met them at the airport and took them directly to the Ministry of Absorption.

Chaim Greenberg, the official in charge of the Ministry, received them in his office. When all were seated, he asked what brought them there.

"We are Hebrews returning to our homeland." Blackwell was the spokesman. "We are here to claim our rights as immigrants."

Greenberg's gaze moved slowly from Blackwell to the others, and they returned his looks impassively. "You are Jewish immigrants?" His inflection betrayed disbelief.

"We are!" Blackwell replied pointedly, a smile spreading across his face.

"What are your names? Where are you from?"

Blackwell supplied the information for himself and the newcomers, stating simply that they were from the United States. "We live in accordance with the teachings of the Torah," he said. "You can ask anybody at *Kibbutz Ayn Tzurim* about me. I have lived in Israel for over a year, but my friends arrived a few hours ago. We need places to live."

Lowering his gaze, Greenberg shuffled the papers on his desk. "We have received nothing, no notification, no report, about you or the others. Ordinarily, immigrants do not come to Israel without notice. The Ministry of Absorption is advised beforehand when new immigrants are coming." He tried to be as pleasant as he could and succeeded in remaining calm.

"This does not change the fact that we are Hebrews and that immigrants' rights belong to us," Blackwell persisted.

"You say you have been here for a year, Mr. Blackwell. Why didn't you come to my office earlier so we could have gone through regular channels before your friends came?"

"I wanted to wait for them. But the facts are still the same."

"But we have made no preparations to receive you. I don't even know whether apartments are available."

Greenberg was vexed; his unruffled calm left him. He scurried from his chair to the office door and called, "Sonya! Sonya! Come here!"

Sonya Peletz entered the office and saw the six blacks. She looked quizzically at Chaim Greenberg.

"Meet Mr. Blackwell and his friends," he said. "I don't remember all your names," he apologized turning to them. "Sonya, they say they are Jews and want immigrants' rights." He paused to allow her to grasp the significance of their claim. "Are there any vacant apartments anywhere?"

Miss Peletz rubbed her chin and bit her lower lip. "Let me think." She excused herself and returned in a minute with some papers. "Yes," she replied excitedly to Greenberg's question. "There are empty apartments in Arad."

Arad, Greenberg explained, was in the Negev between Beersheba and the Dead Sea. It was newly-built by young pioneers to house employees of the Dead Sea chemical factories. It also serves as a rest stop for tourists on their way to Masada, the fortress built by Herod the Great. Chaim Greenberg relaxed a bit. He could not resist the opportunity for a history lesson. "That is where a few hundred Judean soldiers held out for three years against the Roman legions before they were overrun in 73 C.E. When a breach was made in the wall of Masada, the leader, Eleazer son of Jair, persuaded his followers to commit suicide rather than fall into the hands of the Romans. The tale states that 960 women and children died by their own hands. When the Romans finally entered the citadel, they found two women and five children who survived by hiding in a cave. That is why everyone who comes to Israel visits Masada. But I don't believe the story."

Blackwell wondered whether the same skepticism applied to his petition. He was relieved, however, when he heard Chaim Greenberg add, "It appears you can go to Arad."

Miss Peletz enthusiastically offered to drive the six to Arad. She suggested that David Maimon, Director of the Office of Labor, might join them and went to ask him.

Blackwell and his friends exchanged incredulous glances and nervous smiles. Soon David Maimon and Sonya Peletz returned with a minibus for the three hour journey. With thanks for his help and good wishes, Blackwell led his companions out of Chaim Greenberg's office less than five hours after their arrival in Israel.

Alerted by telephone to expect them, Michael Peled of the Arad Absorption Center welcomed the newcomers. With the help of volunteers, dinner was served to them, and they were taken to their apartments. One apartment was assigned to Blackwell; another to Tziona and her son; and, a third to Gabriel and his family.

Within two days, Blackwell was employed as a carpenter

and the two women as office workers at a chemical plant. Gabriel went to work for an oil company.

The people of Arad, themselves recent arrivals from many diverse backgrounds, easily accepted the presence of the American blacks among them. They soon came to respect the newcomers for the quality of their work and their devotion to their jobs.

"I love Arad," the bearded former rock musician exclaimed. "Nobody minds the Negroes' presence."[2] He happily built furniture for his three-room apartment.

Daily encounters were cordial and free from friction, but some felt that the blacks kept a distance between themselves and Dimonians who might otherwise have become close friends. Sabbath visitors were politely turned away and invitations declined, with the explanation that they did not leave their homes or discuss secular matters on the Sabbath. If Orthodox Jews were strict, Aradians shrugged, these black Jews were seven-fold more faithful. Their customs seemed peculiar, but no one in Arad questioned the blacks about their Judaic background. They claimed they were Jews and there the subject rested.

Hezekiah (Charles) Blackwell wrote to the brothers and sisters in Liberia, giving them detailed accounts of all that had transpired on the group's arrival in Israel. The Israelis, he penned, were accepting and trusting people, even a bit naive. It was easier here than anywhere else in the world for aliens to enter the country, obtain food, a job, housing and health care. They would accept anyone who was industrious and willing to devote himself to the well-being of the community. It must have something to do with their religious teachings, he speculated, which holds that each person achieves salvation, an immortality, through the *tzibur*, the community. If their condition in Liberia should become hopeless, he counselled them, they could come to Israel and claim immigrants' rights. The officials are ready, with a minimum of questioning, to open the gates to their country. Blackwell assured them they would be welcome.

The presence of the Black Hebrews in Arad attracted more attention from foreign visitors and the press than from their co-workers and neighbors. Tour guides mentioned them as a point of interest on passing through Arad. They were an example of Israel's diverse population, or of the absence of discrimination, or they were a problem, or a blessing, or a relic or whatever the guide and the busload of tourists could make of this unexpected oddity. Journalists sought out the Black Jews for interviews, with the result that their circumstances became the talk of the country.

As American citizens, Blackwell and the recent arrivals from Liberia had no problem entering Israel. Anyone with an American passport can do so as a tourist. But to secure rights and benefits as Jewish immigrants, the government must be satisfied that their claim to being Jewish can be substantiated and is authentic. The Black Hebrews, however, possessed no documented proof that they were Jews. As a result, they remained classified as tourists. Nevertheless, they were granted special permission to reside in Israel, to secure employment, to join the health care program, and to obtain loans to finance their initial needs. In five years they would be eligible to apply for Israeli citizenship.

Lacking were eligibility to study Hebrew at the *Ulpan*, free education for the children, tax exemptions, and special low-interest loans designed to facilitate permanent settlement. These important aids to assimilation, and automatic citizenship after a relatively short period of time, were reserved for immigrants under the Law of Return.

Status as tourists thus saddled Blackwell and his friends with limitations and caused them to become disgruntled. Although they appreciated the right to live and work in Israel, and were pleased with the praise and approval of their neighbors, friends and co-workers, this soon paled. "It is difficult to be tourists without end," Blackwell complained to a reporter who interviewed him.

"But," the reporter pointed out, "you can be accepted under the Law of Return. All you need do is authenticate or substantiate your Jewishness."

"We have no scientific evidence that we are Jews," he replied with exasperation, "but neither is there any scientific proof that we are not Jews."

It was increasingly apparent that to become fully integrated in Israel, they would need to submit hard proof. Even their American passports were of no help—they make no reference to religion.

To one government official who came to Arad seeking documentation of their Jewishness, Blackwell shouted with resentment, "We are Jews because we were born Jews." The frustrated man posed more questions, and finally asked, "How were you born Jews?" Blackwell replied, "I do not care to answer that question."

Blackwell was depressed. The situation had taken a radical turn for the worse. He wrote to his compatriots in Liberia that his earlier estimation of the Israelis was premature. The Israeli government required verification of their Jewishness, he explained, before it would regard them as authentic immigrants entitled to all the rights and privileges under the Law of Return.

Publicity aroused public opinion in favor of the blacks' claim to the rights of *olim*. Israelis felt a duty toward them as they did to all groups of Jews returning to live in the homeland. Instead of using the Law of Return to free the government of responsibility for the blacks, many Israelis felt it obligated the country to assist them. It was a small group, some argued, and if they were not *olim* neither were they tourists. The red tape should be cut and the status of the blacks clarified. To settle the matter with absolute certainty, the question of their status was turned over to the Ministry of the Interior for a determination.

Chapter V

ARE BLACKS HEBREWS?

The Ministry of the Interior accepted with great seriousness the responsibility to determine the status of the Black Hebrews under the Law of Return. Where there is doubt that a subject is Jewish, as in this instance, the individual's history and that of his immediate ancestors is investigated until a point of Jewish origin is established. Should the inquiry prove fruitless, and should the subject still wish to qualify as a Jew under the Law of Return, he would need to convert to Judaism.

The examination of the Black Hebrews' present and historical Jewishness was assigned to Rabbi Chaninah Dar-ee. An immigrant himself, Rabbi Dar-ee had returned to the land of his forefathers from Morocco, where his family had lived for countless generations. In performing such services for the government, Rabbi Dar-ee combines his profession with the cause to which he has dedicated his life—bringing lost Jews back into the fold. He likens his dedication to that of the patriarch Abraham, who, according to tradition, converted heathens to the belief in One God. Whenever he is told of a Jew who wants to "come home again," or of the child of a Jewish mother who was reared in another faith, Rabbi Dar-ee eagerly carries his mission to them.

At his synagogue in Jaffa, Rabbi Dar-ee conducts classes for prospective converts. He was found there one evening

amidst utter disarray since the synagogue was being refur-
bished. A group gathered around a table in the sanctuary
consisted of two Israeli women who had married Arab men
but wanted to return to Judaism, an American girl who desired to convert because she found Judaism to be the most
satisfying faith, and three adolescent Israeli boys and girls
whose mothers were not Jewish.

At the conclusion of the session, a lean olive-skinned man
in his middle years walked over to the Rabbi and had an
animated conversation with him. Rabbi Dar-ee's parting words
were, "You have eaten the salad, but that is not the meal. A
complete meal includes fish and meat. Study, and you will be
a *mechutan* (relative by marriage) at your daughter's wedding." He explained later that the man wanted to be converted
to Judaism immediately so that he might participate in his
daughter's wedding ceremony, but the Rabbi could not yet
agree to it. "He answers satisfactorily the historical questions,
but not the theological. One must be firm in Jewish belief
before one participates in Jewish ritual."

Rabbi Dar-ee labored vigorously to bring Blackwell and his
friends into the Jewish fold. Together with Sonya Peletz of
the Ministry of Absorption, he made numerous trips to Arad
at his own expense to establish the roots of their Jewishness.
Throughout their long conferences, Miss Peletz served as
interpreter and joined in the effort on the blacks' behalf as
much out of personal as official interest. Her concern earned
for her the designation "guardian angel." Their discussions
opened up a Pandora's box of historical and Biblical questions
that defy resolution by even the most patient scholarship. But
the Rabbi was eager and strove earnestly to remove them from
the category of "doubtful Jews."

Speaking for the group, Hezekiah Blackwell, with a carpenter's pencil protruding from his *kibbutz* tembel hat, stated
with eyes blazing that their tradition holds that they are
descendants of the Falashas, an Ethiopian tribe that performs
many ancient Jewish practices and claims descent from the
Hebrew patriarchs Abraham, Isaac and Jacob. The term
Falasha signifies "exiles" or "immigrants" or "foreigners" in
the Ethiopian language, he claimed, and was applied to the

members of this tribe because they were descendants from the Israelites who fled from Palestine to Ethiopia after the destruction of the Judean state and Temple.

Blackwell was not clear as to which destruction he meant. To the Babylonian destruction of 586 B.C.E., when a number of Jews fled into Egypt from the Kingdom of Judah, and from there possibly migrated to Ethiopia? Or, did he refer to the Roman conquest and destruction in 70 C.E. that began the Jewish exile of about two thousand years, during which time Jews wandered into Africa and into every other continent; or, possibly, to the ten tribes of the Kingdom of Israel the Assyrians drove into captivity in 722 B.C.E.? Due to the lack of clarity, the Falashas are frequently referred to as the Ten Lost Tribes.

In their discussions, Blackwell cited to Rabbi Dar-ee other Biblical bases for the Black Hebrews' claim to be Jews. Scripture itself declares the Hebrews were black, he argued. The Book of Genesis states that Jacob was a "smooth man" (27:11), and do not blacks have smooth skin? Doesn't King Solomon say in The Song of Songs, "I am black" (1:5)? For further proof he referred to Jeremiah 8:21 and Job 30:30. There is no doubt, Blackwell concluded, that the members of his group are descendants of the Biblical Hebrew people.

The first two passages may support Blackwell's claim, but the latter references do not. When Job laments, "My skin is black and falleth from me. . . ," he is ululating that his white skin had become blackened as the result of a severe disease. A black person would not voice such a cry.

As for Jeremiah, he used the term "black" figuratively. "For the hurt of the daughter of my people am I seized with anguish; I am black, appallment hath taken hold of me." "Black" does not refer to a physical characteristic, but to a state of mind. In deep mourning, Jeremiah lamented the fate the Jews were suffering at the hands of the Babylonians. It is similar to Jeremiah's wail that "Judah mourneth, and the gates thereof languish, They bow down in black unto the ground" (14:2). As in the former verse (8:21), it expresses his great anguish and distress at the tribulations his people are undergoing.

Rudolph Windsor, rabbi of a black Jewish group in Philadelphia, likewise strives in his book to bolster the claim that the Biblical Israelites were black.[1] Each of his arguments, however, contains an inherent weakness.

Windsor notes that Pharoah's daughter raised Moses in the palace after Jochebed, his real mother, nursed him through infancy (Exodus 2:1-10). The Egyptians are Hamites, Windsor asserts, and Hamites are black-skinned; therefore, since the Egyptian princess was black the child Moses must have been black too. A white child would have been an oddity in the Pharoah's palace, Windsor reasons, and would have aroused much criticism. This is a specious argument, however. If the princess could raise a circumcized Hebrew child in violation of the Pharoah's decree, she could raise a white or olive-skinned child even if she were black.

Windsor applies the same logic to Joseph. When famine ravaged the area, the sons of Jacob came to Egypt to purchase food. Brought before their younger brother Joseph, they did not recognize him (Genesis 42:8). Distorting the text, Windsor asserts that Scripture narrates that the brothers could not distinguish Joseph from the black Egyptians because he, too, was black. Whether the Egyptians and the Hebrews were all white or all black has no bearing on the story; the brothers did not recognize Joseph because the lad they once knew was now a mature man, and the powerful governor of Egypt, not the slave to which they had reduced him. Never would they have visualized him as attaining such a position of prominence.

Thirdly, says Windsor, Scripture depicts lepers as people whose skin has turned "white as snow." Miriam was affected in this way when she criticized Moses (Numbers 12:10); Moses' hand turned "leprous, as white as snow" when God urged him to action to redeem the Jewish people from bondage (Exodus 4:6); and, when the Prophet Elisha learned that his disciple, Gehazi, had deceitfully taken gifts from the Syrian captain, Naaman, who came to Israel to be cured of leprosy, he was afflicted with the dread disease (II Kings 5:27). In each of these instances, Windsor declares, the people must have been black for leprosy to turn their skins white. The implication is thus that all white-skinned Jews are mutations—the offspring of generations of lepers. It hardly seems necessary to point out that scar tissue on white skin is often whiter than the rest, or that white people may become "pale with fright," or "white with anger," but they become "livid with rage." Descriptions of both physical and emotional traumas are often expressed in figurative language.

The leprosy Gehazi contracted, Scripture informs us, was to affect his reproductive organs because his "seed" were to be lepers "forever." Windsor's conclusion that all white-skinned people are thus the offspring of lepers is an untenable inference because the curse, if it worked, applied only to Gehazi's family. It was not a world-wide or even nation-wide affliction. It is illogical to conclude that the entire Caucasian race is descended from Gehazi.

Two other Scriptural allusions might possibly suggest to a literal reader that the Israelites could have been black. One is Daniel's statement, "I beheld Till thrones were placed, And one that was ancient of days did sit: His raiment was white as snow. And the hair of his head like pure wool . . ." (7:9). The other, when John describes Jesus in similar language, "His head and his hairs were like wool, as white as snow . . ." (Revelation 1:14). Wooly might describe the kind of hair black people people have. Biblically, however, "white wool" is a symbol of wisdom and does not describe a physical characteristic. In its original sense it meant "clear" or "clean" (Isaiah 1:18).[2]

Continuing his case for the historical authenticity of his group, Hezekiah Blackwell picked up the thread approximately 16 centuries after the destruction of the Second Temple and the migration of some exiled Hebrews into Ethiopia. Slave merchants uprooted them and brought them to America in chains, he said. The slave system suppressed their national heritage and their faith. When they were forcibly converted to Christianity to make them more humble and obedient, their leaders buried their Torah scrolls and other sacred objects to avoid brutality. Like the Marranos in 5th century Spain, their Jewishness went underground. Although they were mingled with blacks who were not Falashas and were dispersed throughout America, their secret passed from father to son for more than three centuries—until a number of years ago, he concluded, when our people decided to publicly restore their Jewish identity.

Rabbi Dar-ee was frank to admit that he was enthralled by Blackwell's narration. His experiences in Morocco and Israel and his rabbinical education had not afforded him a detailed knowledge of American history or the experience of black people in America and he wanted to know more.

Before research into black history began to provide ties to their pre-slavery past, black Americans listened eagerly to preachers who bridged the centuries with their Bibles and their imaginations. Basically, four Black-Hebrew theories entered Black American folklore after the Civil War and echoes of all of them were evident in Blackwell's discourse with Rabbi Dar-ee.

To the Ethiopian hypothesis just concluded, Blackwell added a popular theme of black preachers in North Carolina and South Carolina at the turn of the century: that the former slaves were descendants of the ten lost Hebrew tribes. This thesis, propagated throughout the eastern section of the country, was probably a metaphor of their new-found freedom—they were no longer lost—and an attempt to establish an acceptable racial identity complete with culture and history.

Prophet William S. Crowdy[3] was a proponent of this view. The ten lost tribes of Israel are the progenitors of the American blacks, he said.[4] A chef on the Santa Fe Railroad, he organized a black Jewish sect which was located in the village of Belleville near Portsmouth, Virginia, in 1905, to lead God's people, the blacks, to the Jewish faith. Founding the Church of God and Saints of Christ, he maintained that all Jews were originally black, but intermarriage with whites resulted in a strain of white Jews. For all intents and purposes it was a Christian sect with its adherents observing some Jewish rites.

Prophet Crowdy was succeeded by Bishop William H. Plummer who claims to personify "Grand Father Abraham" and is addressed thusly by his followers. A virtual dictator, he takes possession of all the property of his adherents and doles out to them whatever he wishes.[5]

In 1913, two self-styled Abyssian Jews, David Ben Itzock

and Henry Itzoch, promoted their International Peace and Brotherly Love Movement in Chicago. They contended that "the Negro is the right Jew," should "confess his identity," and emigrate to Abyssinia. The movement died a year later when David was exposed as a southern Negro who had never been to Abyssinia.[6]

Prophet F. S. Cherry of Philadelphia taught his followers that they are the descendants of the black man Jacob,[7] and he welcomed all blacks into the congregation he founded in 1915, the Church of the Living God. A seaman and railroad worker with dark brown skin, mixed gray hair and a prominent mole on his chin, he called white Jews "interlopers and fraud(s)." The "so-called white Jews," he proclaimed, deceptively identified themselves as Jews because the true Jews, the black people, were unknown to the world for a long time.

For all intents and purposes, however, Cherry's religious communion was Christian. During services, where Hebrew and Yiddish Bibles graced his pulpit, he would flamboyantly offer $1500 in cash to anyone who could produce an authentic likeness of Jesus to contradict his claim that Christ was black. With great showmanship he would wave a picture of a white Jesus and ask, "Who the hell is this? Nobody knows! They say it's Jesus! That's a damned lie! Jesus was black!"[8]

About the best known black Jewish leader was Wentworth A. Matthews, who alternated between the titles Rabbi and Bishop, and finally settled on the former. Supposedly ordained by Arnold J. Ford, Marcus Garvey's associate,[9] his career was based on the belief that the Hebrews who followed Moses in the Exodus from Egypt were black, and that the "ten tribes of the kingdom of Judah" were scattered in Africa. The white and hairy Jews of today, he asserted, are descendants of Esau described in Scripture as "hairy" (Genesis 25:25), while his brother, Jacob, who had smooth skin, was black. Matthews would thus have us believe that of Isaac and Rebecca's twin sons, one was white, the other black.

Matthews' confusion of Jewish history is readily evident. The southern Kingdom of Judah consisted of only two tribes, most of whom went into Babylonian exile in 586 B.C.E., and then returned to Palestine approximately 50 years later. It was the northern kingdom of Israel that consisted of 10 tribes. They were conquered by the Assyrians in 722 B.C.E. and disappeared in captivity 136 years before the southern kingdom fell. They were dispersed to the north and east of their country.

Learning about Falashas from Arnold Ford, Matthews jumped at the information because psychologically it provided him with a self-image he sorely needed. When he first came to the United States, he had resorted to boxing and wrestling to earn funds. His self-esteem needed to be elevated and a Falasian background did just that. When he founded a synagogue, he referred to it as The Commandment Keepers of the Royal Order of Ethiopian Hebrews, although in the official records of New York City it is named The Church of the Living God, Pillar and Ground of Truth and Faith in Jesus Christ. The term "Ethiopian" held special significance for him; it gave him roots, a sense of identity. And when he established a seminary, he gave it the redundant name of The Ethiopian Rabbinical School of Religion. Being rabbinical, it would surely be religious. In 1936 he proclaimed that he was the "official representative of the Falasian order of African Jews" and "Chief Rabbi with credentials from Haile Selassie."

Like Ford, he too viewed Christianity as a force detrimental to the black people. Not only were the slaves deprived of their language, science and religion, but they were pumped full of Christianity to make them more docile and thus assure their continued subjugation.[10]

Arnold Ford differentiated between "Jews" and "Hebrews." Blacks, said Ford, are descendants of the Hebrew Patriarchs, while whites who profess Judaism are converts to the faith. Whites should therefore be called Jews, and Africans, emanating from the stock of Abraham, should be referred to as Hebrews.

Shaleak Ben Yehuda of Indianapolis, Indiana, and Chargé d'Affaires of Ben Ammi Carter's group, the Original Hebrew Israelite Nation of Jerusalem, has proposed still another theory. As with the others, he begins with the assumption that the Biblical Hebrews were black. The problem, as he sees it, is to determine the origin of the white Jews. He postulates that they are to be traced to Bulan, King of the Khazars, who migrated in the 8th century from the area of Finland and settled in the Tartar region, the frontier between Europe and Asia.

After listening to a debate on the respective merits of Christianity, Islam and Judaism, King Bulan chose Judaism as his faith because, he said, the delegates of the other two religions acknowledged Judaism as their source. Four thousand of his subjects joined Bulan in adopting Judaism. Obadiah, his successor, ardently promoted the new faith among the Khazars. He invited Jewish sages to settle among them to found synagogues and establish schools for the study of the Bible and Talmud, and introduced a religious service similar to those of other Jewish communities. As told by Shaleak Ben Yehudah, however, the Jewish tutors of the Khazars were black, and all the white Jews the world over emanated from this one converted sect. If so, Chinese and Indian Jews are likewise offspring of Khazars. Thus, the first 2800 years of recorded Jewish history would be black history. One wonders how Shaleak Ben Yehudah would explain a red hairy Esau (Genesis 25:25) and a ruddy King David (I Samuel 16:12; 17:42).

Albert Cleage,[11] a bombastic Christian minister, adheres to the Bulan thesis. White Jews, he says, "are the descendants of white Europeans and Asiatics who were converted to Judaism about 1000 years ago" by God's chosen people, the black Jews. The Jewish Bible is thus "the history of Black Jews" for Israel never was a white nation. The Chicago-based United Leadership Council of Hebrew Israelites expounded the same theory.[12]

Cleage, however, is even more expansive than Shaleak Ben Yehudah. He claims that "all religions stem from the black people"—Jewish, Muslim, Christian and Buddhist. The religion of the white man was originally paganism "with a pantheon of gods throwing thunderbolts and cavorting about heaven and earth, filled with lust and violence." He is convinced that "the white man has never created a genuine religion." All he did was borrow religion from the non-whites.

Continuing in this vein, the assistant director of the Mystic Temple of Moses in Philadelphia (otherwise unidentified), declared at a Black Jewish Leadership Conference on October 11-13, 1968, that "all Negroes in the United States are Jews whether they know it or not. They are the real Jews. All Jews were originally black." Jewishness and blackness are thus interlocked with each other; if one's skin is black then he is Jewish. And this relationship has existed from the first moment Abraham founded the Jewish people. This outcry parallels the claim by the Black Muslims that "all Black people are Muslims, whether they know it or not."[13]

In considering the assertion that the Biblical Hebrews were black, J. A. Rogers' *World's Great Men of Color*[14] is noteworthy. This black anthropologist and historian devoted most of his career to disproving the myth that Africans played only minor roles in world history. In this two-volume work Rogers does not include Joseph, Moses or any of the Biblical prophets. Few would argue that they were great men. He devotes sections to Imhotep (c. 2980 B.C.E.), the father of medicine; Hatsheput (c. 1500 B.C.E.), whom he describes as the greatest female ruler of all time; Thatmes III (c. 1500 B.C.E.), the mighty conqueror and administrator Far Antiquity; Lokman (c. 1100 B.C.E.), the most celebrated sage of the East, and Makeda (c. 960 B.C.E.), the supposed Queen of Sheba who bore an offspring fathered by King Solomon of Israel. But Solomon himself is not treated in this manner nor are any other Biblical Hebrew characters. One must therefore conclude that Rogers' scholarship ruled out the Biblical Hebrews from his roster because he did not consider them to be black.

In addition to the theories already mentioned that impinged upon the consciousness of Carter and Blackwell and other blacks seeking a Jewish identity, still more origins of the Black-Jewish movement in America have been suggested. Among these are the affinity many slaves felt for radical Protestantism and its stress upon the ancient Hebrew slaves and their liberation; the belief that they were descendants of Jewish slave-owners in the Caribbean islands;[15] or that Jewish slave-owners converted their slaves to Judaism; and even that blacks living near Jews in northern cities learned and adopted Jewish ritual and belief as a result of residential proximity.

The history of the slave trade does not corroborate the various attempts to denude white Jews of their authenticity, nor does it provide blacks with the Hebrew religious identity they seek. The facts shatter the contention that the Falashas in Ethiopia mingled with West-Africans and were brought to the Americas as slaves.

The great centers of the Atlantic slave trade were located on the western coast of Africa extending from Senegal to Angola. Slaves shipped to the New World came mainly from the tribes who occupied a strip of no more than two to five hundred miles wide along the coast. Most of the slaves belonged to the Twi-, Yoruba-, or Ewe-speaking peoples who inhabit present-day Ghana, Dahomey and Nigeria. Sold from one tribe to another along the way, they eventually reached the coast.

As the slave traffic grew after 1518 and the first Africans were brought to the West Indies, the traders drew the kings of Africa into partnership with them. Fewer natives were kidnapped by foreigners, as was the prior practice, and more were sold by their own rulers. By the end of the 16th century, expeditions no longer found it necessary to make incursions into the mainland risking danger and disease to obtain a cargo of slaves. Instead, "slaves were sold by Negro merchants and caboceers (officials) under supervision of the coastal kings, most of whom were slave-traders themselves."[16] Without the whole-hearted cooperation of many native kings, whose profession and recreation were supplying slaves for European powers, the slave trade would have languished. The rulers of Dahomey, Ashanti, and others were no more principled and tender-hearted than were any of the slave traders.[17]

For permission to trade, Europeans paid the kings in units of goods called "dash" which were equal in value to 150 slaves. The kings' slaves were the first to be offered for sale. Although they were usually the worst of the lot, and were priced far in excess of more desirable slaves,[18] the Europeans dared not refuse to purchase them if they wanted to do business with the kings.

Slavery was a normal African institution, perhaps as old as African society itself.[19] It was an intrinsic part of the African social system and was not introduced by outsiders. All the outsiders did was to increase the value of slaves. Slaves could be sold, exported, or sacrificed by kings in the worship of their royal ancestors. One could become enslaved in any one of eight different ways.[20]

For engaging in criminal activity, the culprit could be sold into slavery by the native chief. Included in this classification were adultery, murder, theft, witchcraft, default on a debt and subversive plots. In the latter instance, not only were the seditionists sold into slavery, but also their wives, children and brothers. If a debt could not be repaid, the debtor's household servants (slaves?) were sold to slave merchants to liquidate it. If the proceeds were insufficient to satisfy the obligation, then the debtor himself, together with his wives and children, was sold into slavery. In the case of adultery, the offended person had a claim upon the man and the woman, upon all their property, and upon their families and slaves. Since the African kings relied upon the sale of slaves for their revenue, accusing and condemning were commonplace.

In times of famine, people sold themselves or members of their families into slavery. Periods of want were especially lucrative for slave trading.

Some were kidnapped (panyared), either by European slavers or, more often, by native gangs who were not averse to selling their own children, relatives and neighbors. Children, especially, were always in great demand.

Wily devices were invented to snare victims. People lured to a gathering might be detained and then sold. Or an intended victim might be hired to deliver a parcel to a ship or to some other spot where he would be seized and marketed.

Native kings routinely turned their own subjects into money. Local African rulers were quoted in 1830 as saying: "We want three things to sell, men, women and children."[21] A missionary reported that he told the son of King Ibo of Nigeria in 1841 that the slave trade was an evil practice, and he replied, "Well, if white people give up buying, black people will give up selling slaves."[22] This might be an example of what the Reverend Albert B. Cleage, Jr., meant when he said that the blacks have been contaminated by the materialistic individualism of the white man.[23]

The kings had a wholesale method of obtaining slaves to merchandise: they would sell whole villages of their own subjects at one time. They would, for instance, order a village set afire, and have the people intercepted and captured as they escaped the blaze. It is also reported that a group of black slave traders destroyed a village of 1,500 people in order to capture 52 women.[24]

The most prolific source of African slaves was inter-tribal conflict.[25] Mungo Park, a Scottish physician and explorer of the Niger, is of the opinion that it was not the demand for slaves that accounted for the large number of Negroes to be exported; they were blacks who had already been enslaved as a result of warfare. Jean Barbot, a French agent, agreed that the Africans who were sold by the blacks "were for the most part prisoners of war."[26] When tribes were at peace, slaves were scarce. When a ship arrived to purchase slaves and an insufficient number were on hand, the king would circulate a message among the village chiefs ordering them to supply him with a given quantity of slaves. If they were unable to provide him with the requested amount, they would engage in warfare, taking prisoners until the desired figure was secured.

As the market for slaves expanded, the West Coast of Africa seethed with perpetual hostilities. At the end of the 15th century, Duarte Pacheco Pereira, the Portuguese pioneer in Nigeria, reported that "The Kingdom of Benin . . . is usually at war with its neighbors and takes many captives, whom we buy at 12 or 15 bracelets each, or for copper bracelets, which they prize more."[27] It was a common sight in Africa to see blacks marching other blacks to market linked together with leather thongs (coffles) tied around their necks.

Some became slaves as a result of gaming or gambling, to which many Africans were addicted. They would stake themselves, first a leg, then an arm, and lastly the head. When they lost, meaning that they were completely bound, they surrendered themselves as slaves.

Slavery by oracle[28] was still another source of acquiring

slaves. Parties found guilty at court proceedings were required to pay the penalty with slaves. Ostensibly, these fines were levied by the deity, the highest court of appeal, which accounts for the descriptive title of this method.

While it is true that many of the African blacks transported to the New World as slaves had already been enslaved in their own countries, the case of the Falashas is different. Some, including the Black Hebrews of Chicago, believe that they either migrated, or were forced to traverse the continent below the Sahara Desert from Ethiopia to the west coast of Africa,[29] and from there were brought to America as slaves. Hailu Moshe Paris, the unordained rabbi of Mount Horeb Synagogue in The Bronx, New York, admitted to the author that this theory is a "romantic supposition without historical basis." Although he was born in Ethiopia, he does not claim to be a Falasha. His parents, he acknowledges, were Copts who were probably in touch with Falashas. When they died in 1935-36 in the Italian-Ethiopian War, Falashas in Addis Ababa contacted members of Rabbi Matthews' congregation, The Commandment Keepers, and a West Indian couple adopted him. Although he was admitted to the high school associated with Yeshiva University, he was unable to enroll in the rabbinical seminary.[30] He stated in a letter that "not any Falashas came to this country before the Ethiopian-Italian War."[31]

When the Axum dynasty of Ethiopia adopted Christianity in the fourth century, the Falashas, persecuted because they remained faithful to Judaism, retreated from the coastal region of the Red Sea into the more hospitable and more inaccessible mountainous regions of Ethiopia. There they remained in isolation from the outside world for a very long time, enjoying political independence under their own rulers.[32] The first person to tell of the existence of the Falasha community was the ninth century merchant and traveler, Eldad ha-Dani (the Danite). Professing to belong to the Hebrew tribe of Dan, he claimed that the Danites together with the tribes of Naphtali, Gad and Asher, sons of Jacob's concubines, Bilhah and Zilpah, formed an independent Jewish kingdom in Eastern Africa.[33] Most scholars accepted Eldad's claim. Thereafter, the Falashas were regarded as descendants of the tribe of Dan.

This decision may have been prompted by the consideration that as a sea-faring people, a number of Danites were among the crews of King Solomon's Red Sea trading vessels. Some of them may have developed an affinity for Ethiopia and settled there.[34]

There are still other explanations as to how Jews may have come to Ethiopia. One theory maintains the Falashas are descendants of Hebrews who left Egypt at the time of the Exodus and migrated into Ethiopia. Another theory suggests they are descended from native Hamitic tribes who were converted to Judaism by Yemenite Jews, or they are Yemenite Jews who crossed the Red Sea into Ethiopia. Still others believe that as a result of the destruction of the Judean State by the Babylonians in 586 B.C.E., a remnant of Jews fled to Egypt taking the Prophet Jeremiah with them. There they joined other Jews who had already established flourishing Jewish communities. Many Jews served as mercenaries in the armies of Psammeticus I and still others resided in the Elephantine region of Egypt. From there, they drifted southward until they reached Ethiopia. Again, some may have gone there during the Maccabean period in the second century B.C.E. or as a result of the war with Rome in the first century C.E. Maccabean coins have been found in Natal and Zululand which indicates Jewish people carried on a lively trade relationship with East Africa prior to the Christian era.[35] Living in Ethiopia, the Jews may have converted some of the natives and intermarried with them.

Another theory concerning the origin of the Falashas is based on the pseudohistorical *Kebra Nagast*, which means "The Glory of Kings." The most cherished book of the Amharas, it was apparently written by an Ethiopian at the close of the 13th or at the onset of the 14th century, when the political disturbances of the preceding centuries came to an end.[36] The *Kebra Nagast*, probably written to glorify the newly restored "Solomonic" dynasty, contains the verse, "The will of God decreed sovereignty for the seed of Sem and slavery for the seed of Ham." It is not surprising that the Amharas, a Semitic Christian literate group, expressed racial prejudice because of the fundamental character of Ethiopian Christianity.[37]

In this ancient book, an Ethiopian queen, Makeda,[38] (Sheba), "a woman of splendid beauty," undertook the long and arduous journey to Jerusalem to learn the wisdom of Solomon, King of Israel. A love affair blossomed and the two married. Upon her return to Ethiopia, Queen Makeda gave birth to a son, David. When he attained manhood, David visited his father in Jerusalem. Solomon urged his first-born son to remain with him and to eventually succeed him on the throne, but the young prince insisted he must return to the country in which he was reared. Acceding to his wishes, Solomon sent him home with an army of Israelite warriors and ordered the first-born sons of priests and nobles to accompany the prince to Ethiopia to serve in his court and to teach the Ethiopians the Jewish faith. When David ascended the throne as Menelik I, he founded the Solomonic line of emperors in Ethiopia who bore the title "Lion of Judah" and made Judaism its official religion.

This tale underlies the claim that a line of Ethiopian Hebrew kings could be traced to the late monarch, Haile Selassie, even though Ethiopia was converted to Christianity in 330 C.E. Ethiopian Christianity then became dependent on the Coptic Church. It is quite evident that there was a strong Jewish influence in Ethiopia before the appearance of Christianity. The fact that the Falashas have no trace of Talmudic influence would further indicate that many Jews arrived there before the destruction of the Second Temple in 70 C.E.

Some doubt that the Queen of Sheba ever existed, finding her life more legendary than real.[39] The Biblical version of the above narrative (I Kings 10:1-13) describes the queen as a real person, with allusions to material incorporated in the *Kebra Nagast*. Scripture relates that Solomon withheld nothing from Sheba. Overwhelmed by the magnificence of his surroundings, his wisdom, wealth and regal manner, her relationship with Solomon was so satisfying that she extols him and praises the God of Israel. It is conceivable that when she returned to Ethiopia she brought with her some Israelite practices, or she may have adopted Judaism as her faith.

The twelfth century traveler, Benjamin of Tudela, presents a hearsay account of Ethiopian Jews, never having visited Ethiopia. It was not until the Scottish explorer, James Bruce, stumbled upon them in Gondor in northwestern Ethiopia that a first-hand account of the Falashas comes to our attention. In his descriptive book,[40] Bruce mentions the Falashas by name and writes knowingly of Jewish history, Scripture and customs. Their practices resembled Jewish observances. Bruce reports that they refrained from work on the Sabbath, abided by the dietary laws, practiced circumcision, prayed in a community building that served as a synagogue, and proudly identified themselves as Jews. Contrary to Ethiopian practice, they adhered to the Biblical law, "ye shall not cut yourselves . . . for the dead" (Deuteronomy 14:1). Bruce also mentions the "Jews Rock," a large area where the Falashas maintained their ancient sovereignty and religion.

Having been brought to the world's attention, the Falashas soon became the object of Christian missionaries' attempts to convert them. A German-born converted Jew, Henry Stern, who described himself to them as "a white Falasha," failed in his efforts to achieve this aim. More successful were the missionaries of the London Society for Promoting Christianity Among the Jews. Under strict control of the Ethiopian officials the missionaries were instructed to bring the Falashas into the Ethiopian Coptic Church. Although they viewed that church as pagan, they felt it was better to cooperate than permit the Falashas to remain unsaved as Jews.

Due to these proselyting efforts, Joseph Halevy, a professor at the University of Paris, was sent to Ethiopia in 1867 as a representative of the Alliance Israelite Universalle, to counter the missionary activity and help the Falashas survive as Jews. Halevy gathered much information about them and brought two Falasha youths with him to Europe for an education so they could become teachers of their co-religionists in Ethiopia. It was, however, through the exceptional efforts of another French Jewish professor, Jacques N. Faitlovitch, who continued with the work of his teacher, Joseph Halevy, that the Falashas remained Jewish and were brought to the attention of the world. He opened a school for them in Addis Ababa in

1924, and during the 1920s and 1930s sent 22 young Falashas to Europe and Palestine for study. The school was short-lived, however, because the Italian Fascists closed it when they occupied Ethiopia in 1936. Again the Falashas went into obscurity, only to come to the attention of the world once more with the establishment of the State of Israel.

Dr. Edward Ullendorff, professor of Ethiopian Studies at the University of London, adamantly adheres to the position that the Falashas are non-Jewish Ethiopians of Agaw stock who resisted conversion to Christianity in the 4th century. Fully conversant with the many impressive arguments that have led some scholars to conclude the Falashas are Jews, he dismisses them as limited in value. He suggests that all Ethiopian tribes performed some Jewish practices that had infiltrated their country from Southern Arabia where sizable Jewish communities were established. The Falashas, Ullendorff points out, embody a mixture of pagan-Judaic-Christian beliefs and ceremonies, and he contends that the reflection of transplanted Judaic practices and beliefs does not make them Jews.[41]

The Falashas remained virtually inaccessible during the slave trading era, and were unknown even to most Africans. When American slavers, ever in search of better and cheaper sources of slaves, began to do business with the Royal African Company's slave factory in the southern part of Mozambique in Delgoa Bay in 1721, Falashas were not involved. Although the Americans were trading regularly along the east coast of Africa by the beginning of the 19th century, they confined themselves to the lower half of the continent, away from Ethiopia.[42] Whenever Falasha slaves are mentioned, they are in oriental countries. This is because the captives the three kingdoms in Ethiopia took from each other during continually recurring warfare, were sold as slaves in the eastern part of the world.[43]

Other Africans also observed customs that correspond to Jewish practice, but that would no more make them Jews than the wearing of a skullcap (*yarmulke*) would make a Jew of a Cardinal in the Catholic Church. From the 8th to the 2nd centuries B.C.E., North Africa was molded by Semitic influences—Phoenicians—and by Jews who came there under Phoenician influence.[44] Some of the people in the Maghreb, the Moslem countries west of Egypt, embraced Judaism, and the Punic language is so closely akin to Hebrew that both peoples are believed to share a common ancestry. The North Africans were thus closely connected to the Hebrews of Palestine. Although common practices and common verbiage exist between Jews and North Africans, there is no history of Jews residing in Black Africa, south of the Sahara Desert. Ethiopia is not in this area. The Hamitic (African) language, however, is closely related to the Semitic language and as in North Africa there is a similarity of words.[45]

Thus, Blackwell's claim that the original Jews were black is open to considerable dispute as is his assertion that black slaves were compelled to convert to Christianity.

Prior to 1725, little if any pressure was applied to the slaves to become Christians. The slaves were brought to the New World to be exploited and the slaveowner cared little about their religion as long as it did not interfere with their work.[46] From then until the end of the century, efforts to convert them were sporadic, though it resulted in the slaves adopting some of the surface forms of Christianity.[47] With the dawn of the 19th century, however, the whites began to proselytize among the slaves energetically, attempting to impose formal religion as a means of maintaining tighter control over them.

Pushed to adopt a Christian sect, the slaves inclined toward the one whose practices and rituals resembled most the mode of worship to which they were accustomed. Of the various denominations that strove to win their souls, the Baptist church appealed to them most. Locally autonomous and run democratically, the Baptists approximated their African tradition of local self-direction. It granted the oppressed slave the freedom to express himself, which slavery denied to him. The Baptist church permitted less restrained behavior and provided them with opportunities for greater participation in religious practices. Permission was granted them to preach and the manner in which communion was administered did not discriminate against them. Furthermore, the Baptist practice of total immersion for baptism satisfied their desire for the spectacular and was closely associated with African ritual.[48]

At first the slaveowners were skeptical about the undertaking. Assured by the missionaries, however, that converting the blacks would not cause them any loss, but would benefit them greatly, they agreed. To assuage the masters, the missionaries reduced Christian theology and ethics to simplistic and harmless affirmations. Painstakingly avoiding the New Testament emphasis on "the freedom of the Christian man," they concentrated on the text, "Servants, be obedient to them that are your masters according to the flesh, with fear and trembling, in singleness of your heart, as unto Christ" (Ephesians 6:5). They drafted a catechism that would indoctrinate the slaves with humility, patience, acceptance of God's will and their station in life—attitudes that would diffuse rebelliousness among them.[49] If they were obedient and honest and truthful, they were taught, they would be rewarded in the hereafter.[50] The missionaries concentrated on the children since the adults might possibly revert to old heathen ways or combine the new with the old.[51]

While the slaves were prompted to become Christians, they were restricted from practicing their religion fully. Various states imposed limitations upon them; Maryland prohibited them from holding independent religious meetings and Georgia permitted no slave assemblies. In their own way, however, the blacks resisted these restraints and gradually evolved their own distinctive African-American form of Christianity, condemning slavery and condoning their struggle against their sorry lot. Utilizing the resources they brought with them from their native lands, they were encouraged to cope with the many new problems that faced them as slaves and to adapt to their new environment. Not interested in a religion that served merely as an opiate to assuage their suffering, they selectively accepted the white man's heaven and apocalyptic visions for the emotional relief these concepts provided them.[52]

The "African cult" did much to influence the slaves' style of religion and encouraged them to reject the despotism of the white man. While they developed Christianity's inner meanings to suit themselves, their own heritage continued to flourish among them creatively and potently, and it contributed greatly to their struggle for freedom. It made their daily lives bearable and enabled them to surmount their adversity, if ever they were to break their shackles. Black Christianity prior to the Civil War was thus flavored by African religions that slavery never obliterated.[53]

E. Franklin Frazier, on the other hand, contends that the process by which blacks were captured, enslaved and inducted into plantation life, loosened all social bonds among them and destroyed the traditional basis of social cohesion.[54] It does not appear to be so.

Slaves from neighboring plantations often gathered together for weekly prayer meetings. Crowding into huts, they sang, prayed and shouted to "get happy." Forming a circle, they would place a hand on the shoulder of the person next to them and would glide into a slow dance as they sang. These sessions solidified the bond between them. "The Africans became American slaves while the American-born slaves affirmed their contact with the African experience through the exchange of ideas with newly arrived vassals."[55] These religious gatherings were substantially pervaded by an air of African devotional practices.

Perhaps the most valuable function of the meetings was as group therapy sessions. The camaraderie enabled them to express their innermost yearnings and fortified them against the debilitating effects of slavery. They discussed the events of the week and planned joint strategies and tactics. The prayer service also served as a social institution to a degree unknown in white churches even in rural communities. It functioned as the information dispensing agency, intelligence bureau, and entertainment center. And it introduced newly arrived slaves to those already here on various plantations. At times it seemed the prayer meeting was more social than religious.

The prayer meeting also provided the slaves with a semblance of community life. It gave them hope that they would eventually overcome their situation. And since it was the only place where they could attain positions of prestige, importance and dignity as preachers and functionaries, attendance was consistently good. Even the children attended.

Many contemporary churches, lodges and social organizations, which play important roles in the black community, trace their origins to these meetings and the African influence. As in the past, these affiliations help blacks adapt to a status, in this case a freer one. Despite the marked skepticism of our day, religious belief within the black community is much stronger than it is among the general population of the United States. As underprivileged members of society, blacks readily accept the supernatural as consolation for their social and economic frustrations.[56]

No such evangelical pressure was exerted by Jewish slaveowners. Historical records contain only one reference to a black, "Old Billy," who was converted to Judaism by his master in 1857.[57] A newspaper vendor, Billy attended services at Congregation *Beth Elohim* in Charleston, South Carolina, but was not affiliated with the synagogue since it did not accept blacks as members.[58] In an article for a German periodical, the rabbi of the Charleston community, Maurice Meyer, indicates his high regard for Billy as the "most observant of those who go to the synagogue."[59] When Billy died, the *London Jewish Chronicle* noted that he attended services on *Yom Kippur* (the Day of Atonement), the holiest day of the Jewish year, "in a ruffled shirt."[60]

It appears that except for Old Billy, a black Jew was a rarity. Some synagogues required their members to "be free" and not "people of colour," discouraging Negro slaves who might want to adopt the religion of their masters.[61] These facts undermine the contention of blacks who regard themselves as descendants of slave converts to Judaism. It also weakens Blackwell's argument that the slaves who were brought to the United States were Falashas who were compelled to relinquish their faith. As stated above, slaveowners paid no attention to the religion of their slaves as long as they did their work properly.[62]

To their African heritage and Christian indoctrination, the slaves added another religious expression that sprang from their own experience—the spiritual. A significant contribution by blacks to American life, the spiritual was their musical declaration of independence. These original hymns voiced their innermost feelings and were understood only by themselves. Thomas Wentworth Higginson, the New England abolitionist, recorded a number of the songs his black soldiers sang.[63]

Many spirituals were deliberately clouded in ambiguity to conceal their meaning from the masters. "I am bound for the land of Canaan," for instance, held the code name for Canada, where they hoped to gain their freedom. Egypt generally referred to the South, Pharoah to the slaveowner, cruel Egyptians to harsh slaveholders, hell to being sold farther south, Israelites to themselves, Moses and Joshua to their leaders. Other hymns that were quite clear in their intent, such as "Go Down, Moses . . . let My people go," were banned by most slaveowners.[64]

Spirituals also described attitudes held by slaveowners. For example, when their masters prohibited their holding religious services because they feared they might incite rebellion, the slaves assembled by stealth, and the spiritual "Steal Away" resulted. During these clandestine get-togethers, they put turned down pots over their heads believing that they caught the sound of the singing and prevented the noise from escaping. Their masters would thus be unable to hear them when they engaged in their forbidden activity.[65] West Africans use pots as part of their ceremonial paraphernalia, viewing them as special symbols of the gods who protect men and women. Repatriated slaves may have introduced this practice into Liberia and from there it spread into neighboring countries.

Rabbi Robert Devine of Chicago sees the Scriptural source of the spirituals as proof that the slaves were originally Jewish. "Do you imagine," he asked with a smile, "that slaveowners allowed Christian missionaries to teach them a hymn like 'Let My People Go?' No," he answered his own question, "they wanted to keep them as chattel. This hymn came out of the slaves' Jewish heritage!" Devine overlooks the impact the Biblical description of the Jewish Exodus had made on them, and the particular circumstances in which the slaves found themselves.

Patiently and attentively Rabbi Dar-ee listened while Blackwell told of the various theories about the origin of black Jews in the United States which he insisted supported the group's claim to be Jewish. From his limited knowledge of American history, Rabbi Dar-ee knew that he could not ascertain the validity of Blackwell's claims. Yet he listened, and asked questions out of sympathy for the blacks' experience and for clues to the man's character. Finally, he led Blackwell away from the subject of history and asked about observance. "Tell me," he said, "which *mitzvot* (religious commandments) do you accept and how do you observe them? Perhaps in this way," the Rabbi added hopefully, "we shall be able to relate you to one of the groups already living in Israel." A soft-spoken and kindly man, Rabbi Dar-ee hoped to untangle the past and thus substantiate their claim.

"Our ties to Judaism are firm and deep," Blackwell assured the Rabbi, "but some of our practices differ from those of other Jews, even other black Jews. For instance, we observe Shabbat strictly. We do not allow anybody or anything to distract us from the holiness of the day.

"Then there is the wearing of *tzitzit* (a four-cornered fringed shawl usually worn as an undergarment). Among Orthodox Jews only the men wear them; with us the women wear them, too. Also, our *tzitzit* differ in cut and design from those worn by the Orthodox." Since he was not wearing *tzitzit*, Blackwell could not demonstrate the difference.

Rabbi Dar-ee smiled, aware that some Jewish women in the past did wear *tzitzit* and even donned *tephillin* (phylacteries). "Tell me, what were your marriage practices in the United States?"

Blackwell glanced toward Tziona and Gabriel, then at his hands. Finally, he looked up and replied, "This is where we were lax."

"What do you mean?" the Rabbi asked.

"I must admit," Blackwell said, throwing his hands upward, "many of our people married non-Jews. Some were married in churches and others were even baptized." Blackwell found it painful to make these admissions, when his friends were seeking to be recognized as Jews.

Rabbi Dar-ee pondered a moment, then asked, "Did your sons have a *brit* (circumcision rite)?"

"Of course they did!" Blackwell responded with gusto. He was animated again.

"A *mohel* (circumcisor) performed the *brit*?" the Rabbi queried.

Blackwell replied softly, "No."

"How then?"

"A doctor performed the operation."

Rabbi Dar-ee shook his head. "Is this how this *mitzvah* is performed in America?"

"Many do it this way. Reform Jews especially."

The frown on the Rabbi's face indicated that the information displeased him. He asked no more questions but sat quietly, deep in thought, until Blackwell broke the silence.

"Well, what do you think, Rabbi?" Blackwell asked expectantly.

"Mr. Blackwell," the Rabbi started slowly. "I feel that whatever knowledge you and your friends have of Judaism did not come to you from your parents or uncles—I mean, your families." He paused and glanced benignly at Tziona and Gabriel. "Nor did you learn it from a rabbi. In your search for a religion, you may have read the Bible, some history books, maybe other literature." He paused again, then fixing a steady gaze on Blackwell, he said, "I am unable to find any proof that a relationship ever existed between yourselves and the fountain of Judaism."

The sting of repudiation pained them. Blackwell and his friends had not expected Rabbi Dar-ee to rule against them. Blackwell was most visibly affected. His eyes darted from side to side and he passed his fingers through his hair. His muscles bulged tautly with each movement of his hands and beads of perspiration dotted his forehead. He had been so confident that the State of Israel would accept them as readily as it had welcomed them. Instead, there was total rejection. "I can't believe it," he muttered. Then frustration gave way to anger. "What are you telling us, Rabbi, that we are not Jews?"

"I take no pleasure in telling you this, Mr. Blackwell," the Rabbi said softly. "It pains me to say this, but I cannot do anything about it. Hebrew law is not to be trifled with."

"Is this all there is to it? Is this the whole thing? Is there nothing we can do?" Blackwell was desperate.

"I recommend that you and your companions convert to Judaism. Then you will all be recognized as Jews with full immigrant rights, and you will have no problem."

"But converting would be an admission that we are not Jews." Blackwell stood up abruptly and paced the floor. "But we are Jews!" He emphasized his comment with a downward thrust of his fist.

"Mr. Blackwell," the Rabbi said consolingly. "You claim a relationship with the Falashas. But you ought to know, Mr. Blackwell, the State of Israel does not accept the Falashas as Jews under the Law of Return."

"It doesn't?" Blackwell asked incredulously.

"No. There are too many doubts about them. That is why the Law of Return does not apply to them. The Falashas who wish to immigrate to Israel under the Law of Return must first convert. You and your friends, Mr. Blackwell, are in the same situation."

Blackwell was at a loss. He had assumed that associating themselves with the Falashas would open the door wide for them.

Rabbi Dar-ee continued. "Should any of them come to Israel in surreptitious ways—as tourists, or sailors who jump ship, or in other devious ways—they will find themselves in great difficulty, because they are not eligible for assistance from the government or The Jewish Agency."

"Why does Israel treat the Falashas this way?" Blackwell asked greatly annoyed.

"For a number of reasons," the Rabbi commented.

"What are they?" Blackwell persisted, hoping in this way to find a loophole to bolster his case.

"Briefly, they are as follows. They adhere to the Torah only; they know nothing about the *Talmud* or Oral Law. As a result, the Judaism they practice is more like idolatry. Besides, their Torah is the Ethiopian version.

"Then, a number of their women have Coptic crosses tattooed on their foreheads. They say it means nothing, that they merely copy what their neighbors do to beautify themselves.

But to us, they are introducing a foreign element into our faith.

"Their divorces present a further problem. They are not granted in accordance with *halachah*, Hebrew law. They simply announce their separation in the presence of two witnesses and swear to it in the name of the Emperor. There is no *get* (a document of divorce in accordance with Hebrew law). Consequently, if a divorced Falasha woman remarries and bears children, there is a question whether they are *halachically* legitimate. It may be that they are all *mamzerim* (illegitimate) in the Biblical sense and are therefore forbidden to 'enter into the congregation of the Lord' (Deuteronomy 32:2). The religious legitimacy of all Falashas must thus be questioned.

"Here are three fundamental reasons, Mr. Blackwell. You know, you and your friends are like the Falashas in the way you observe the Shabbat. They do no work whatsoever on Shabbat and nobody even leaves the village. You are also alike in your divorce proceedings. You do not give a *get* either."

"Aren't they circumcised?" Blackwell countered.

"What difference does that make?" the Rabbi said turning up his palms. "Do you think everybody who is circumcised is Jewish? This is foolish. Many non-Jews are circumcised. There is more to Jewishness than circumcision; there must be a *brit*, a holy ceremony.

"Also, there must be some proof. The *Midrash* (narrative commentary on the Bible) tells that when God gave the *Torah* to the Jewish people, the nations of the world wanted to be included. They also wanted to receive God's word and to be part of the Sinai experience. God dismissed their petition, the *Midrash* continues, by telling them: 'Bring Me the record of your pedigree as My children are doing.' By means of this anecdote the Rabbis tell us, Mr. Blackwell, that documentary proof or witnesses are necessary to support one's claim to Jewishness."

Blackwell and his friends cast hopeless glances at each other.

"I'll tell you something more, Mr. Blackwell," the Rabbi continued. "The Falashas have a better case for being Jews than you do. Chief Rabbi Kook (of Israel) recognized them as Jews."

"Impossible!" Blackwell retorted loudly. "We are Falashas too!"

"Not quite," Rabbi Dar-ee smiled. "Let me explain. The Falashas claim to Jewishness rests on the accepted belief that they are descendants of the Hebrew tribe of Dan. They have a tradition of Jewishness recognized by many scholars. Other black Jews today emanate from ancestry that has no identification with Jews, and they do not conduct themselves as Jews. Members of your group, for instance, have identified themselves with Christianity. You told me so yourself. Nothing like this can be said about the Falashas. That is why I compared you to them.

"Your only claim to recognition as Jews would be if your parents had converted to Judaism. You have not made this claim, and you regard it as abhorrent; yet, you claim to be the direct descendants of the original Jews which cannot be proved. This connection is spurious and must be dismissed."

Blackwell looked dejected. He saw that his case was weak. He put his face in his hands and shook his head. "Can't we work something out?" he asked in a weak voice.

Rabbi Dar-ee stroked his beard. Deep in thought, he began slowly. "Maybe, maybe we can arrange a *giyur chelki*. This means a partial or simple conversion. Its use is reserved for certain situations. For example, should a Jewish woman marry a non-Jew, she may drift into living as an adherent of her husband's faith. If for some reason she later decides to return to Judaism, she would then be expected to undergo a *giyur chelki*, a partial or simple conversion, since she never renounced Judaism, nor did she formally adopt her husband's religion. Maybe the same thing can be worked out for all of you."

The Rabbi implied that even if their claim to Jewishness were valid, there was little doubt that whatever identification they had with Judaism was lost in the course of time. During the hiatus of several centuries since their enslavement, erosion of religious practices and beliefs had undermined any *halachic* basis for granting them Jewish status without conversion.

The same principle applies to the descendants of Jews who intermarried with Christians generations ago and raised subsequent generations of children in the church. Separated from whatever Jewish roots their ancestors had, they can no longer claim Jewish identification. If they wish to reclaim the faith their forebears had relinquished, they must convert. Regardless of any other considerations, the rabbinic authorities have consistently maintained that when doubt exists about one's Jewishness, one must prove he is a Jew; if proof is impossible, conversion is necessary. If one is not a Jew, conversion is a very serious undertaking; but, if one is a Jew, he cannot have too many opportunities to affirm it.

Blackwell realized that Rabbi Dar-ee still had not slammed the door shut on his hopes. He had mentioned a partial or simple conversion. "Are there other types of conversion?" Blackwell asked.

"Yes. *Giyur chumri*. It is full conversion, for someone who has never been Jewish. It entails studying the Jewish faith and Jewish history from the very beginning, and the performance of certain rituals."

The Rabbi expected Blackwell to inquire further, but he did not.

Throughout the entire interview Tziona and Gabriel had been silent. Now a decision must be made, and Blackwell felt he must have their support. He turned his chair and pulled it closer to theirs. They spoke in hushed voices at first, and then with increasing animation they argued loudly for a quarter of an hour while Rabbi Dar-ee eyed them, unable to determine what direction the discussion was taking.

When Blackwell turned his chair around and the three faced the Rabbi, Blackwell spoke with great solemnity. "We will not agree to conversion. It would be a confession that we never were Jews. We can't do that."

"I cannot agree, Mr. Blackwell. *Giyur chelki* does not mean you were never Jews, only that you followed non-Jewish practices for a time. Give the matter further thought before you make a final decision," the Rabbi pleaded. "I will give you every possible assistance.

"Let us spend some time together. Come to my home on

Chanukah (The Festival of Lights). We will light the candles in the *menorah* (candelabrum), and celebrate together. We will sing songs, tell the story of the celebration, and eat *latkes* (potato pancakes). You will come on other *yomin tovim* (holidays) and at still other times. We will work it out." In this way the Rabbi sought to clarify his own doubts concerning *halachah* and their Jewishness. "Please accept my advice for your own sakes—and for the sake of the children."

"I still can't believe what's happening," Blackwell exploded.

"Mr. Blackwell," the Rabbi reassured him, "converting will only confirm what you already profess. You will merely clarify and affirm your customs and beliefs. The Rabbinate will be satisfied, and it will speed your recognition as *olim* and guarantee the rights you seek."

"We'll think about it," Blackwell said curtly. "We'll see."

With that, Rabbi Dar-ee and Sonya Peletz, who performed well as interpreter, returned to Jaffa.

Upset with the Rabbi's verdict, Blackwell claimed he wrote to Zalman Shazar, then President of the State of Israel, and requested a meeting to discuss his Jewishness and that of his friends. He received no reply, Israeli officials said, because no letter was ever received from him.

Blackwell was deeply disturbed and apprehensive to find himself at an impasse. The fate of his brothers and sisters in Liberia hinged upon the successful outcome of his discourse with Rabbi Dar-ee. He knew first-hand the hardships they were experiencing and worried about Carter's faltering leadership. He feared for the future. His confreres would be permitted to enter Israel as American citizens, but their acceptance as Jews entitled to assistance and rights outlined in the Law of Return was now impossible unless each one was willing to convert—something he considered unlikely. Moving to Israel thus held all the same portents of failure as the Liberian experience. He had warned Carter that if the group experienced failure again, it would be totally demoralized.

Blackwell's consternation was fully justified because things went from bad to worse with the pioneers in Liberia. By November 4, 1969, an article in *The Liberian Age* quoted Attorney General James A. A. Pierre to the effect that the

American immigrants were "undesirable aliens" and were "asked to leave the country within seven days for failure to file their declaration of intention." According to law, an immigrant must declare his intention to become a Liberian citizen within two years after his arrival, or he must leave the country. When they first arrived, President Tubman could have granted them citizenship immediately, but they either refused to accept it or neglected to request it. Now, after residing in Liberia for two years, only about 25 of them had filed declarations of intention. Thus, approximately 100 souls were affected by the deportation order. Regarded as non-useful, non-productive aliens, and as "parasites" whose living conditions were "deplorable," they would either start denizenation within seven days "or get out." The government would no longer tolerate the situation.

Furthermore, the newspaper stated, the government's immigration policy requires immigrants to disperse themselves throughout the country and become assimilated among the Liberian population. A few did spread out; most, however, clustered in a ghetto-like enclave, where is was inevitable that the Liberian "people will always regard them as strangers." J. Newton Garnett, secretary of the Commission to investigate the needs of the American blacks, revealed there were 5 farmers among them. The government planned to settle them in 3 different counties in two pairs and as a single, but they begged off claiming they were not trained farmers. They preferred to remain together, none of them feeling secure enough to go it alone or in pairs.

The Liberian Age, which again referred to them as "Black Muslim Priests" as it had on September 18, 1967, explained further that Pierre had complained that "They don't even make gardens for themselves," and few of them had any skills listed as necessary for immigration. Pierre failed to understand why even those who had filed declarations of intention to become naturalized two years before had neglected to follow through and assume citizenship. The newspaper article further reported that the Americans had been advised that "the United States Embassy will pay their passage back to America."

Not all government officials shared Attorney General Pierre's view that the American immigrants were "undesirable aliens." Several were at a loss to explain it. Garnett said he had never heard anyone express such an opinion about them. Shown the newspaper article, he read it with disbelief and challenged Pierre's assertion. Quite the contrary, he said, the government felt they were making a good adjustment to Liberian life. With pride he pointed to King Craig who served at coach of the local boxing association, to another man who was instructing police officers in the art of self-defense, and to two young women, an elementary school teacher and a bank employee, who were making valuable contributions to the country. Some wanted to return to the United States, he conceded, but only to acquire additional training that would help them better to establish themselves when they returned, and to assist in the development of the country. He pointed out, in support of his position, that they had requested visas before they left to facilitate their return to Liberia.

Winston Tubman, Deputy Minister for Foreign Affairs, concurred. To his knowledge, all went well after the Commission that visited The Camp secured the help they needed from the Cabinet. He knew of no reason for the Attorney General to categorize them as "undesirables."

These two gentlemen, working in their offices in Monrovia, seem to have been unaware of conditions in Gbatala. When John Barnes of *Newsweek* visited The Camp, he cabled the magazine that he saw "no one tending the camp's vegetable patches. Instead, about a dozen men lolled in the opensided hut that served as community center, synagogue and school. One bearded brother told me: 'Why man, we don't have to kill ourselves for anyone, never again. We get up when we want and we work when we want.' "[66] Apparently the Attorney General was better acquainted than they with the true condition of The Camp.

Basically, the reason for their poor performance as settlers was their defective self-evaluation. They deluded themselves with enhanced self-concepts. As a group, they assumed they had knowledge and skills which they in fact lacked. They thought they could live in primitive fashion, but their limitations were too great. Over-estimating their abilities doomed their colony to failure, and the Liberian government could not provide for their needs.

Also, attitudes brought with them from the United States undermined their resolve. After the first blush of enthusiasm for Liberia wore off and their situation continuously deteriorated, they blamed the government for providing too little help. They attempted to get as much money as they could out of Liberia without doing anything in return. Some Liberians felt the Americans viewed them as ignorant, backward and incapable of shaking off the jungle. Beyond this, the Liberian government feared they might be the vanguard of a large migration from the United States that would upset the political balance of the country.[67] As a result, officials did not extend themselves as they otherwise might have.

Above all, the American blacks suffered from lack of good leadership and from poor social organization. Ben Ammi Carter had returned to the United States several times, leaving in charge deputies who were ill-matched to the responsibilities thrust upon them. Without a strong leader exercising control over the group, individuals were compelled to shift for themselves. Disorganized, they were unequal to the task of building a new life in a strange country.

Beyond this, some members of the group rejected Carter's leadership. James T. Greer, who had scouted Liberia with Carter and Blackwell, withdrew from the group. Carter tried his best, one loyal supporter observed, but he was too haughty and authoritarian for some of the people. Rumor also endowed him with as many as 4 wives at one time. This may be doubtful, but he assuredly set a poor example for his followers when his wife, Patricia, was granted a divorce in 1972 in Rockville, Maryland, on the grounds that he deserted her and their children for another woman. But, even so, despite his shortcomings, the majority of the group readily followed Carter's leadership.

Internal feuding may also have contributed to the failure of the colony. When Asiel Ben Israel and Ben David visited on the campus at Johnson C. Smith University, neither of them admitted knowing King Craig, although they lived together in The Camp and had received stipends from the Liberian government. Nor would they say anything about the Buie family, who are related to Craig. When Craig was interviewed in Monrovia, he claimed no knowledge of elementary facts about group members.

A seriously detrimental factor from the beginning was Carter's shallow research on Liberia, or the one-sided way in which he described Liberia to the congregants at Alpha Beta.

He said nothing about the interviews Harold Isaacs had conducted in 1958-59 on attitudes about Liberia among blacks who had returned to their ancestral homeland in search of freedom from racism and prejudice. Isaacs cites such statements as, "Liberia is corrupt," "Liberians have all negative standards of Negro Americans and none of the positive features," "I think of Liberia as a mistake . . . Liberia is like Mississippi. I try to block out Liberia when I think of Africa," and "American Liberians . . . the ruling class in Liberia (were) hostile to American Negroes."[68] American Liberians kept American blacks from establishing businesses there and prevented them from improving their position. Like Richard Wright, they found their paths studded with difficulty and even danger.[69]

The Liberians, not surprisingly, were unwilling to allow newcomers to move ahead faster than natives. They outspokenly told American blacks that to get along in their country they would need to adopt the proper attitude—to reconcile themselves to the fact that they would not become president of the country or enter the political and educational arenas. Most of them had no such ambitions. The American blacks merely wanted to be accepted as human beings with freedom to be what they are and to become what they can. "A black skin does not make everyone an African," the American blacks were told quite frankly. And if they were light-skinned Negroes, they had great difficulty convincing Africans that they were blacks. Lighter skin indicated that they were not racially pure and could thus not belong to the accepted group.

The American black thus found himself no freer in Africa

than he had been in the United States. Still fighting prejudice, he was perplexed to find that he was more of an alien in Africa than in America, perceiving himself as an expatriate, an American-in-exile.[70] Thus, he was disappointed in his search for solace and a sense of identity and achievement in a land where all inhabitants are black. The pleasurable sensation of residing in a country where the white man was not the master, was fleeting.

Similarly, the American Jew who had settled in Israel did so because he felt himself to be an "outsider" in American society. Desirous of becoming an "insider" among fellow Jews in the land of his fathers, he was disappointed to find that he continued to be an "outsider"—an American.[71]

The black American's disillusionment was further enhanced by the horrible manner in which African blacks treat their black servants. They freely state that their menials are not human, are not concerned about them, call them uncomplimentary names, yell at them and feed them scraps from the table.[72] To him, this was not escaping to freedom, but was a poor trade-off.

Oddly enough, the Liberian experience had a reverse effect upon the American black. It confirmed his American identity and made him appreciate more fully the American way of life. This manisfestation has already been indicated in the case of Eldridge Cleaver.[73]

Apparently, American blacks are especially aware of this situation. For today, even with the emergence of Africa as the home of the blacks, no "back-to-Africa" movement has developed as it did in the days of Marcus Garvey. And even then, in spite of his fiery personality, no blacks were repatriated. Perhaps the earlier unfortunate experiences from Paul Cuffee to Bishop Henry M. Turner discouraged them from pursuing this approach as a solution to their problem. They undoubtedly came to realize that if they are to attain a good life for themselves, it must be based on their achieving successful integration in the United States as Americans, not as blacks.

Ban Ammi Carter should have been aware of these and additional factors concerning Liberia. Illiteracy abounds there.

Although a compulsory education law was enacted in 1912, it is estimated that only about 15% are literate.[74] Living, health and welfare conditions are poor.[75] Furthermore, Carter surely knew of Liberia's noxious traffic with slavery, but he chose to ignore it. It was primarily because of American pressure that an international commission began to investigate this condition in 1929. Distraught that the practice might still be persisting, Secretary of State Henry Stimson was prompted to write Liberian officials, "It would be tragically ironic if Liberia, whose existence was dedicated to the principle of liberty, should succumb to practices so closely akin to those which its founders sought to escape."[76]

The findings of the commission were so mortifying that some of the country's highest officials resigned their positions.[77] They had promoted forced labor and derived financial gain from its practice. Even as late as 1962, a fourth of the country's labor force was still recruited involuntarily.

Carter should also have known that snobbism is pronounced in Africa. A visiting scholar at a West African university related that not a single colleague invited him to his house during the first 9 months he was there, and in two years he received but two or three invitations. A black American who had lived in Ghana for 8 years has claimed that he still does not have the feeling of being "inside" with Africans. Many American blacks are turned off by this. They have no intention of trading a second-class status in America for a second-class status in Africa.

When word reached President Tubman that the Americans had been ordered out of the country, he rescinded the decree. He personally saw to it that if they wanted to remain in Liberia, they could. Carter and Blackwell, however, had long concluded that the Black Hebrews needed to go elsewhere—to the State of Israel. Their unique identification as blacks and as Jews prompted a shift in emphasis from their blackness, which brought them to Africa, to their Jewishness, which now turned their interest to the Promised Land.

In retrospect, it appears that Rabbi Devine of the House of Israel Cultural Center in Chicago adjudged the situation correctly when he said that moving to Liberia was not the solution to the problem with which the members of Congregation *B'nai Zakin Sar Shalom* were wrestling. He warned members of his congregation who contemplated moving to Liberia with Carter that the time was not ripe for their redemption, Biblically speaking, and they lacked the training necessary for the venture. As the direct descendants of Abraham, Isaac and Jacob, they must fully reenact the prophecy of Scripture, the Rabbi insisted. God assured Abraham that he would have numerous progeny, but foretold "thy seed shall be a stranger in a land that is not theirs, and shall serve them; and they shall afflict them four hundred years" (Genesis 15:13). The "land" in which they are "stranger(s)" is the United States, the "modern Egypt," Devine explained, because Deuteronomy 28:68 states, "And the Lord shall bring thee into Egypt in ships . . ." Since ships are not needed to go from Palestine to Egypt because they share a common border, he reasoned that Deuteronomy 28:68 refers to the enslavement of African blacks in the United States to which they were brought in ships. Now, since the first true Hebrews (the African slaves) arrived in the United States in 1619, the Scriptural 400 year period will not be completed until the year 2019. God's timetable cannot be pushed ahead or delayed. "You just can't fight prophecy," he stated with confidence. And those who had left for Liberia "were doing just that."

Rabbi Devine is indulging in sophistry. He interprets "Egypt" figuratively, claiming it refers to "servitude" wherever it is practiced. Yet he insists dogmatically that the phrase "400 years" is to be taken literally, rather than as an extended period of time. The impracticality of his position is further compounded by the remainder of the sentence in Deuteronomy. It reads: "There ye shall sell yourselves unto your enemies for bondmen and bondwomen, and no man shall buy you." The fact of the matter is that the Africans did not sell themselves into American slavery but were sold by others, and plantation owners purchased them almost as soon as they alighted from the ships.

Rabbi Devine was delighted that his prediction that the Black Hebrew expedition would end in failure had been vindicated. The hardships the American blacks were experiencing in Liberia and the difficulties Blackwell was encountering with the officials in Israel, were clear evidence of their blunder. Furthermore, Blackwell and his confederates were living in Arad, not Jerusalem, the seat of government, because they attempted to force the hand of God. "No one can do this and succeed," Rabbi Devine said triumphantly, jutting forth his chin.

Then, one day, without advising anyone, 39 of the American blacks left Liberia for the Jewish State. Liberian officials were mystified. The only one who cared to speculate about their hasty departure was Winston Tubman.[78] The American blacks, he said, had expressed dissatisfaction with the large number of white people in the country, feeling that they wielded too much power. They may have wanted the government to adopt a more militant stand against whites, Tubman suggested. The officials, however, did not see it their way. Liberians, he said, have no axe to grind.

Chapter VI

IMMIGRATION TO ISRAEL

The sky was filled with stars and a soft wind blew across the landing field when a Trans World Airlines plane dipped down uneventfully onto the runway at Lod (Ben Gurion) Airport in the State of Israel. The passengers busily gathered their belongings, scurried off the plane and headed for Passport Control. They mistakenly believed the sooner they were cleared for entrance into the country, the sooner they would collect their baggage and head for their hotels. It was about 8:00 P.M. and they were tired, having spent many hours in the air. They did not know that thirty minutes or more usually elapsed between landing and leaving the airport.

Among the more than 100 passengers who deplaned were the 39 American blacks from Liberia. They cleared Passport Control and proceeded into the baggage claim area. Their American passports facilitated their entry into the country since Israel requires no visas from Americans. Before proceeding to the baggage ramp, they gathered in the middle of the room around a tall bearded man with braided hair.

"Brothers and sisters," he said to them softly, "we have arrived safely in the Lord's country. We are fulfilling God's promise to our people. December 12, 1969, is an historic day for our nation."

"Praise the Lord," many of them uttered, their voices muffled.

Huddled together, they waited uneasily for the luggage to arrive.

"Scan the waiting people and see if Brother Blackwell is among them," the tall bearded man said.

"I can't see him," a few responded simultaneously.

At the appearance of the first suitcases, all the people in the area converged on the luggage ramp, and some were not gentle. Hesitantly, the erstwhile Liberian residents also moved toward the ramp and collected their battered suitcases and cartons held together with knotted string. They moved haltingly toward the exit. Their unsure gait and searching looks indicated they were looking for a familiar face. Reaching the door, one of the men yelled, "Brother Blackwell! Brother Blackwell!" Breaking from the group, he ran to Blackwell and embraced him. "You are a sight for sore eyes," he said admiringly. "It's so good to see you." Tears welled up in his eyes.

Blackwell returned the embrace and smiled broadly. "It's so good to be with you again," he managed. He then moved from person to person embracing the men, kissing the women and hugging the children.

Blackwell had come to meet them as he had earlier met Tziona and Gabriel and their families. He would assist in settling them as he had the initial arrivals. Familiarity with the Hebrew language and the procedures of the country, placed him in a favorable position to render them expert assistance. "I've been waiting for this moment," Blackwell said earnestly. Inwardly, he was troubled. Turmoil seethed within him as he contemplated the difficulties that would assuredly soon confront them.

The warm expressions of fellowship continued unabated until one of the men asked, "What happens now, Brother Blackwell?"

"That's why I'm here," he replied reassuringly. "I'll take care of everything." With that he ambled over to the young guard standing at the door and asked loudly, "Who's in charge here?"

Automatically the swarthy-skinned guard's hand moved to the revolver that hugged his hips. Looking at Blackwell with fixed eyes he asked softly and unemotionally, "What do you want?"

"I want to speak to the man in charge."

"Why do you want to speak to him?"

"I want the man in charge," he repeated. Nothing would deflect him.

The guard did not stir. Then, eyeing Blackwell closely, he said as he turned, "Wait here." Slowly he walked toward a door near the passageway through which incoming passengers enter the customs inspection area of the terminal. After taking a few steps he would veer around to see what Blackwell was doing. This action was repeated several times. Finally, he stopped next to an unpretentious looking man of medium height who was examining some papers. After a brief exchange, the two started towards Blackwell.

"I'm *Mar* (Mr.) Gershom," the newcomer introduced himself to Blackwell. "Who are you and what do you want?" Israelis get to the point with a minimum of words. As *Mar* Gershom spoke, the entire group of blacks encircled him, the guard and Blackwell.

"I'm Hezekiah Blackwell. My companions here have returned to the Promised Land."

"Hallelujah!" erupted spontaneously from the group.

"They," Blackwell started again motioning to the group surrounding them, "have returned to the land of their fathers." Heads nodded in agreement.

Mar Gershom was either oblivious to what Blackwell had said or if he heard, paid no attention to him. Such declarations are heard at the airport almost every time a plane brings another mass of people into the country. Besides, Gershom was straining to view the other passengers who had already gathered up their baggage and were exiting from the hall.

"Mr. Gershom!" Blackwell said with exasperation. "You are not listening to me."

"I'm sorry, Mr. Blackwell. What did you say?"

Pointing at his friends he said, "They are Hebrew immigrants who have come to their homeland to be free. They have no money and cannot return to Liberia from where they came. They demand all the rights that belong to Hebrews returning to the homeland. They want what is due them in accordance with the Law of Return."

Gershom's grimace indicated the State of Israel had a problem on its hands.

As Blackwell had discovered in his earlier studies, the Law of Return, passed in 1950, provided aid to Jews returning to their homeland. "Every Jew," the Law states, "has the right to come to this country as an *oleh* (a Jew immigrating to Israel permanently)." When he expresses a desire to settle in Israel and is cleared by the Minister of the Interior, he is given an *oleh's* visa and certificate and immediately becomes a citizen of the country by virtue of the Law of Nationality passed in 1952. This procedure operates automatically unless he indicates within three months of acquiring an *oleh's* status that he wishes to waive the privilege of Israel's citizenship or the Minister of the Interior has reason not to grant it.

The Law of Return and the Law of Nationality operate jointly when the immigrants are Jewish, but they do not apply to non-Jews, unless the Minister of the Interior determines that a non-Jew is entitled to the right of *oleh*. A non-Jew may become a citizen of Israel, according to the Law of Nationality, by applying for citizenship after having been a resident of the country for three years within a five year period.

Gershom scratched his head and contemplated the people before him with disbelief. He was visibly shaken. Did he hear Blackwell correctly? Are they really claiming immigrants rights? There was no mistake, however, when Blackwell repeated the demand, "They insist on immigrants' rights."

Blackwell's tactic was plainly evident. He aimed to get all the benefits of newcomers for the group and through them for himself, Tziona and Gabriel.

Gershom was at a loss. The Law of Return applies to Jews. But were the blacks standing before him Jews? The issue of who is a Jew is so complicated. He felt helpless. His face brightened when he resolved that the issue did not concern him. He had no authority to make the determination that they were or were not Jews. But why did they come? Doesn't Israel have enough problems? Now this. If only they had not come. If they had to come, why didn't they arrive when he was not on duty.

Enough of this foolishness, he thought to himself. Some determination had to be made regarding them. But what could he do at 9:00 in the evening? An hour had passed already since they got off the plane. None of the ministries were open. What was he to do with them?

"Were they in contact with the government before they came?" Gershom asked Blackwell.

"They were!" Blackwell was emphatic.

"They were?" he asked unbelievably. "Then why is there no notice that they were coming?"

"But they have been in touch!" Gershom's mind was racing. His darting eyes conveyed the quandary he was in. "Wait here, Mr. Blackwell," he said crisply. "I will call Moshe Shapiro, the Minister of the Interior, and ask him what to do. I know he does not like to be disturbed at home, but I don't know what else to do." With that, Gershom turned and walked toward an office at the other end of the waiting room and disappeared behind its door. The guard returned to his station. It was meaningless to stand in the midst of the group by himself.

"What is going to happen to us?" one of the women asked Blackwell with great concern. "What if they send us away? Where will we go? What will we do?"

Blackwell smiled confidently as if to indicate he had the matter wholly under control. "Don't worry, Sister Miriam," he replied loudly enough for the entire group to hear. "The Lord of Abraham, Isaac and Jacob is watching over us. We have come home and here we shall stay." Blackwell aimed to calm the fears that were contagiously engulfing the group. And he was successful. They were all comforted, convinced he spoke knowingly.

About fifteen minutes later Gershom returned.

"*Mar* Shapiro says the Ministry of the Interior has received no communication from them. No application for immigration has come to his office from them."

"But that's impossible," Blackwell raised his voice.

"Do not shout, Mr. Blackwell." Gershom had no desire to

let hysteria reign. "The Minister is fully aware of all correspondence that comes to the Ministry. When he says they did not hear from this group, you can believe him." Sighing to relieve some of his own tension, Gershom threw out the question, "To whom did they write?"

"We were in correspondence with one of the *kibbutzim*," the man with the braided hair spoke up. "We wrote to them and they sent us letters in return."

"Which *kibbutz*?"

Silence. He shrugged his shoulders and shook his head to indicate he could not remember the name. Neither could anyone else. They looked at Blackwell, but he remained stone faced.

"Maybe," Mr. Gershom continued, "you wrote to a friend at the *kibbutz*, or even to the secretary, but the *kibbutz* is not the Israeli government." Blackwell's face betrayed the unspoken question, "How did you know that this is what happened?" It was he with whom the Liberian group had been in contact. Fortunately, none of them gave him away.

"Writing them about your intentions," Gershom went on, "is not preparing an application. You failed to apply through proper official channels. So now you have a problem and you have given us a problem."

The man with the braided hair persisted. "But six black families came here from Liberia in August—this year—under circumstances similar to ours. There was no problem then, we were told. Why should there be a problem now?"

Gershom furrowed his brow as he stared at him intently. So this is the situation. Others supposedly did the same thing and got away with it. Now they are trying it too. They are playing a game with us. They shall not get away with it, if I have anything to do with it, Gershom said to himself. He felt anger well up within him. Instead of exposing his thoughts, he shook his head from side to side and said softly, "No such thing has ever happened before. If others had arrived here as you have, we would know about it. No group ever came to Israel like this before."

Blackwell stared at Gershom for a number of seconds. He knew that two families, Tziona and Gabriel and their families, not six, had entered Israel earlier that year. In fact, he was the one who was instrumental in getting apartments in Arad for them and himself. Should he speak up and tell it all? While he pondered what to do, Gershom asked, "Do you know the procedure of how immigrants come to Israel?"

They all looked blank.

"It works this way." Gershom then launched into an explanation. A Jew may enter Israel in one of three ways: as tourist; as temporary resident; as *oleh*. Tourist visas are valid for three months but may be extended up to two years. Since tourists are visitors, they are not entitled to most of the benefits and rights granted temporary residents and *olim*. Temporary residence visas are given to those who come to Israel with the thought that they may possibly settle in the country. *Olim* visas are given to newcomers who plan to settle in the country permanently.

"Of the three," Gershom pointed out, "your group is in the category of tourist .You may have been able to enter Israel as temporary residents or as *olim* if you had gone through proper channels. But you didn't."

Blackwell looked defeated. So did the members of the group. He had felt something like this might happen. And it had, before they even left the airport. Should he tell his brothers and sisters he caused their uncertain plight? If they found out, how would they react to him?

His thoughts were interrupted when the man with the braided hair moaned, "We were given incorrect information. We were misled." Blackwell felt himself cringing inwardly.

"This is the correct procedure," Gershom said, and he explained the history and present practices of Israel's immigration policy.

When a Jew decides to emigrate to Israel, he declares his intention to a representative of The Jewish Agency, *ha-Sochenut ha-Yehudit l'Eretz Yisrael*, in the country in which he lives. An international, non-government body, centered in Jerusalem, The Jewish Agency is the executive arm and representative of the World Zionist Organization. Between the time it came into existence in 1922 (when the League of Nations ratified Britain's Mandate to Palestine) and the establishment of the State of Israel in 1948, it served as the sole representative of the Jewish people. It also played the principal role in relations between *Eretz Yisrael* and world Jewry, on the one hand, and the officials of the British Mandate and other powers on the other. The Jewish Agency then relinquished many of its functions to the newly created Israeli government, but it continued to be responsible, among other things, for the immigration and absorption of immigrants into Israel. As a result, it set up departments in each of the areas it was delegated to handle.

In 1954 an agreement was entered into between the government of Israel and the World Zionist Organization that legally recognized The Jewish Agency as world Jewry's representative for immigration and absorption, Youth Aliyah, education and culture in the Diaspora, agricultural settlement, and other functions. The Immigration Department of The Jewish Agency operates a network of facilities in Europe and elsewhere to process immigrants at their points of origin and in transit. It arranges for medical examinations, supplies transportation, and is involved in other formalities.

"As you can see, Mr. Blackwell," Gershom noted, "a rather complete picture of the person is gathered by The Jewish Agency. The assembled information is then submitted to the Israel Embassy of the country in which the immigrant resides and a visa, either as a temporary resident or as an *oleh*, is granted the prospective immigrant.

"Your group did not do this. If they had, their reception here tonight would be altogether different."

Gershom continued with his explanation. When a newcomer arrives in Israel, the Department of Absorption receives him, and sends him to one of the many absorption centers throughout the country to help integrate him culturally. He is given grants of cash, housing accommodations and some household goods. He is also provided with Hebrew instruction in its *ulpanim*, vocational training and, in conjunction with the economic department, a loan if he needs it. Health insurance and welfare services are also granted him.

"Over a year ago, I think it was in June of last year," Gershom said with furrowed brow, "the Israeli government created a new Ministry of Immigration Absorption and thus assumed direct responsibility in this sphere. Nevertheless, The Jewish Agency's departments of immigration and absorption have continued to register new immigrants, bring them to Israel, supervise the *ulpanim* and reception centers, and care for the needy newcomers. The Ministry of Immigration Absorption, however, deals with most areas of absorption in Israel itself."

Blackwell knew that Gershom's explanation was correct. He had lived in Israel long enough to become acquainted with the accepted procedure. His cohorts had not followed the prescribed course and he was guilty of not giving them proper guidance. But what could they do under the circumstances, he rationalized. They had to leave Liberia.

"Now, Mr. Blackwell," Gershom said with a soft smile, "you don't expect me to believe that these people had been in contact with officials of the government. If they had, members of the Ministry of Immigration Absorption would have been here to greet them warmly."

Gershom and Blackwell stared at each other.

"You might also be interested to know," Gershom said as he narrowed his eyes, "should a non-Jew choose to settle in Israel, a Special Committee of The Jewish Agency not only investigates the individual's personal life, but also inquires into his motives. Why does he want to renounce his country for Israel? Why should he be accepted by Israel, and so forth. When the investigation is completed satisfactorily and all documents are in order, arrangements are then made for him to enter the country as a resident and after three years he can apply for citizenship.

Gershom then added, "You know, Mr. Blackwell, your friends could have saved themselves a lot of money in coming here."

"How so?" Blackwell asked wearily.

"Immigrants who come to Israel under the sponsorship of The Jewish Agency, can arrange their transportation through the Israel Aliyah (Immigration) Center. They then get a special air fare rate and are even allowed an excess baggage weight allowance."

Blackwell snickered.

Gershom had a purpose in meticulously explaining this procedure to Blackwell and the arrivals. He saw through their machinations. They had ignored the accepted procedures—as Jews or as non-Jews. Because they had not applied to enter Israel other than as tourists, the representatives of The Jewish Agency were denied the opportunity to investigate them. They aimed to present Israel with a *fait accompli*. They must have reasoned, he thought, that the Israelis would not dare refuse them admittance because Israel is claiming it is absorbing Jews from more than "seventy nations." To turn blacks away would bring Israel a bad press and make her appear reprehensible in the eyes of the world. They therefore concluded, he assumed, that they would breeze easily into the country. He would not be a partner to their plot.

"I don't know what we can do for them," Gershom addressed himself to Blackwell.

"What are they going to do?" Blackwell pleaded. "Where are they going to go?"

"The man at the information desk," he said pointing to a long counter against the far wall in the baggage claim area, "will help them get hotel rooms."

Blackwell walked away from Gershom and was followed by his group. Their faces were expressionless as Blackwell spoke to them. Would they be allowed to stay or would they be put back on the plane and returned to Liberia? Since they had no return tickets, it would be the responsibility of the airline to fly them back to the point of embarkation.

All at once Gershom's face lit up and he called to Blackwell. "Come here, young man. I think I know what you were referring to," he said, smiling.

Hope spread across Blackwell's face as he approached Gershom.

"Only you have the facts twisted," Gershom continued. "About a year ago, five blacks came here—a family of three and a mother and a son. I don't know whether it was exactly that way, but five people came, not families. None of them, however, said they were Jews when they entered the country. They came as tourists. Then they claimed they were Jews and requested rights as Jewish immigrants. They were written up in the newspapers. That's why I remember it.

"But their case was not like these people," he said with a wave of his hand. "They entered the country as American tourists. I was right. No group ever came to Israel as this one here demanding the rights of the Law of Return at the airport."

After a long pause he added, "Why did they do it?"

Silence.

Blackwell's face fell; his self-assurance crumbled. He hesitated to rejoin his people. With effort, he dragged himself away from Gershom. What was going to happen to them now? He had betrayed them. The possibility of their returning to Liberia made him shudder.

This thought, however, was sufficient for him to brace himself, walk back to Gershom and speak forcefully. "I don't care what you said. Your lecture on immigration is meaningless. They are Jews and we are not budging from here until they are given their rights as *olim* under the Law of Return. So they didn't follow the rulebook. This doesn't mean they are not Jews."

Blackwell's outburst and defiant stand took Gershom aback momentarily, but he stood his ground. "I don't know what more I can do for you. I can get some rooms for you," he reiterated.

"Rooms be damned," Blackwell exploded. He was losing face in the presence of his brothers and sisters and he had to turn it around. "We want apartments like all other *olim*," he demanded.

An impasse had been reached. Gershom felt himself inadequate to handle the situation. He was tired. Stymied, he agreed to call Jerusalem again "and whatever they decide, I'll do. I have no alternative," he said to Blackwell with resignation.

Again he disappeared behind the door of the office at the other end of the waiting room.

"*Mar* Shapiro," Gershom said upon reaching him, "the blacks won't leave the airport. They want apartments—all immigration rights. What am I to do?"

"What have you found out about them?"

"I am not pleased with them. I feel they are aiming to back us into a corner and take unfair advantage of us. They are playing a game with us."

"Why do you think so?"

"Because of the things the leader has said to me. It seems they are trying to do what other blacks did earlier this year. They are copying them."

"Wait at the telephone, Gershom," the Minister said. "I'll call you back."

There was no precedent for handling large numbers of people, whose status was unclear, suddenly appearing at a port of entry. In the absence of prior notification so that due consideration could have been given to the needs of the new arrivals, the Israeli officials had to grope through their laws in order to deal properly and humanely with these unexpected arrivals from Liberia.

Gershom sat impatiently at the telephone. When it rang about twenty minutes later, he grabbed it so hastily he fumbled the receiver out of his hand. Snatching it up he yelled into it, "Is it you, *Mar* Shapiro?"

It was. The Minister told Gershom the arrivals would have to spend the night at the airport and a decision about them would be made the following day. In the meantime, Shapiro instructed Gershom to make arrangements for them for the night. "Regardless of the merits of the case," *Mar* Shapiro said, "it is late and men, women and twenty-one children are involved. They are tired. Compassion requires that we do this."

When informed of Moshe Shapiro's telephone call, Blackwell said, "All we ask is to live in Israel, to work and to study. We are Jewish, we have always been Jewish and we came here for the same reason any other Jew comes here. We waited four hundred years; I guess a day or two more won't matter."[1]

The Kenesset was convened the next day and the Rabbinate was consulted concerning the new arrivals. Later that day, Deputy Prime Minister Yigal Allon called and advised that although their exact status had not yet been determined, the group members were to be given three-month visitors' visas, which is automatically granted to anyone carrying a United

States passport, issued *cartes tipul* (a sort of *carte blanche* to claim many immigrant rights), and given temporary housing, employment, sick fund and other considerations. He also said they were to be taken to Dimona,[2] a development town in the Negev where the Absorption Center was expecting them.

This disposition of the group was misunderstood by many. Moshe Yeger, the Israeli Consul in Philadelphia, for example, assured the Philadelphia Association of Black and White Jews that, since their case was similar to the black Jews of India who are settled in Israel permanently under the Law of Return, they would be accorded the same treatment. They would thus be entitled to automatic citizenship, he said.[3] On the other hand, *The Chicago Tribune* reported that they had been given tourist status for three months.[4] Later events proved them both to be incorrect.

Gershom was displeased with the decision. He knew a flim-flam when he saw one. The blacks were to be handled as tourists, as temporary residents, and as *olim*. What a combination! But orders are orders, and he had no alternative but to obey. He was relieved that the matter was resolved even though he did not agree with the solution.

Before Gershom informed Blackwell of the government's decision, he was overwhelmed by the urge to set the record straight with Blackwell. He did not want him to feel that Israeli officials were naive and unaware of what was transpiring.

"There is no doubt, Mr. Blackwell," he said forthrightly, "no government official or ministry was advised of your friends' coming to Israel. If they had been, then the hassle stirred up yesterday and today would have been avoided. Certainly we would not have had to suffer through the past twenty-four hours for a hasty decision to be made.

"I just wanted you to know, Mr. Blackwell, that we are aware of what is afoot. Anyway, the government has decided to allow your people to enter the country." Gershom then filled in the details.

Blackwell felt restored. He was all smiles. Never had he expected the State to submit to his demand—not after his dialogue with Gershom. The brothers and sisters patted him on the back when he broke the news to them and they called him "Moses."

Gershom arranged all the details with dispatch and the blacks were on their way to Dimona.

It all happened so rapidly that the city fathers of Dimona were not apprised of what was taking place. Israel Navon, the Mayor of Dimona, remarked, "I arose in the morning and found them in my city. The municipality was not even notified of their coming."

The two-hour ride to Dimona began with an air of excitement. The people talked incessantly. They yelled to each other, laughed and joked. "I knew it. I knew it," one of the men kept repeating. It was a far cry from the despondency that had settled on them the day before. They had gained a foothold in the land; they had overcome. But would Israel be their permanent home? Would it be another Liberia? Better? Worse? Nothing could be as difficult as the two and one-half years in Liberia. But, then, even Liberia was better than racist America.

Gradually the women and children drifted off into fitful naps; the men stared into the dark countryside with watchful eyes, trying to absorb as much of the terrain as was visible. And as they stared into the night, they thought back to the "why" and the "when" of their leaving the United States. But for now, they had stormed the "gates of Jerusalem" and were looking forward to the future.

Chapter VII

TO CONVERT OR NOT TO CONVERT

Dimona, a heterogeneous, growing and dynamic factory town in the south of Israel southeast of Beersheba, proved to be an ideal site for settling the newly arrived American blacks from Liberia. Of its approximately 30,000 inhabitants, half had emigrated from North Africa, and the remainder included immigrants from India, America, Iran, Roumania, Poland, Hungary and Russia. In addition to their varied skin colors, each group came with its own language. Vast cultural differences abounded.

Composed as Dimona is of myriad elements, the American blacks encountered no hostility. Although they were a curiosity because of their colorful African clothing, the residents of the city accepted them immediately. They were truly overcome by the warm welcome and cooperative attitude that greeted them. Conditions were so amicable that it led a member of the group to state when interviewed, "It is wonderful to be in a free country and to be among one's own brothers who behave so kindly to you."

"That there is no discrimination in Dimona because of skin color," said Yehuda Yaffet, the Histadruth Secretary in charge of employment in Dimona, "is evident in how people marry." Dark-skinned residents from India marry light-skinned Roumanians, as do members of other immigrant groups. In fact, said Yaffet, the people of Dimona encourage the integrative process. They all place their children in the same schools, attaching no significance to their own place of origin or to the color of their skin. The Israelis have learned from settlement programs in other cities that immigrants from the same country should not be settled exclusively in one area. Such a situation perpetuates the living conditions and social problems that had prevailed in the countries from which they came. It hinders the integrative process. To encourage people to adapt quickly to life in Israel, immigrants are dispersed throughout the country and are intermingled throughout the towns in which they are settled. In this way, adults and children learn to understand each other and to compromise with each other, which encourages and promotes the assimilation process.

Photographers sought them out and reporters interviewed them frequently about their relationship to the original ten lost tribes of Israel. They were the focus of attention and greatly enjoyed being in the limelight. Things were looking better for them with each passing day.

Soon, however, they slipped into the routine life of the city and photographers and reporters came less often to quiz them on their views concerning the Creator and about other subjects that would interest their readers.

Their eight or ten apartments and furnishings were of the same standard received by all immigrants, and whatever else was provided them was on a par with that of most Israelis. "They had received much better housing in Israel than they had dreamed of, they said."[1] They were given immigration certificates, working permits, and *tipul* cards. They attended Hebrew courses, and their children did well in school though they had to do their homework in Hebrew. Nor did prejudice impinge on Dimona from other parts of the country. The Tel Aviv labor exchange offered jobs and housing to two members of the group. The offer was declined, however, because it meant moving to Tel Aviv and they wanted to stay with their brothers in Dimona.

As soon as they were settled, they sponsored a "Soul Festival" to enable the people to get better acquainted with them and to help them raise some needed funds. It was a gala event. The program included a sing-along and each member of the group who possessed any kind of talent performed. One of the blacks spoke to the audience in halting Hebrew. A Tel Aviv group provided music and Indian immigrants danced to the sitar. There was also a fashion show, and young and old modeled handmade African garb. It was a "sort of hello," said El Kannan, a leading member of the group.[2] Their neighbors enjoyed the performance and made them feel even more welcome. No Israelis were yet aware of the black Americans' newly evolved belief that the country belonged to them.

Although their absorption and adjustment were proceeding well, the problem of their Jewishness remained. This was a crucial issue. It needed to be clarified if they were to receive the rights of *olim*. Consequently, they were open-mindedly requested by the government to prove their Jewishness. In this regard, they were again treated like everybody else in their position.

The request made of the blacks was not related in any way to their social level, said Dr. Joseph Burg, the new Minister of the Interior. Cave-dwelling Jews from North Africa were brought into the country and the Israelis felt a compelling responsibility to accept them as *olim* under the Law of Return and to assist them. When an authentic Jew comes to Israel, he must be helped. This is their debt to him, the Israelis say, and they accept this responsibility without equivocation.

When immigrants are not Jews, the State feels it has no special obligation to them. It need not assume additional sacrificial burdens on their behalf when it is already over-burdened by the heavy task of absorbing true Jews who are settling in the country out of necessity. Nevertheless, said Dr. Burg, although not one Israeli believed then that the American blacks were Jews, Israel gave them housing, work, food, medical attention, and other things as needed. Moshe Shapiro, the Minister of the Interior in 1969 when the blacks came from Liberia, had set the tone when he said that a nation of refugees must treat others with compassion. If anything, color was in their favor and it made the Israeli authorities more liberal in their attitude. Admitting them into Israel was a purely humane act to meet human needs.

It was quite conceivable that they might be able to establish their claim to Jewishness even though none of the government officials had ever heard of a Liberian Jewish community. Had the blacks been able to provide the necessary proof, the question would have been resolved then and there. Unable to do this, the problem was further compounded by the fact that members of their group are not accepted as true Jews by the Jewish community in the country of their origin—the United States.

In addition, a Hebrew law commonly referred to as the principle of presumption, operated against them.[3] From the earliest times, the Jewish community had been known to be composed of white-skinned people. This fact led to the recognized doctrine of presumption. When a white person claims to be a Jew, he is accepted as such unless there is reason to doubt the validity of his claim, as with the Samaritans in Israel and the Karaites. Thus, a Caucasian immigrant who comes to Israel and identifies himself as Jewish is accepted as such unless there is grave suspicion about his claim. This was the case, for instance, with Father Daniel, a white-skinned Catholic priest who was born of a Jewish mother and wished to enter Israel as an immigrant under the Law of Return. Another example concerns a group of people who saw themselves as Jews while they believed in the divinity of Jesus. All were denied admission into the country under this law. Conversely, a person of black or yellow skin is not accepted as a Jew because no such presumption can be made about him, unless the group from which he comes has a documented history of being Jewish and an association with the Jewish people, as did the Yemenites, the B'nai Israel of Cochin-China, and others. All people, however, regardless of original faith or skin color, can become fully accepted as Jews if they formally embrace the Jewish faith by conversion.

Modern support for this principle comes from Robert Coleman, a black who converted to Judaism some years ago after serving as a minister of a Baptist church. He later functioned as Director of the Division of Social Justice for the Synagogue

Council of America and is president of *Taharas Yisrael* (Purity of Israel), an organization concerned with the claims of American blacks identifying themselves as Jews. Coleman claims that "there is not one genuine Black synagogue or rabbi" in the United States, and that most members of groups composed of American blacks who call themselves Jews have "no legitimate claim to Jewishness whatever." Writing in *The Jewish Observer*,[4] he asserts that the only blacks who are true Jews are those who have formally embraced Judaism by converting to the faith. Those who call themselves Jews because they are black and trace their origin to the early Hebrews are spurious.

Coleman maintains that the leaders of black Jewish groups "have perpetuated nothing short of fraud on their unsuspecting black followers, as well as those of the Jewish community who have given sympathy and support to their Black brothers." He feels it is imperative that the question of the Jewishness of the blacks be settled once and for all. The uncertainty of their status and the conflict of claims can be harmful emotionally to black youngsters who are taught by their parents and the members of their groups that they are Jews, while the Jewish community as such reads them out of the faith. Besides, he adds, this furor is unnerving to the Jewish people too.

In similar vein, Coleman's attitude is applicable to the consequences of the unclear position of the Israel government toward the Black Hebrews. Its indecisiveness is causing concern among genuine black American Jews and Falashas, lest Israel's differences with the Black Hebrews boomerang against them. Furthermore, the Black Hebrews are harrassing the Falashas in Israel calling them Uncle Toms and traitors for following the white man's religion.[5] It is therefore imperative that the government arrive at a decision soon with regard to this sensitive matter.

On the other hand, Rabbi Wolfe Kelman, executive vice-president of the Rabbinical Assembly of America, the organization of the Conservative rabbinate, argues "there is no need to assume there is any question of (the black Jew's) Jewishness. If he says he is Jewish, he should be accepted as such, unless evidence contrary to his claim is presented." His position is diametrically opposed to the traditional principle of presumption and Robert Coleman's support of it. Rabbi Kelman feels that assumptions regarding an individual's religious affiliation should not be made on the basis of color. "There is no *halachah* that applies to Black or white people only." If this should be the case, then the *halachah* is "racist." The Jewishness of some black Jews may be open to question, but it does not hold true for every black Jew. Every person must be considered individually "in the context of his personal history."

Coleman's response to Rabbi Kelman is that *halachah*, not race, determines Jewish status.[6] Whenever any individual's status as a Jew is suspect, and he can furnish no proof to support his claim, then *halachah* requires that he undergo conversion if he wishes to be regarded as a Jew. He agrees with Kelman, however, that each individual should be treated on his own merits, as with the blacks who came to Israel from Liberia and a white group from Italy. The Israeli rabbinate required that each individual submit supporting evidence for his own claim. Should they be unable to do that, they must undergo conversion.

Rabbi Moshe Sherer, executive president of *Agudath Israel*, a very traditional group within Orthodox Judaism, took strong issue with Rabbi Kelman averring that his charge of racism against *halachah* was "insulting and totally devoid of substance." Such an accusation, he claimed, can only inflame passion and distort the issue. Rabbi Sherer reiterated Coleman's premise that *halachic* proof is the only method by which black Jews can authenticate their Jewish identity.[7]

Rabbi J. David Bleich,[8] Professor of Philosophy and Talmud at Yeshiva University, which supplies rabbinic leadership to most American-born Orthodox Jews, is of the same mind. Judaism is color blind in determining the status of black Jews, he asserts. The crucial problem is that of Jewish identity which involves the all-encompassing question of "Who is a Jew?" and is intimately associated with the problem of Jewish survival. Thus, the sole pertinent factor concerning the status of black Jews is whether they have a valid claim to Jewish identity through birth or conversion.

In pursuit of this view, Coleman founded an interracial synagogue in the Crown Heights section of Brooklyn, New York, in September 1975,[9] consisting mostly of black converts to Judaism. He insists that most black Americans who claim to be Jews and who have established congregations lack *halachic* validity. His congregation, he said, is the only one with black members that meets *halachic* requirements since every adult member who is a convert had been converted by an Orthodox rabbi. The *halachic* authority of the congregation, since it has no rabbinical leadership, is Rabbi Bleich.

Blacks contend that the reason the *halachah* imposes restrictions upon them is that the *halachah* is white oriented. For instance, the *Shulchan Aruch*, the traditional code of Jewish law, was formulated by white people and blacks had no hand in developing it. *Halachah* is thus viewed as a white conspiracy to exclude blacks from their "rightful heritage." But such a claim is self-defeating. If white Jews had devised *halachah*, then the early Jews could not have been black, since Hebrew law has been in the process of formulation for thousands of years.

The literature of various black cults is replete with anti-Semitism and black supremacy themes, Coleman claims. They allege that they alone are the "original Jews" and accuse white Jews of "stealing their religion," asserting they emanate from sundry foreign sources. Yet, continues Coleman, these same men who unhesitatingly assail white Jews freely appeal to the white Jewish community for financial help. And they get it—from individuals and from the organized Jewish community, especially in New York City and Chicago which have the two largest black Jewish communities in the United States. They have also received, as outright gifts, Torahs and fully equipped synagogues, or have been able to purchase them for nominal sums. Furthermore, said Coleman, some black children are accepted as students in *Yeshivot* (Jewish parochial schools) and *Talmud Torahs* (Hebrew schools) even though they are not true Jews. The leadership is aware of this, but the schools do not want to be accused of prejudice. He bewails the fact that true black converts to Judaism are threatened with bodily harm by parents and group leaders if they say that wearing a *yarmulke* (skullcap) and *tzitzit* (a fringed shawl undergarment) does not make a black Jewish child.

Since the State of Israel operates in accordance with traditional law, Israeli officials presumed the American blacks were not Jews and mistrusted their claim that they are the offspring of the ancient Hebrew exiles. Nevertheless, they permitted the blacks to enter the country and even extended to them special privileges. Humanitarian consideration was involved as well as the concern that the country might be vilified as racist if the blacks were deported. Besides, they reasoned, the blacks would soon weary of residing in Israel, as they had of Liberia, and would leave the country on their own. Then no one could accuse Israel of being racist.

To bring the matter to a head, Joseph Geva, the Minister of Absorption, dispatched Rabbi Dar-ee to investigate their claim that they were Hebrews and to discuss conversion with them, if necessary.

The Rabbi undertook the mission with enthusiasm, as he had done about two years earlier when he investigated the Jewishness of Hezekiah Blackwell and the five others who arrived in Israel in 1968. Anxious to bring these "lost sheep of Israel" back into the fold, he visited them and they visited him.

The Rabbi was disappointed by the outcome of his mission. As with Blackwell, he reported the blacks were not Jews. With each conference it became more evident that their Jewishness had no relationship to Hebrew law. In addition to the differences in customs, some admitted they had been baptized as Christians and that they came to Judaism as a result of reading the *Tanach*, the Hebrew Bible, and Jewish history in their search for the true faith. Even then, Rabbi Dar-ee was prepared to recommend a *giyur chelki*, a partial conversion. However, they rejected his counsel.

Geva then went to Dimona to personally explain to the blacks that since their Jewishness was unsubstantiated, they should convert to Judaism in order to benefit from the rights of immigrants under the Law of Return. Otherwise, he explained, permission to work would be withdrawn and their status would revert to that of aliens.

They were in a dilemma. Why must they convert? They

were Hebrew Israelites, direct descendants of the Hebrew Patriarchs, who had returned to the land of their ancestors. "What will I convert to or from?" asked El Kannan. "I am a Hebrew. I have been a Hebrew all my life. Why should I convert to what I already am?"

In the meantime, two incidents occurred that cast even greater doubt on their claim to Jewishness. The League for Aiding Proselytes went to Dimona on Purim[10] to welcome the new black immigrants, to inquire about their needs and to bring them and their children *shalach manot* (gifts of food). This is a traditional practice of the Purim celebration. The members of the League were greeted by the women, who soon disappeared, and they met with about a dozen of the male members.

When the visitors explained their mission to the blacks, they did not know what Purim was and had no idea what *shalach manot* meant. When the holiday was explained to them and the Biblical source was shown to them, they asked to be excused from accepting gifts of food because they observed their own dietary restrictions.[11]

The second incident that added doubt to the black Americans' claim of being Jewish occurred when visitors asked a few black 15 and 16-year-olds their religion. The young people replied, "Protestant," and then volunteered that they were not religious and had never attended a synagogue service.

Nevertheless, despite their claim that they were original Jews, they continued to consult with Dar-ee and reluctantly acceded to the Rabbi's suggestion that they convert on the ground that it would be to their own benefit to formally adopt Judaism. Thereupon a number of the arrivals opened conversion portfolios with the Rabbinate. "We felt they wanted to assimilate themselves as quickly as possible in the country," one of their friends said.

A number of Israelis disagreed with the tactic adopted by the government officials. The government had committed a serious blunder, they felt; it had erred in judgment. Since the government knew they were not Jews, as Interior Minister Burg had admitted, then the officials had no right to give them immigration certificates and immigrants' rights. But having done so, they had led the immigrants from Liberia to believe that they had been accepted as Jews. It was unreasonable, the Israelis felt, to demand their conversion now. Having made a mistake, they contended, the State should live with it. With as many minorities as there were in the country, Israel could surely absorb one more small group.

With this see-sawing of opinion within the country, an unnamed official involved in handling the matter concerning the blacks was critical of the government's policy of "wait and see" in such matters. The State needed a firm and immediate policy to avoid similar occurrences, he said. If the government did not take necessary measures, he was convinced the State would be confronted with many other serious problems to its own detriment. He counselled that Israel halt the unacceptable practice of giving immigrant privileges to tourists, especially to people whose Jewishness is problematical. As he put it, they were not tourists and not immigrants; not-Jews and yes-Jews.[12]

Time soon proved him to be correct. In March 1970, three months after the 39 had arrived, word reached the government that Ben Ammi Carter, the *Moreh Tzedek*, the Righteous Teacher of the American blacks in Liberia, was planning to come to Israel with another group. Their pattern of moving into Israel was similar to their earlier migration into Liberia—by stages.

On the recommendation of Rabbi Dar-ee, the Israeli officials advised Carter by letter not to come with his group directly to Israel. Rabbi Dar-ee wanted those with whom he was working to convert before Carter arrived. The officials suggested that he and his followers go to an immigrants' camp in Marseilles and convert to Judaism there. Then they could enter Israel as authentic Jews and be entitled to all the benefits of *olim*. Carter's reply was bitter in its rejection. Quoting Hillel, the ancient Jewish sage, he wrote back, "What is hateful to thee do not do to your neighbor."

One day that month, according to Aryeh Shmerlik of Dimona's Absorption Center, the atmosphere among the blacks in the city was charged with expectation. The blacks made changes in their work schedules, and the officials were unable to figure out what was brewing. By nightfall the matter was clarified. The brothers and sisters of Dimona had gone to the Lod Airport to welcome Carter and his fellow travellers.[13]

Again Israeli officials were caught on the horns of a dilemma. How should they handle the newest black arrivals? The determination had already been made that they were not Jews and were thus not entitled to enter the country under the Law of Return. At best, they might be regarded as a "Mosaic sect which is close to Judaism." But this was not sufficient reason to merit permission to enter the country. When, however, the arrivals claimed to be the fathers and husbands of Black Hebrews living in Dimona, they forced the government's hands. It did not want to be accused of breaking up families, even though in some instances the claim was suspect.[14] Weren't Jews using the claim of reuniting families as a reason for emigrating from Russia and other countries? Thereupon the officials permitted the blacks to enter Israel as tourists, but were not given housing or work permits as were the earlier arrivals.

Undeterred, Carter and 47 of his devotees joined the earlier arrivals in their apartments in Dimona. This brought their number to 92 and caused considerable over-crowding.

Despite his erratic performance, Carter had maintained his leadership role and continued to exert a powerful influence on the Hebrew Israelites. Joseph Lapid, senior editor of Israel's leading daily, *Maariv*, attributes his effectiveness not so much to his ability as to the primitive state of social development within the group. Although some of the group members were on a higher economic and social level, they lacked patterns of organization. Having floundered since 1967 outside the United States—and all their lives in the United States—the Hebrew Israelites were dependent on his control and authority, Lapid suggests.

Once again, the unclear position of the Ministry of Absorption and the Ministry of the Interior facilitated the entry of the blacks into the country, giving rise to a truly ambiguous situation. Three sets of members of the same group arrived at the airport and each was treated differently. Responsibility for this inconsistent behavior had to be placed somewhere. The recognized practice, an official explained, was as follows: First the Ministry of the Interior was to stamp the passport with the appropriate seal and then the Ministry of Absorption handled the immigrants. "If the Lubavitcher Rebbe came to Israel," said a member of Absorption, "we would not begin to handle his absorption as long as he did not have an immigrant's certificate from the Ministry of the Interior." Mysteriously, something went awry. How had it happened? Since most of the communication was handled via the telephone, it caused misunderstanding to be heaped upon misunderstanding with contradictory results. This blundering may have suggested to blacks in the United States that one can start a new life in Israel with comparative ease and thus motivated some of them to go to Israel.

Realizing that another error had been committed as a result of inaction, government officials were especially eager for the blacks to convert. If the conversion issue were settled, the pressure would be off them and the rights of *olim* with its benefits would accrue to the blacks. Their integration would be facilitated. When the proposal was presented to Carter, he retorted that he and his followers would first examine the Talmud and the rabbinical laws and would then decide whether or not to submit to conversion.

Isaiah Winters, Carter's kinsman and former clerk in the Chicago Post Office, expressed it this way: "I was a soccer player in America. I played American style. Should I be asked if I know how to play soccer, I would reply, 'Positively!' But if I were sent to play Israeli soccer—I would be lost. I would be totally confused.

"So it is with conversion. I know how to play soccer—I am a Hebrew. But I do not know how to play your soccer—your Judaism. Give me time to contemplate, to study, and then decide if I want to play."[15]

Like the Karaites of old, the Black Hebrews accepted only the laws written in the Torah (the Pentateuch or the Five Books of Moses), but not the additions and interpretations Jewish sages have later promulgated. They knew nothing about rabbinic Judaism. Neither *halachah* nor the *Talmud*

had any validity for them, nor did any other Hebrew literature, for that matter. The Bible was all-encompassing, they
said. No one had the right to add to or subtract from the
Torah, Carter asserted. Notwithstanding, the Black Hebrews
were selective. They did not adhere to all the commandments
in the Torah, but chose what they wished to observe and
ignored the rest. Furthermore, asserting they would first study
the *Talmud* and rabbinic writings before deciding on whether
to convert was a dodge. Since they did not accept these
writings as valid, studying them would have no influence on
the blacks.

At an assembly of Black Hebrews in Dimona where Carter
was the only speaker, they agreed unanimously not to convert.
All their lives, Carter told the Israelis, they had served God in
one way and now they were being told to change their religious practices. To convert would constitute a rejection of
their tradition and belief that they are the true Israelites. As a
result, those Hebrew Israelites who had already started the
conversion process instructed Rabbi Dar-ee to close their files.
Winters, who had earlier decided to study toward conversion,
was one of them. Whatever progress Rabbi Dar-ee had made
to bring the Black Hebrews to the status of full immigrants,
and all the assistance Sonya Peletz had rendered, were suddenly aborted. The problem that had been laid at the doorstep
of the government of Israel months ago was thus intensified.

Carter contended that the earlier arrivals had not intended
to convert. Rabbi Dar-ee, however, had records to support
his position that they did. It is further reported that the Rabbi
had sent two religious teachers to Dimona to give them instruction.[16] El Kannan Ben Israel, who was Carter's assistant
in Liberia and was now one of the Twelve Princes in their
movement in Israel, attempted to mediate the conflict. He
explained that because of the friendly relationship that prevailed between the blacks and Rabbi Dar-ee, the Rabbi assumed they were going to convert, but that they never
publicly declared that they would.

El Kannan's well-intentioned efforts, however, were futile
since Rabbi Dar-ee was actually working with the blacks
toward this end and had promised them every assistance to

speed their acceptance as Jews by Israel. When El Kannan was pressed[17] as to why, if his explanation were correct, they had misled the Rabbi into believing they were going to convert, he bowed his head in silence.

Carter freely admitted some of his followers had been baptized in churches. How could they, therefore, claim to be Jews? The Jewish community in the United States, he explained, does not accept the Black Hebrews as belonging to the body of the Jewish people. But, in order to be a part of American society, one had to belong to a church. Baptism, or attending a church, does not disqualify anyone from belonging to the Hebrew people, he said. The important thing was whether the person accepted Judaism as his faith. All of his followers did just that, and they observed strictly the *mitzvot* (commandments) of the *Torah*. Consequently, they belong to the Hebrew people despite their baptism. He dismissed as unimportant the differences in their observance of the *mitzvot*.

Here again, Carter was entangled in his own rhetoric. He claimed the blacks were Hebrews by nationality, not by religion. Yet, he argued, because his followers accepted Judaism as their religion, they could not be ruled out of the Jewish people.

Carter and his adherents also discarded the traditional concept of community as expressed in public worship. Every family prayed at home, so they had no need of a *minyan* (a quorum of ten people for public worship), though they did have public services in Liberia. They did not drink or smoke, and some of the men had two wives. Carter himself was reputed to have two families in Israel.

With the arrival of Carter in Israel, the amicable relationship that existed between the Black Hebrews and the residents of Dimona underwent a marked change. Where there had been cooperation, disharmony increased and conflict erupted. Carter alienated many of their friends. Even when Dimona's spiritual leader, Rabbi Elmaliach, attempted on numerous occasions to become involved with them, unofficially, the group was unresponsive.

Carter had an abrasive personality which had already manifested itself in Chicago. He had several unhappy encounters there with the Jewish community and its leaders. He proposed a number of projects to them through Rabbi Ralph Simon of Congregation Rodfei Zedek, which continues to function in the south side of Chicago where many blacks reside. Each project called for the Jewish community to give him huge sums of money.

Rabbi Simon tells of Carter coming to him with a proposal that he open a kosher delicatessen. Determining that the idea had merit, the Rabbi put Carter in touch with a committee of small businessmen organized by the Jewish Federation of Metropolitan Chicago to assist people going into small businesses. Not only did the group offer some financial help, but it provided practical advice from people successfully engaged in the type of business under consideration. Thus, the new entrepreneur received the benefit of experience, assistance in the purchase of furniture and fixtures at fair and reasonable cost, advice concerning businesses with whom to open accounts, and in Carter's specific case, where to purchase the meats he would sell, and on what terms. Upon examining Carter's proposed expenditures, the committee found them to be excessively high in each category. But most unreasonable was his demand that the Jewish community give him personally all the money he had requested. They refused. Later, Carter told Rabbi Simon that he had scrubbed the idea because the advisory committee pried too much into his business. They insisted on being kept fully informed and Carter would have none of that. He refused to be subservient to anyone, he exclaimed.

Another of his proposals was to establish a *kibbutz* in Liberia and he spoke with Rabbi Simon about the plan. This project coincided with his plan for the members of his congregation to move to Africa. He estmiated the cost at $750,000 and he asked Rabbi Simon to get the Chicago Jewish community to finance their emigration. In return for their support, Carter promised there would be less trouble between blacks and Jews. His proposition had all the earmarks of blackmail.

"If you are a Jew," the Rabbi said to him, "why don't you go to Israel rather than to Africa?" Carter replied, "I am also a black man and I must establish my blackness. I'm going to Africa." When the Rabbi offered him a token contribution explaining it would be impossible to raise the amount he requested, Carter refused the money and stalked out in anger.

Carter's interest in material benefits continued unabated. He had angled for monetary assistance from the Liberian government and evinced the same attitude in Israel. Although he accepted money from the Ministry of Immigration Absorption in Israel, he refused to discuss conversion, upbraiding the officials, "Don't be like the rich man giving alms to the poor and asking for their souls in return."[18]

The government officials, Rabbi Dar-ee, Joseph Lapid and others were convinced that Carter lacked sincerity and that his motivation was personal. Should he and the group convert, they would become adherents to traditional Judaism. Carter would be stripped of his authority over his followers and prohibited from promulgating his own rules and interpretations. The Israeli rabbinate would not regard him as a religious leader since he had neither the education nor the proper credentials. Lest he be deprived of his constituency, he stubbornly maintained there was no need for his followers to convert. They were Hebrew Israelites, he said. It was a national designation, quite different than the term "Jew" which is a religious designation.

Rabbi Dar-ee foresaw nothing but trouble and additional problems resulting from the arrival of the last group of blacks. When the earlier blacks came, he was a true friend to them and was instrumental in breaking down the hostility of the rabbinate against them. Carter's presence, the Rabbi admitted dejectedly, had altered the situation. He began to doubt the seriousness of the entire group. They became more materialistic and contradicted their earlier contentions. Whereas they had originally claimed they wanted to study Judaism as it is practiced in Israel, they later said they would select those aspects of the faith they would accept. If they really wanted to study Judaism, he said, "they would come to me and I would guide them with all my heart." In spite of all that he and Sonya Peletz had done, the group now refused to have anything to do with them.

Rabbi Dar-ee says he suggested to the Ministry of the Interior that no more Black Hebrews be permitted to enter the country unless they converted prior to arrival. And as far as he knew, the Ministry accepted his recommendation.

Despite the existing state of affairs, the government still took no action to prevent the situation from recurring. The "wait and see" policy remained.

Chapter VIII

THE GATHERING STORM

A wonderful atmosphere pervaded Dimona when the blacks first arrived. The neighbors of the blacks in *Shikun Nitzachon*, the apartment complex in which they lived, agreed the relationship was first-rate. They believed Ben Ammi Carter was earnest when he said soon after he arrived, "We do not want complications. We are anxious for one thing: that you understand that we love the country, that we want to be good citizens, to be friends with everybody." The Dimonians agreed they conducted themselves in upstanding fashion. Their manners, politeness and industriousness were beyond reproach. Their women were pleasant and modest.[1] When Israel Independence Day was observed, they participated in the celebration with a band and vocalist. "They sang 'We Have Returned to Jericho' with such enthusiasm," said one of the inhabitants, "that we sensed they seriously meant it." Their performance was one of the main attractions at the observance.

But after they had been in Dimona for only a few weeks, the pendulum of public opinion began to swing in the opposite direction. Their very first interview with a newspaper reporter about two weeks after they arrived, incurred the wrath of Liberian officials in Israel. When asked about their stay in Liberia, they complained the Liberian government gave them paltry assistance and even less advice on how to cope with the climatic conditions and the terrain. They were especially crit-

133

ical that some of their people were denied work because they refused to work on the Sabbath at Lamco.[2] It was then they decided that Liberia "was not the Holy Land to which Jews traditionally yearned to return, just a stop-off."[3]

When the interview appeared in *The Jerusalem Post*, Milt Greaves, the Liberian Public Information Officer, happened to be in Jerusalem. Angered by what they said, he wrote a blistering letter to the "Readers Letters" section of the newspaper,[4] and denied vigorously the slur against his country. He expressed shock at "the absurd claims" made by the "American Negroes who recently arrived in Israel, that they left Liberia because it is 'hard to be a Jew' in Liberia." They thus implied, he said, that in their search "of a life free from discrimination" they were disappointed "at not finding it in Liberia." Pointing to the Liberian Constitution, he wrote that it "guarantees complete . . . freedom of worship. In addition, it is illegal to practice discrimination in Liberia and there are stringent laws against it."

Greaves' anger could well be understood for the Constitution does state: "All persons demeaning themselves peaceably, and not obstructing others in their religious worship, are entitled to the protection of the law, in the free exercise of their religion; and no sect of Christians shall have exclusive privileges or preferences over any other sect, but all shall be alike tolerated."[5]

Greaves was so irate at the American blacks that in his letter to the newspaper he went beyond merely refuting the charges against Liberia. He wrote that the Liberian government gave the black Jews "free housing for three months, free land at a place of their choice upon which to build and live, and set up a special commission to help them assimilate and get adjusted in so far as jobs are concerned. The plea then, as now, was that they came looking for a place 'free from discrimination.' I know this for a fact because I attended several Presidential press conferences in Monrovia at which the 'Black Jews' problems were discussed and dealt with.

"It might interest you to know that after nearly three years, most of these self-styled Black Jews have not bothered to find jobs or in any way improve their lot.

"For this and many other reasons, the Attorney-General of Liberia recently issued an expulsion order against the Chicagoans who, after nearly three years, still had no visible means of support. The order was stayed by the President, however, so as to give the immigrants still another chance. Apparently those who came to Israel think they will live on 'Easy Street' here. They are going to be surprised when they find out that the Israelis, too, work hard."[6]

To further discredit their claim, Greaves said, "Liberian offices are closed on Saturday, and Seventh Day Adventists, because of their particular religious convictions, are not required to work on the Sabbath."[7] To claim discrimination when there was none was a poor way for them to justify their failure in Liberia, Greaves felt.

Greaves made still another scathing comment about them. When they arrived in Liberia, "they stated that there were others in Chicago interested in coming to Liberia. The basis of identification then was that we were 'all black soul brothers' who had to stand together. The basis of identification in Israel is probably that they and the Israelis are religious soul brothers. When they discovered that Liberia, a developing country, could ill afford parasites merely because they were 'soul brothers,' they decided to seek greener pastures. The logical place was Israel. Where they will go next is a little harder to determine."[8]

Despite the public airing the matter received, the blacks withstood Greaves's onslaught. The Israelis turned neither from them nor on them. From then on, the blacks ceased referring to their Liberian experience. When asked about it, they pretended they had not heard the question or shifted the conversation to another subject.

They were still confronted by the problem of authenticating their Jewishness. When Carter convinced the earlier entrants to halt the conversion process, the relationship between the blacks and the government became strained. Though many Israelis still sided with them, the blacks lived in limbo. Enraged that they were denied the benefits of the Law of Return which they claimed were rightfully theirs, black leaders made intemperate public pronouncements and engaged in ill-conceived actions that made the burdens of the Black Hebrews heavier.

Anxious to be legitimatized, the Black Hebrews attempted to circumvent the Israeli Rabbinate and the Ministry of the Interior by issuing their own "Certificate of Nationality." Signed by Ben Ammi, Carter, L. A. Bryant, and a third person,[9] the document averred that the individual named thereon was "born an Israelite." In this way, the Black Hebrews aimed to achieve the status of legal immigrants without converting. All that they did accomplish, however, was to antagonize friends without altering their status. While not all Israelis are religiously observant, and some would have the government limit the authority of the Rabbinate over certain areas of their personal lives, rabbinic jurisdiction over the question of who is a Jew is generally accepted. Here was an illustration of how far removed the Black Hebrews were from the "Jewish way of doing things."

This was one in a long series of blunders, errors in judgment, and outright viciousness the leaders of the Black Hebrews practiced. Comparing Israel to the United States, they were convinced that by indulging in proscribed antics, they would bring Israel to its knees. When American authorities are confronted by demands from segments of the population, regardless of how outlandish the demands may be, the officials are usually ready to compromise, even to yield totally. They were confident Israel would react similarly because of its delicate and sensitive position among the nations of the world, especially the Third World nations.

But they were mistaken. Israel stood firm against their demands, and it was the Black Hebrews who were compelled to retreat. Their actions alienated their followers from the sympathies of the Israeli populace and weakened still further their precarious presence in the country.

All the while, many blacks infiltrated Israel illegally from various parts of the United States. Arriving singly, they attracted no attention, went directly to Dimona and moved in with the families already living there. It soon became difficult to determine the number of Black Hebrews in the city. According to municipal officials, by 1971 the unofficial tally had climbed to about 250, while the blacks themselves claimed it had risen to 500 with thousands more on the way. Their apartments became overcrowded, with reports that as many as 16 people occupied a one-bedroom flat. Gabriel Katan, one of the blacks and father of two children, told a reporter that three additional families lived in his apartment, with others occupying bathrooms, balconies, shower rooms, emergency shelters, "wherever it is possible to put a mattress."[10] Carter said 350 people were sharing 19 flats in Dimona.[11] The local residents couldn't explain how it all came about, but the uncomfortable fact was that the complexion of the community had changed so much that many found it difficult to continue to live in the city.

Serious health, social and behavioral problems develop when people with no income are without comfort and privacy. They become nervous and angry, foment trouble, and disturb the peace of the community.

By ignoring the laws of the country, the blacks in Dimona interfered with the government's plans for improving housing. The officials were upset because it was obvious to them that the blacks were transplanting to Israel the sub-standard living conditions they had endured in the United States and Liberia. They were disturbed because of the seemingly stubborn desire of the blacks to foster unwholesome living in their country.

Adding to the unreality of the situation was their secretiveness. The blacks would not talk to strangers or allow themselves to be photographed. The men warned reporters not to talk to their wives or children. If they wanted information, the reporters were told to contact the group spokesmen, Ben Ammi Carter or Hezekiah Blackwell.

The tension that this attitude produced in the city was demonstrated one day when neither Carter nor Blackwell was seen in Dimona. The non-black residents began to whisper about their whereabouts. Before long a rumor circulated that they had gone to the airport to bring additional black newcomers to the city. The residents were conditioned to expect such a possibility because Carter long had threatened to inundate the country with millions of blacks within the next six years. He had warned that "maybe two million, maybe many more" would come from the United States to wrest Israel away from the Jewish inhabitants, for the Lord had "personally ordered (him) to take possession of Israel."[12]

Asiel Ben Israel likewise boasted at a conference in 1971 in America that more than 1,500 black Americans already were living in Israel and more would be coming by the plane load to "run out the Europeans."[13] All white Jews, Carter declared, would be deported to the countries from which they came to Israel—Germany, Poland, Morocco or elsewhere—to make room for the new black arrivals. A special exception, however, would be made for those born in Israel. They would be permitted to remain in the country, but would be expected to join the blacks and adopt their practices.

El Kannan fanned the flames when he proclaimed that the Black Hebrews had come "to liberate Israel from the false Jews—the white Jews." The founders of the modern State of Israel had deceived the people of the world, he claimed, by declaring they were the descendants of the people of the Bible. This is impossible, he said, since all the early Hebrews had black skins. The people in that section of the world have skins of various hues, but none are white. Only blacks, therefore, can be authentic Jews, he said. The Black Hebrews are thus not hesitant in invoking the post-Biblical principle of presumption—in reverse. Since they assume that Abraham, Isaac and Jacob were black, they presume that authentic Hebrews must also be black. White people cannot be Hebrews because they do not have a genetic connection with blacks.

Apparently El Kannan and others who claimed that the original Jews were black were not aware that the peoples of the Middle East and in countries of Africa north of the Sahara Desert, which includes Egypt, belong to the European or Caucasoid (white) race. Their skins are of lighter hue and are not part of the African or Negroid (black) race, which is a collection of related races in Africa south of the Sahara.[14] The effort by the Black Hebrews to locate "the land of Canaan-Israel" geographically in "Northeast Africa"[15] and thus claim that its inhabitants were black, is futile. Even if Palestine were joined to Africa as they claim, it is situated in that part of the continent where the people are regarded as European, not

African. The Patriarchs were not blacks nor were the Israelites who dwelled in Egypt. Racially they are classified as European or Caucasoid, while American Negroes are mostly of African origin.

Soon thereafter, a black spokesman prophesied that if the country were not turned over to them, all the plagues that befell Pharoah would be visited upon the Israelis and Russia would destroy the country.[16] And when another black leader declared publicly, "We do not need visas; we came at the command of the Lord," he sorely tried the patience of the Israelis. "We may let the Jews stay in the country," he said magnanimously, "if they come to terms with us. We have 15 million adherents in the United States and about two million of them are preparing to immigrate."[17]

Israelis heard this and were afraid. It awakened within many, memories of centuries of Jewish wandering accompanied by fear and anxiety. The officials of Dimona were shocked and alarmed. Israel attracts various kinds of sects, "but never before have any staked out their claims, belligerently and threateningly, and offered nothing in return."[18] Although the city "did not get any advance notice," Mayor Israel Navon said, the people of Dimona had welcomed the blacks graciously and had extended themselves on their behalf despite the unusualness of their case. How disconcerting it was to see the blacks repay them in so dreadful a manner. The townspeople were so demoralized as a result of their statements that the Mayor felt obliged to warn the Foreign Ministry and the Ministry of the Interior that the city administration feared violence. The blacks were breeding instability. Something had to be done, Navon emphasized, because the situation "is like dynamite. It can explode one of these days."[19] In reply, the Foreign Ministry advised that it was fully aware of the problem and was attempting to resolve it.

The Israelis viewed the blustering statements by the blacks as an attempt to transform a pan-Negro nationalism into Jewish form. To the Israelis, Jewishness is more than a gesture.

In addition to national identity, Jewishness means the acceptance of the entire Jewish community as an historical, cultural and religious aggregate. When the blacks steadfastly refused to accept this view, the Israelis felt they were playing a game with Judaism to win a national home for themselves.

"No Israeli would exclude a Jew from Israel," an irritated Israel spokesman remarked, "but the Black Hebrews would do just that. They would exclude Jews only because they are white."

When these blacks left the United States, they vociferously denounced America as a practitioner of racial discrimination, he said. Yet they made racial discrimination their own overriding consideration in Israel. Surely they would have strengthened their position and portrayed themselves as more authentic if they had said, "We will all live here together."

Unlike American cosmopolitanism which often takes on an air of anti-Americanism, Israelis are frankly nationalistic, but not chauvinistic, he continued. They see nothing wrong with loving one's country and people, as long as it does not call for the extermination of others.

Joseph Lapid of *Maariv* explained that national feeling is similar to the family tie. Parents love their own children more than those of others. When a terrorist bomb explodes in a public place, Lapid readily admitted that his first thoughts are for the safety of his own wife and children. Similarly, he felt that Israel's first concern is itself. The nation cannot afford the luxury of giving first thoughts to others. Security, absorption and development, therefore, should take priority over a self-declared Jewish sect of Chicago blacks attempting to force itself upon the Jewish people. The Israelis, in fact, are concerned about humanity, Lapid insisted, citing the medical and agricultural assistance missions in African, Asian and South American countries. But when the country is threatened, as it has been continuously since its founding, and when Jews are in jeopardy in North Africa, South America, Middle Eastern countries and Russia, Israel must concentrate its energies and resources on the survival of the country and on the ingathering of Jews in need, Lapid said.

Carter, defending himself, denied that he ever made the statement that the Black Hebrews would drive the Jews out of the country. Reporters made it seem that he said that, but "it is a lie," he protested. He admitted, however, that he felt that Israel's present government would not last long because it was not a government of truth.

"We will not destroy the government by force of arms," he averred. "God will fight for us the same as He fought for Joshua and with a trumpet caused the walls of Jericho to topple. For it is said: 'Out of Zion shall go forth the law.' When a government of truth is established, relief and success will come to all the inhabitants of this country.

"The Palestinians? We will deal with them according to just law. But, neither will they be able to dwell in this land if they do not recognize our truth."[20]

To complicate matters further, the blacks in Dimona played music from early afternoon into the wee hours of the morning. In sharp contrast to their hard-working neighbors, most of the blacks had no routine to keep, so they played their musical instruments whenever the spirit moved them. The sounds overflowed their crowded apartments and were amplified by the bare stone and concrete structures in a treeless courtyard. One resident related that he was awakened frequently in the middle of his sleep by shattering noise from thunderous tambourines accompanied by guitars. He complained that he could not go back to sleep, and he needed his rest because he worked very hard with phosphates in Oran. "I didn't complain to the police," he said, "because it would accomplish nothing. Besides, why should I be the one to complain? Let the other neighbors do it."

Dudu Chered, a lad who lived in the same complex and who sometimes played with the dark-skinned children in the playground, said the same thing and was quite sad about it. "They make terrible noise at night," he related. "They sing and dance and this draws me to watch them through the window. Because of this, I am unable to concentrate in class during the day and the teacher is angry at me."[21]

"It is like living in a carnival," another resident complained. "We can't live this way." Still another neighbor who protested the loud music at 2:30 in the morning was told, "We're singing because we are happy to be in Israel." With a characteristic shrug she replied, "Why not during the day?"

Adding to the problem, black children ran noisily back and

forth in the courtyard and made it impossible for the residents to benefit from the hours set aside for afternoon rest. Through the open shutters of the apartments came the cries of children in their mothers' arms. No one, however, dared tell the children to quiet down or ask their parents to control them. Some described the scene as the visitation of a plague.

In a press release dated August 1971, the blacks called the Israelis racists who maintained "Jim Crow policies similar to what we left behind," impairing the weakened relationship still further. To substantiate this claim, El Kannan, a machinist with a background in architecture, said he was given a supervisor's job at a Dimona fiber works factory. When he reported for work, he found he was to supervise only members of his own group. El Kannan accused the foreman of discrimination, which the foreman denied. Unable to get the foreman to alter the situation, El Kannan and his men walked off the job.[22]

In another incident, about ten black women entered the Dimona supermarket and filled baskets with food worth hundreds of dollars. When they came to the check-out counter, they told the manager they had no money to pay for the food, and asked for credit. Shocked, the manager called the police and the blacks were persuaded to return the food. The blacks then claimed they were denied food because of racism.[23] Whenever they could not get what they wanted, they resorted to the cry "racial discrimination."

Carter explained the supermarket incident in the following way.[24] Every brother contributes a minimum of ten per cent of his earnings toward the support of the community. He can give more if he chooses, but it is voluntary. They were experiencing hard times. "Hunger lurked at the door," he said in a clear strong voice. They were not permitted to take jobs. If they did find work, they would be compelled to quit. So they decided to call attention to their plight and to put public pressure on the authorities, he said.

One day in October the leaders of the Black Hebrews sent their women into the supermarket to fill their baskets with food while the men waited outside to see what would happen. They also invited American reporters and photographers to observe what took place. The net effect, however, was not what they had intended. The newspapers described the incident as "an unsuccessful attempt at robbery by women." The authorities in Dimona did not say, Carter observed, "it is forbidden for people who live among us to go hungry." Instead, they declared, "the blacks are hungry. Hungry people are capable of anything. You must be on guard against them."

The Israelis resented the audacity of the blacks in calling American television cameramen to record the contrived incident. "The blacks aimed to hurt us in the eyes of the world," they complained bitterly. Since a bad press in the United States usually altered the position of American officials, the blacks assumed the unfavorable publicity would force the Israelis to become more amenable to their demands. The ploy did not work. As one Israeli put it, "Americans feel publicity is more important than substance. We do not."

To a degree, however, they were successful. At a convention in Rome, Egyptian socialists proclaimed publicly that the Black Hebrews who were being expelled from their homes in the Jewish state would be welcome in Egypt.[25]

Mayor Navon reported that the day before the supermarket incident, some black families met with him to work out details to improve their situation. They astounded him by requesting a welfare dole, the distribution of free food, and other kinds of assistance on a continuing basis, similar to what some had received in the United States. Predictably, Mayor Navon refused. Apparently it was then that the blacks decided upon the supermarket ploy.

During another discussion with the Dimona Mayor, they requested that he ask The Jewish Agency to grant them permission to establish an agricultural settlement in the *Negev* so they could grow their own food. They then swamped the offices with petitions and announced openly, "If you will give us land, we will establish our own settlement." They even proposed to "relinquish immediately our apartments in Dimona" if this were done. They claimed to have spoken about it with a representative of Golda Meir. Before a reply came, some of them started to build houses on a site not far from *Kibbutz Beth Kama*. Chancing upon what they were doing, Bedouins of the El-Huziel tribe in the northern *Negev* reported it to the Ministry of the Interior. The Ministry contacted the police who ordered them to leave.[26] They then attempted to settle in a refugee camp in Jericho, but it soon became evident to them that living conditions were much better in Dimona.[27] In yet another incident, they illegally entered two vacant apartments reserved for new immigrants and carried out a "sit-in" to underscore their shortage of living space. The police gave them two hours to vacate the premises.[28]

The public image of the Black Hebrews was further tarnished when, frightfully reminiscent of the Arab threat "to drive the Jews into the sea," they proclaimed they would not fight in the Israeli Army, but would enthusiastically join a military force to drive the Israelis out of the country. Their image was damaged even further when Carter threatened that if Jerusalem's plot against the Black Hebrews was not discontinued, then the anti-Jewish resentment that already existed among blacks in the United States would grow. "We do not represent just a small remnant of Hebrew Israelites who are presently residing in *Eretz Yisrael*, but we represent some two million Hebrew Israelites."[29] More speculation arose when Carter was seen coming out of a Mosque in Old Jerusalem. Asked his purpose in going there, he stammered, "I sell rugs." Amid the prevailing mood, this incident led to suspicion that Carter was planning some conspiratorial act to harm the State.

The toll was tremendous. Old-time residents of Dimona, unwilling to wait for the pressure cooker to explode, left the city. More intended to follow. Immigrants were unwilling to settle in Dimona because of the blacks, it was claimed, and it was reported that a woman had suffered miscarriages because of them.[30] The fear of violence was very real. Police had already been compelled to intervene a few times to restore law and order.

These many encounters led to feelings of animosity between Mayor Navon and the blacks. Since the Rabbinate and the Mayor were members of the same political party, the National Religious Party, and it was the Rabbinate that refused to recognize them as Jews, the blacks accused Navon of personally conspiring against them. They threatened him, declaring publicly, "Today you sit here, but tomorrow you will no longer sit on this chair," and boasted that violence and calamity would occur in the country if their problems were not resolved.

Navon explained, however, that the decision concerning their status was not his to make and that he did not discriminate between one inhabitant and another. But since they were dissatisfied with their personal condition in the eyes of the law, he advised them to turn to the Supreme Court to secure what they sought. Nevertheless, he did not take their threat lightly, and had a permanent guard stationed at his home.

Convinced that the blacks had no future in Dimona or elsewhere in Israel, Navon foresaw only continued havoc and upheaval in the country because of them. He cited Asiel Ben Israel's unrestrained remark: "If we all can't work and see our children in school, then none of us will."[31] Their voluntary unemployment, said the Mayor, resulted in a crime wave and proved they were "undesirable." As if to demonstrate his point, a black from Dimona, Israel Lee Harris, was arrested as a suspect in the robbery of a gas station in Mitzpe Ramon. Cash and gas coupons worth hundreds of *liras* (Israel pounds) were reported stolen.[32] Confessing his guilt, Harris was fined and given a prison sentence.[33]

Navon was further convinced that, because they had nothing to lose, the blacks would go to any length to discredit the Israeli government for denying them the status of *olim*. He was hopeful, however, that an authoritative solution would be found that would "put an end to this situation so that Dimona could return to peaceful existence."

Apparently, the residents of Dimona shared the Mayor's view. When Rabbi Meir Kahane of the militant Jewish Defense League spoke at the local movie house in Dimona in the Fall of 1971, 700 people reportedly went to listen to his tirade against the blacks. He called them racists and anti-Semites, and it was reported that about 300 of his listeners joined the Jewish Defense League.[34] When he spoke a year later at the Zion Hotel in Jerusalem, where the JDL was headquartered, Kahane called the blacks "con men," "frauds," "vicious Jew haters, psychopaths and dangerous people" who migrated to

Israel because they believed they could live off the sympathy of the Jews.

Angered by what was transpiring, Mayor Navon asked the Ministry of the Interior why, despite all they had done, Black Hebrews were still being permitted to enter the country. The ministers explained to him again, as they had in the past, that they could not deny entry to a tourist who satisfied the officials at the port of entry that he would not be a burden on the country. "But they are a burden," he protested, "and yet you are renewing their visas every three months."[35]

At first, the government was reluctant to take any action on visitors' privileges. But in October 1971 the admittance policy to the country was toughened. The Ministry of the Interior directed that every black who sought entrance into Israel had to be thoroughly questioned about the purpose of the visit and whether or not he had a return ticket and sufficient funds with which to support himself while in the country. Although new to Israel, the procedure was the established practice in countries the world over. Tourists may be refused entrance if they do not have return or continuing tickets. This explains why a traveller entering a country must complete a landing card designating his next destination. Should no card be completed, the official at passport control usually will ask this question or request the tourist to show his airline ticket. Blacks who were permitted to enter the country were issued only one month visas, and the routine extension of transit visas was discontinued. The government felt it had the backing of its citizenry in issuing these directives. And it was right. Polls showed that 78% of the population was so upset with the blacks that they wanted them deported.[37]

In that month of October, the State of Israel refused entrance to three groups totaling twenty-four blacks, because they had insufficient funds with which to support themselves or because they did not have return tickets.[38] With only seven dollars in its possession, one family told the agent at passport control that comrades in Dimona would care for them. They were returned the next day to the United States.[39] When a group of 18 Chicago blacks returned home after being refused entry by Israel, they accused the country of being "the same as South Africa." They identified their headquarters as 1643 W. Roosevelt, the central base of Levi Israel, and claimed that his organization had no relationship with the Dimona group.[40] They gloated they "want the world to know that the white European Jew in Israel is racist."[41]

When word reached the Black Hebrews in Dimona that some blacks had been barred from entering the country, they locked themselves in their apartments and prepared to resist deportation. Since they were tourists, they feared they would be deported at the will of the State when their visas expired. This led Carter to declare that he and his followers were ready to lay down their lives to remain in Israel.

The charge of racism against Israel by the Black Hebrews is discredited by a black graduate of Talladega College, Larry Lewis, who entered Israel as an immigrant under the Law of Return; and by a black psychologist, Dr. Sandra A. Garcia, an associate professor of psychology at the University of South Florida, who spent 15 months in Israel to study the assimilation of Moroccan Jews into Israeli society.

While active in the civil rights movement, Larry Lewis[42] converted to Judaism in 1965 at Temple Israel in Boston, Massachusetts. Ascribing fully to its goals, he joined the Student Zionist Organization, which advocates "the unity of the Jewish people . . . the ingathering of the Jewish people in its historic homeland, the land of Israel . . . (and) the strengthening of Israel, which is based on the prophetic vision of justice and peace."

When he emigrated to Israel in February 1972, he was met at the airport by a representative of The Jewish Agency who arranged overnight accommodations for him. The following morning the Agency provided a car to take him to *Kibbutz Gat*, a democratically organized collective community where he was to live. Three months after arrival, being a permanent immigrant, he was granted automatic citizenship as are all Jewish newcomers. He then applied for membership in the *kibbutz*, whose motto is "From each according to his ability and to each according to his need." Candidates for admission to the *kibbutz* must serve a probationary year to give members an opportunity to know them before voting on them. Lewis waited the year and was elected to membership in November 1975.[43]

Fully accepted by the State of Israel, Lewis served in the Israel Defense Forces. He was ordered to report for induction on October 24, 1973, which later turned out to be the day of the final cease-fire of the Yom Kippur War (the war in which Egypt attacked the State of Israel by crossing the Suez Canal). Because he had done a four-year stint in the United States Air Force, he was to remain in the military forces for only three months. Due to the Yom Kippur War, however, his assignment was extended for three additional months. Like all Israelis, he was a member of a reserve military unit, subject to an annual call to active duty of 50 to 70 days.

Lewis affirmed his complete acceptance into *kibbutz* life, experienced no prejudice and was quite happy living in the State of Israel. "Those Blacks who condemn Zionism," he has written, are uninformed since "the early champions of the African cause" were "influenced by the example of Zionism." When blacks learn the facts, he states, "Black support for Israel will be second to none outside of the Jewish community." His own experiences and those of other black Jewish men and women he has known, as the Orthodox black Jewish girl who worked as an x-ray technician at the Hadassah Hospital in Jerusalem, illustrate the absurdity of the Black Hebrews' charge that the State of Israel is racist. All that is needed is to abide by the requirements of the country.

Larry Lewis is not associated with the Black Hebrews in Israel. He disagrees heartily with the beliefs which they set forth in a manifesto published in December 1974,[44] i.e., that Israel belongs to them, that they are not to "be identified as Jews or Jewish," and, that they "have not returned to Jerusalem to live together with the European-Jewish community presently occupying our land."

Black psychologist Dr. Sandra A. Garcia was interested in the conflict between *Ashkenazic* (western) Jews and *Sephardic* (eastern) Jews who live in Israel, and sought to determine whether their relationship could be compared to the American race problem.[45] The *Ashkenazi* Jew would be comparable to the white American; the *Sephardi* to the black American. She chose to study the Moroccan Jews because they are the largest *Sephardic* group in Israel.

Dr. Garcia states emphatically "there is no color prejudice in Israel in the American terms." The conflict that exists in Israel society, as she sees it, is not based on color but on cultural differences—the Jews of North Africa and Asia (*Sephardi*) come from cultures different than the Jews who immigrated from Europe (*Ashkenazi*). She thus correctly concludes that the social conflict in Israel has greater similarity to the conflicts that erupt between different immigrant groups in the United States than to racial problems. For example, *Ashkenazi* Jews dominate Israel's power structure and hold the better jobs; *Sephardi* Jews live in slum areas similar to American ghettos. *Sephardi* Jews also score lower on IQ tests and are held responsible for the increased crime rate in the country. Yet, there are other factors that mitigate these indicators. Dr. Garcia notes that in Israel there is no hatred of other ethnic groups and everyone is committed to closing the social gap. Since both groups are Jewish, they are interested in assimilating and becoming Israelis. In a few generations, as the groups intermarry and the various ethnic groups assimilate into Israeli society, the problem will be resolved. No such possibility exists between blacks and whites in America.

About the only potential source of racial disharmony is the immigration of the black Falashas into Israel from Ethiopia. Approximately 400 of them reside in Israel today,[46] working in a variety of occupations. On February 9, 1973, the *Sephardi* Chief Rabbi, Ovadia Yossef, ruled that as descendants of the tribe of Dan,[47] the Falashas are *halachically* entitled to enter Israel under the Law of Return. To placate those who doubt the authenticity of the Falashas' Jewish origin, he stipulated that, since they may have fallen away from the Jewish covenant during centuries of isolation, they should undergo simple or symbolic conversion. Rabbi Yossef's decision was in consonance with earlier rulings by two Chief Rabbis: Abraham Isaac Kook, the first *Ashkenazi* Chief Rabbi of modern Palestine from 1921 to 1935, and Isaac Herzog, the first *Ashkenazi* Chief Rabbi of the State of Israel. Rabbi Herzog began his tenure in 1937, before the State was established, and continued in that office until 1959. Rabbi Yossef was interested in hastening Falasha immigration to Israel and to enhance their knowledge of Torah.

When he was Chief Rabbi of Tel Aviv-Jaffa (1968-1972), Rabbi Yossef had converted 70 Falashas,[48] so he anticipated no resistance to conversion on their part. A lone voice, however, was raised in opposition to it. Yona Bagale,[49] a Falasha leader in Addis Ababa, adamantly insisted conversion was not necessary since they were already Jews, but many Falashas did not share his view. The *Ashkenazi* Chief Rabbi, Shlomo Goren,[50] announced that he, too, would accept a symbolic conversion ceremony as sufficient to erase any doubts about Falasha ancestry or belief.

Despite their emigration into Israel, no racial problem is anticipated. It is remote, Dr. Garcia believes, because their numbers are relatively small, 25,000 at the most, and they would be easily absorbed into Israeli life. "There will be no color problem if more Falashas come," a *kibbutz sabra* (Israeli-born native) married to a Falasha woman said confidently. "Falashas are no darker than some other Jews. Israelis will take it in stride."

Like Larry Lewis, Dr. Garcia admonishes blacks not to put a black-white racial conflict tag on Israel. Before blacks call Israelis "imperialistic racist white pigs," they should acquaint themselves with the facts.

Three women who returned to Chicago from Israel likewise refuted the accusation by the Black Hebrews that Israel is racist. One day, Mrs. Brenda Ross, Mrs. Odessa Washington, and Mrs. Renee Kirkpatrick heard Warren Brown, a Black Hebrew, on Wesley Smith's WVON "Hot Line" Radio Show. He was soliciting funds for the blacks in Israel. Since WVON is a black oriented radio station, Brown attempted to stir up his listeners and thus loosen their purse strings by condemning Israel for practicing racism toward black Americans in their country.

Infuriated by what they heard, the 3 women decided to expose Brown and to challenge his charge as baseless.[51] The real reason for the existing unrest among the Black Hebrews in Israel, they said, was that Brown himself was locked in a power struggle with Ben Ammi Carter and Louis A. Bryant for leadership of the group.

When the blacks first arrived in Israel, the women asserted, the Israelis received them "with open arms." Strained relations developed because of violent political outbursts by the leaders of the group. Supporting Dimona Mayor Israel Navon's contention that the blacks "exploited our hospitality," the women said that the unemployment of the black Americans in Israel was largely voluntary; they simply refused to work.[52] (This was substantiated by Edward Lynne who wrote,[53] all Black Hebrews left their jobs with the Dimona Cotton Mills and lived without visible means of support.) Therefore, the women contended, the straits the Black Hebrews were in was brought about by their own actions.

The dogged position Israel took with regard to immigration was not aimed specifically at blacks, but at all non-Jewish immigrants who might attempt to enter Israel on pretenses similar to the ones used by the Black Hebrews.

Meanwhile, two black children died and the question arose as to the place of burial. Non-Jews may not be interred in Jewish burial grounds. Where were they to be laid to rest? Humanely and without fanfare, their burial was arranged close to the Jewish cemetary, but a low fence was erected so that technically they were buried "outside the gate," while it appeared that they were interred "within the gate."[54]

In December 1971 when tourist visas ran out on 8 Black Hebrews, a Leona Clark family of 7 and a Paul Cramer, the government shed its timidity still further and initiated deportation proceedings against them. They had arrived in September for a regular three-month stay and then had applied for an extension. The Ministry of the Interior denied the extension and ordered them "to make necessary arrangements to leave the country within 5 days of receipt of this letter." Unfortunately, they were arrested before they received the letter of rejection. It was handed to them while they were being detained.

Thereupon, the 8 sued the State to prevent their expulsion and that they be granted the status of immigrants.

They argued first that the term "Jew" has different meanings. As Hebrew descendants of Abraham, Isaac and Jacob, they came within the definition of that term. Although they did not regard themselves as Jews in the same sense as the white Jews did, they observed the laws of the Torah and were, therefore, sufficiently Jewish to benefit from the provisions of the Law of Return.[55]

Secondly, they contended, the law required that when visas were not extended, the Ministry of the Interior had to give just cause, and the spokesman for the Ministry had refused to do that. The government explained that because they had not applied for temporary residence visas while abroad, they were in Israel as tourists. The government also indicated that they had promised not to apply, at a later date, to be considered immigrants. In violation of this agreement, they then asked for housing and other benefits.[56]

The High Court of Justice granted them an order *nisi*, calling on the Minister of the Interior to show cause why he should not rescind his decision to refuse to renew their tourist visas or to grant them the status of immigrants.

Israel officials felt they had nothing of which to be ashamed. They dealt fairly with all people, including the Black Hebrews, but the group's provocations and attendant unfavorable publicity had brought them discredit in the eyes of the country. When the Black Hebrews called the citizens of the country "white Israeli racists," the Ministry of the Interior felt it necessary to retort, "This is a most unfair slur on a people that has never been racist."[57] Israel was established and recognized internationally as a haven for all Jews who wish to settle there. It was not intended to serve as a refuge for all humanity. Should the Irish or the Eskimos proclaim themselves descendants of the ten lost tribes of Israel, Israel would not feel bound to provide them with the rights of immigrants. They could enter the country, but they would be required to adhere to the laws of the land in all respects, including immigration and citizenship. The officials thus concluded that Israel had no legal or moral obligation to the Black Hebrews as non-Jews; and that, by declaring themselves enemies of the State, the Black Hebrews nullified the humanitarian basis for accepting them. Furthermore, when they first entered the country, they specifically referred to themselves as Jews who had returned to their homeland. By changing their designation from Jews to Black Hebrews or Hebrew Israelites, they undermined their already shaky status because they then reflected a national political outlook, not a religious orientation. By doing this, they set themselves up as an invading nationality.

That the Israeli officials were justified in their feelings was borne out by other actions by the Black Hebrews.[58] Earlier, in the United States, they already had established themselves as the "Representative Government of the Immigrants." In April 1970 they had petitioned the Sub-Committee on Human Rights at the United Nations to enable them to settle in Israel, to recognize them as a third party in Israel in addition to the Jews and Arabs, and to assist them in assuming authority in Israel. And then, on November 16, 1970, at a convention in Philadelphia that was attended by two delegates from Dimona, they had unfurled a new national flag, depicting the Lion of Judah surrounded by the symbols of the twelve tribes on a blue background.

In 1971, some government officials suggested that it would be beneficial to the State and the blacks if they were deported as a group to end the impasse. "It's better to get rid of them now rather than we be the ones put on buses some day," said Mayor Navon.[59] The blacks could then make a new start elsewhere. The officials realized that the news media would sensationalize such a mass deportation, ignoring the fact that dozens of whites are asked to leave the country each month for similar reasons. Also, when Liberia expelled them, there was not a murmur in the media. But if Israel should expel them en masse, it would stir a hornet's nest. Those who favored this course of action predicted the incident would be forgotten in a few days, and the government could then turn its attention to the country's truly pressing problems.

While deportation proceedings were pending, the blacks, concerned about their public image, decided to present a low profile. Little was heard of them or from them. Impressed by their change in behavior, Israeli officials began to believe that the Black Hebrews might have a future in Israel after all.

When Joela Har-Shefi[60] of *Maariv* went to Dimona with a

crew of television cameramen and broadcasters to do a story on the Black Hebrews, she dramatically portrayed the modification that had taken place. From reports she had read in preparation for meeting them, she had expected the residents of Dimona to tell her the Black Hebrews had made their lives a nightmare, that "violence peers forth from their squinting eyes," and that they had "spread like a cancer in the blooming body of the desert city." She was also admonished before leaving Tel Aviv to be extremely careful in the presence of the blacks.

To her astonishment, she found the atmosphere was not poisoned; the blacks roused no attention nor were they cursed by anybody; nobody hit them; there was no "gnashing of teeth"; white children did not flee from them; and, rocks were not thrown at them.

When outbreaks occur in Tel Aviv, they usually originate at the movies. So she went to the Dimona movie only to find that all was quiet.

Television cameramen roamed the apartment complex and broadcasters asked the tenants such questions as: Do you have any problems with the blacks? Do they disturb your sleep? Do they empty the garbage in your backyard? Do they disturb your children? Do they block the entrance to the house and crowd the staircase? Except for a few people who expressed some resentment, all replies were in the negative. The Black Hebrews had effectively avoided all confrontations with the residents of Dimona, and the residents, with tensions relaxed, were apparently willing to let bygones be bygones.

Steering a middle course between the extremes of mass deportation and settlement, the Ministry of the Interior arrived at an out-of-court understanding with the blacks. No Black Hebrews would be deported and no others would be permitted to enter the country. If equilibrium could be maintained and the blacks fomented no disorder, the government would allow the matter to rest. Should provocations continue, or should the Black Hebrews attempt to weaken the country or portray it in false light before the world, they would be deported forthwith. In effect, the blacks were placed on probation.

Mayor Israel Navon disagreed with the government's settlement. While he admitted quiet had settled over his city, he regarded it as the quiet before the storm. And amidst this calm, suddenly, a murder was committed within the Black Hebrew community.

Chapter IX

END OF THE ROAD

With the fear of deportation hanging over them, the Black Hebrews were sensitive about their public image. To their chagrin, the behavior of three of the brothers received unfavorable publicity. One of them, Cornell Kirkpatrick, was arrested for publicly beating his wife; Israel Lee Harris, found guilty of robbing a gas station, was also suspected in the theft of photographic equipment which led to a humiliating police search of the entire Black Hebrew community; and Oliver Williams, was believed to be a homosexual.[1]

The Black Hebrews chose a committee to deal with their errant members. The committee found the three men's actions brought shame and disgrace upon them and endangered the welfare of the entire group. The committee ruled they should be expelled from Dimona with permission to visit their relatives on occasion. "We can't have any thieves among us; we can't have any wife-beaters among us; and we can't have any perverted people among us," said one member in justifying their banishment. "They interfered with God's reason for our being here," said Ben Ammi Carter.

On January 29, 1972, Kirkpatrick, Williams and Harris returned to Dimona to gather up their possessions.[2] As they left the bus depot and headed toward the apartment complex, they encountered five Black Hebrews on their way to the depot. A fight broke out between them and Kirkpatrick was fatally wounded. He died later at the Negev Central Hospital. Arrested and charged with manslaughter were Thomas Whitfield (Yehuda Ben Israel), John Boyd (Shabbat), James Coats (Ben Kahal), Charlie Clark (Shlomo), and Thomas Glober (Ahiezer Ben Israel). Whitfield's Hebrew name appears with an American singing group called The Pharoahs on their first album, "Awakening." Friends in Chicago were surprised to learn of his involvement because he went to Israel only to visit his pregnant wife, who was living there with her parents.[3] Glober was the so-called Press Counselor of the Black Hebrew community; it was he who issued several press releases accusing the Israeli government of Jim Crow discrimination.[4]

The trial in Beersheba was covered by the American Broadcasting Company and the Columbia Broadcasting System, in addition to the press. It was alleged that Kirkpatrick had said he and his friends came armed to "fight the community." Oliver Williams testified that Kirkpatrick did carry an axe and Harris carried two, each equipped with a leather thong for swinging; also one of them had a dagger. The five defendants were also armed, Coats testified, but he claimed their thick black and yellow staves, engraved with ancient Hebraic designs—a lion of Judah, a *menorah* (candelabrum),[5] and a High Priest's breastplate[6]—were carried to emulate their forefathers.

During the fight, Kirkpatrick fell to the ground, still clutching his axe. The pathologist, Dr. John G. Meyersohn, testified that Kirkpatrick died from repeated blows to the head delivered by a "sharp, heavy instrument, used with great force"[7] that fractured his skull in several places.

Whitfield and Boyd disclaimed any connection with the crime, declaring it was a coincidence that they were on their way to Beersheba when Kirkpatrick, Williams, and Harris arrived. They refused to sign a police statement describing the incident because it was written in Hebrew and they could not read it.

The other defendants testified that their sole purpose in approaching the trio was to convince them to leave without causing any trouble. They were fearful lest any further bad publicity would hasten the deportation of some members of the group.

The evidence failed to establish who were the aggressors and who killed Kirkpatrick. Williams asserted he saw both Clark and Coats strike Kirkpatrick, but when Kirkpatrick fell to the ground, he and Harris ran away. Israel Lee Harris, the main witness for the prosecution, failed to appear in court. Apprehended in an abandoned refugee camp in Jericho where 12 Black Hebrew families lived,[8] he was taken into custody and his American passport impounded. It was Ben Ammi Carter who speculated at a press conference that Kirkpatrick accidentally fell on his own axe.

The prosecution called for a finding of guilty because the facts did not indicate accidental death. Even if the victim fell on his own axe, the prosecutor argued, the defendants were still responsible for causing his death. Joseph Ben Menashe, the defense attorney, argued for acquittal because the prosecution was unable to prove who killed Kirkpatrick.

The five defendents were found guilty of homicide, but their sentences were suprisingly light.[9] In the State of Israel, which has abolished capital punishment, the sentence for homicide usually carries a 10-year prison term. James Coats was sentenced to two years and each of the other four defendants to six months in jail.[10] This, despite their accusations of discrimination during the trial, and Carter's claim that local agitators influenced Kirkpatrick to create a disturbance in the Black Hebrew community. Apparently, the court did not hold them fully accountable.

Ironically, the murder and trial revealed that a change was taking place among the Black Hebrews. Assuming a low profile, they were striving to conform to Israeli standards of behavior and to acquire an acceptable image. When Ben Ammi Carter testified at the trial, although he refused to take the oath, he spoke slowly and with dignity. "The God of Israel made us realize," he said, "we had to make order in our household."

Despite the effort by the blacks to swing public opinion in their favor, the fact that manslaughter had been committed within the group aroused apprehension. It frightened them sufficiently for some Israelis to regard the Black Hebrews as too troublesome to remain in Israel, diverting energies needed for more serious problems. Once again, the government decided to rid the country of them by instituting regulations that would reduce the colony by attrition. They were:

To be admitted, a tourist of any race or religion must have a return ticket, means of support while in Israel or proof that he would be adequately cared for.[11] This would exclude newcomers, as it did on November 13, 1972, when four Black Hebrews arrived from the United States to settle in Israel. They were denied entry because they had not applied for immigration before arriving, and the individual who came from Dimona to welcome them was denied permission to meet with them.[12]

Black residents who left the country for any reason would not be permitted to return.[13]

Blacks would be required to leave when their visas expired, even though they had been renewed before.[14]

No work permits or apartments would be made available to Black Hebrews. No longer would they be given preferential treatment.

During the first six or seven months of 1972, approximately 65 Black Hebrews were repatriated to the United States, some at American expense. Another 28 were ordered deported in August 1973. Thy secured a court injunction to delay their expulsion and requested permanent residency, instead of immigration. Their request was rejected. They apealed, but withdrew the appeal in January 1974 because they did not expect a favorable ruling. Three were granted stays of deportation for "humanitarian reasons"; the other 25 left.

As the Black Hebrews felt increasingly isolated, they decided to sponsor a Summit Conference in Jerusalem on November 13-16, 1972, to bolster their public image. They invited conferees and speakers from the United States and several African nations. Interestingly, one who attended was Kenyon C. Burke, Urban Affairs Consultant to the Anti-Defamation League of B'nai B'rith.

For an agenda, they produced a weighty brochure, "For Profound Men of the United States and Africa." It set forth a "New World Plan" that dealt with seven subjects: Industrialization, Non-Exploitation and Non-Pollution; Light on

⁺he Middle East's Dark Past; Education Based Upon Knowledge; Monetary System Based on a Scale of Equality for all Nations; The Everlasting Non-Competition Between Men and Women in their Proper Roles; Divine Marriage; and, Health and Hygiene.

Frequent use of the term "divine" throughout its pages— "divine teacher," "divine living," "divine hygiene," "divine woman," and so forth provided a rare expression of humor during a visit with Shaleak Ben Yehudah in Dimona. "Here," said our host extending a glass, "is divine orange juice."

Of special interest was a section on "A Divine Woman" which helps to understand how females were enlisted and kept loyal to the sect. According to the document, a woman should renounce "all competition between man and woman and between woman and woman."

Before a woman marries, her father directs her life and provides for her. When she marries, it is for the purpose of bearing children, and for this "her mind must be . . . disciplined to doing right." Subservient to man, she is his "reflection" and her duty is to uplift him. She is her husband's "pillar of strength" and for this he provides her necessities. In pleasing her husband "she pleases God."

Ben Ammi Carter explained that although women are equal before God, in the Black Hebrew community they are one step below men. Therefore, strict rules limit a woman's behavior. For example, a woman may not initiate a conversation with a man, and make-up and perfume are forbidden, except those compounded from plants by Charles Blackwell.

The lack of clearly defined male and female roles, Carter admonished, is one indication of a decaying society. The blurring of the sexes prevents the home from functioning as a stabilizing influence and causes the delinquency of youth.[15]

The restrictions the document placed on women went much further, complained Brenda Ross, Odessa Washington and Renee Kirkpatrick, widow of the slain Cornell Kirkpatrick, who returned to Chicago. They and their children had been beaten because they failed to comply with the dictates of the brothers who call themselves "gods" and "princes." They also revealed that the Black Hebrews, "broke up the husbands and wives and families" (sic) and compelled the women to accept polygamous relationships. Some women apprised the American Embassy that they were detained in Israel by force and that the Black Hebrews shaved the heads of women who expressed a desire to leave the country. Nothing was done to assist them.

A visit with Shaleak Ben Yehudah in Dimona demonstrated that women "aren't allowed to say anything," as Brenda Ross put it. A young woman, asked about her alleged imprisonment by the authorities, was ordered to leave the room, and Shaleak undertook to answer all questions about the incident.

Families in the United States also expressed concerns about their relatives living among the Black Hebrews in Israel. At the same time, their grievances shed light on how the blacks support themselves in Israel.

From the beginning, government officials wondered how funds seemed always available to the Black Hebrews. They were so destitute they staged the scene at the Dimona supermarket and demanded a dole from the municipality; yet they had money to charter buses for trips to Tel Aviv and Jerusalem. Since 1973, however, the coffers apparently are filled by preying on unsuspecting young women with good jobs and money in the bank.

Here is the story of a woman whose divorced daughter was victimized by a group which called itself "The Original Black Hebrews." In 1973, the daughter moved to Israel with her three children without telling her mother. When she called her daughter's home, a man answered, saying she was away on vacation and he was looking after the house for her. Each time she called, the same male voice repeated the same story. Two months later, the mother received a letter from her daughter saying she was in Israel and planned to remain there. The mother wrote, asking what her daughter intended to do with her two homes, valued at about $50,000, the furniture, and an automobile. She received no reply. Later she learned the Black Hebrews disposed of the property. Distraught, she wrote in care of Charles (Hezekiah) Blackwell in Arad, telling her daughter she planned to visit. The daughter telephoned instructions for finding her in Arad.

With her eleven year old son, the woman arrived for a two-week stay in Israel. Her daughter was living under deplorable conditions, she said. In a small apartment with little furniture, as many as 12 people slept on quilts and comforters, which were rolled up during the day to serve as couches. Bedbugs abounded. Her son was bitten so badly, she feared he would become feverish. Suitcases littered the porches, and the scene was in total disarray.

Her grandchildren she learned, were living away from their mother in another city, and she was barred from seeing them until she threatened drastic action against the leaders of the Black Hebrews. When she finally found them, they were very unhappy, were forced to perform strange customs, lacked adequate clothing, and were not receiving proper education. They begged their grandmother to send their father for them.

The father had tried unsuccessfully to get his sons returned to him. Now the grandmother asked her daughter if the children could return to Chicago with her. The daughter had no objection, but permission, she said, must be obtained from the *Nasi* (prince), since women neither made decisions nor did anything without permission. The *Nasi*, the grandmother said, emphatically declared he would never allow the children to return to "Babylon."

She attended a Sabbath Service where the subject discussed was the doom of America in 1976. Concluding that the Original Black Hebrew Nation was founded on hate, the grandmother was concerned that her grandchildren were being infected with malevolence.

An equally painful situation befell another family whose daughter withdrew all the money from her $3,000 bank account, wrote almost $2,000 in worthless checks, and left Detroit. She called home from Israel, but the family sensed she could not talk freely. She then wrote her mother that she had become pregnant by a man still living in Detroit, and that she wanted to come home. Her mother did not hear from her again until months later when she received word that a son had been born. The child was not delivered in a hospital, and there was no birth certificate. (It is impossible to determine how many such births have occurred.)

The girl later requested clothing for the baby from her sister. Although some was sent, she wrote that she did not receive it and that she wanted to come home. After that her family never heard from her again.

A newspaper report told of a James O. Williams who was searching for his estranged wife, Karen Celeste, and his 2-year old son, Damien.[16] He learned they were expected to leave Detroit, possibly for Israel. A Mrs. Delaney also said she had sent packages to her daughter in Israel in care of Charles Blackwell. Although the mother heard from her, there was no mention of receiving the packages.

Yaakov Keiman, attached to the Israeli Consulate in Chicago, said Israel had requested the United States Department of State and other American authorities to investigate these situations. Israel, he said, did not want "to be blamed if United States citizens are cheated out of their money and property because of some group's false promise of paradise in our land."[17] He added "the situation had caused disputes and delicate problems within our land which we fear might be misunderstood in other countries or turned into Arab propaganda against us." In fact, he wondered whether the Arabs might not be behind the whole affair. Keiman was anxious that Americans be warned about the ploy. He was distressed that Detroit blacks were selling their homes to migrate to Israel. He described "the true picture" of the living conditions of blacks in Israel as "dirty buildings, clashes with neighbors, rebellious activities, internal strife, homicides and enforced polygamy."

The blacks were also suspected of joining in a conspiracy with a foreign power,[18] as they had been in Liberia, where it was rumored that they displayed pictures of Mao Tze Tung in their synagogue.[19] The rumor proved to be groundless.

Soon after the Summit Conference of November 1972, the Black Hebrews began to circulate epistles on an international level, hoping to gain recognition for themselves and a foothold in Israel.

Israel was always depicted in an unfavorable light. The more they were thwarted, the more caustic the letters. Earlier, they petitioned the United Nations Human Rights Commission to turn the State of Israel over to them. When no reply was received, Carter accused the Israeli government of intercepting their proposal, charging the Israel Security Forces conspired to combat the Black Hebrew Israelites' "messianic aspirations" to establish "God's Kingdom in Jerusalem." Nevertheless, a "friendly" nation agreed to support their case before the United Nations Human Rights Commission, but Carter refused to identify the country.[20]

Despite the earlier decision not to antagonize Israel, Carter's actions had that effect. On November 28, 1972, in an open letter to Kurt Waldheim, Carter charged that by turning the State of Israel over to the Jews from Europe, the United Nations was thwarting the prophecy of God concerning the eventual return of the true Hebrew people to the Holy Land. "The Zionist elements of world Jewry perpetrated the idea that they (Jewish people by religion only) were the descendants of the Biblical Hebrew Israelites." But this was false because blacks were the rightful heirs to the land that became the State of Israel. It was this error by the United Nations that enabled the Zionist manipulators to violate the blacks' basic human rights and usurp their culture and identity. The United Nations must bear full responsibility for this trespass, the letter said, and for thus throwing the world into chaos and confusion. The United Nations must hear their case and satisfy their quest for the right of nationality.

On December 7, 1972, the Israel High Court of Justice finally ruled that the expulsion order by the Minister of the Interior against the eight blacks was not unlawful.[21] Judge Zvi Berinson, who spoke for the court,[22] noted that the Black Hebrews had arrived in Israel as tourists and requested permission to settle permanently only after the Minister of the Interior refused to extend their tourist visas. At no time did they claim to be Jews or regard themselves as Jews; consequently, they were illegal aliens.

The 1952 Entry into Israel Law accords the Minister of the Interior absolute discretion to extend visitors' visas up to two years or to reject them without explanation. Under the Law of Return, a non-Israeli citizen may neither enter nor reside in Israel except by permission of the authorities. Even if a person entered the country lawfully, the Minister of the Interior could cancel his permission to remain without giving reasons. Furthermore, since 1955 regulations required tourists to leave the country before the expiration of their visas. When extensions of their visas were refused, the eight should have left the country. When they failed to do so, the Minister properly issued an expulsion order.

Permitting other members of the sect to remain in Israel, did not obligate the Minister to do the same for them, nor was his refusal discriminatory. If they proved that the Minister acted corruptly, fraudulently or without good faith, then his ruling could be disqualified. Every country reserves the right to restrict foreigners from entering its borders and to expel aliens whose presence is viewed as undesirable. In no country are the authorities required to give reasons for their decisions, Judge Berinson went on.

When the Law of Return was amended in 1970, the word "Jew" was defined as "a person who was born of a Jewish mother or had become converted to Judaism and who is not a member of another religion." It was impossible, however, to draw any conclusions concerning their roots in Judaism, Judge Berinson said. Nor could any member of the sects claim a "Jewish" mother.

Their belief in the God of Israel could inspire a highly moral and ethical life, but by accepting only the Torah and denying the remaining books of Scripture, they were not adherents of the Jewish religion as it had developed throughout the centuries.

Nor could Judge Berinson accept a claim that they be viewed as converts to Judaism. While the Law of Return does not specify a procedure, conversion implies an overt act of accepting Judaism and joining the Jewish people. The Black Hebrews never claimed their forefathers had converted, and they themselves refused to participate in such a ceremony. The Black Hebrews had remained distant and separate from the traditions, culture and heritage of Judaism, and calling themselves Hebrews and not Jews was meaningless as it pertains to the Law of Return.

Withal, compassionately aware of their quest for a home, the High Court of Justice recommended that if the Minister of the Interior deemed it proper, he might permit the eight blacks to remain in the country. The decision, however, denied categorically their claim to being Jews or authentic Hebrews.

The seriousness of their plight was plainly evident to the leaders of the colony. In desperation they drafted a leaflet, "Journey of the Hebrew Israelite Nation in Liberia," that described in graphic language the hardships they encountered there. Although they had not referred specifically to their Liberian experience since the Liberian Minister of Information, Milt Greaves, attacked their poor record there, they hoped to win sympathy to their cause.

The land they purchased, they wrote, could only be used on a limited basis because it was alive with wild creatures and infested with venomous insects and reptiles.[23] It was inadequate, even by Liberian standards, to grow sufficient food for their needs. Also, urban life in America had not conditioned them for rural living in Liberia. Between buying food and hiring taxis to transport them to Monrovia, their money ran out. To ensure their survival, natives taught them how to identify and prepare safe foods that were plentiful in the jungle. Seven days a week their diet consisted of rice and margarine or flour and gravy, causing them to grow leaner and gaunter. Although they were visited by one tragedy after another in the form of illness and accidental death, their spirits remained high, the leaflet stated. A number of immigrants, however, unable to endure the hardships, returned to the United States.

The failure of the tract to stir the Israeli populace in their favor, prompted them to enlarge their letter writing program to include international personalities and American congressmen and senators. They wrote United Nations Secretary-General Kurt Waldheim, complaining of a "morally revolting situation . . . mounted against our people in Israel."[24] Specific grievances were enumerated: they claimed Thomas Glober was seized by the local police of Dimona when he sought to cash a payroll voucher and was never heard of again. The same thing allegedly happened to another Black Hebrew in Mitzpe Ramon when he reported to local police with regard to rental obligations on his apartment. Other grievances were catalogued: a woman was deported; women were beaten; their adherents were awakened during the night and carried off to police headquarters.

Copies of this letter were sent to all permanent missions of African and Asian nations to the United Nations, to newspapers in England, France and Germany, to American academicians, senators and diplomats, and to individuals such as H. L. Hunt of Dallas, Texas. Undoubtedly, they hoped Hunt would favor them with a grant of money since it was felt he was not favorably disposed toward the Jewish people.

Questioned about these incidents, Michael Buchner of the Special Duties Division of Israel Police in Jerusalem, explained that a number of blacks who had been ordered deported because they were in the country illegally, could not be identified because they had destroyed their passports. When they came to the police department to register complaints and had to identify themselves, it was found that they were the ones to be deported. So they were detained and expelled from the country.

Thomas Glober was deported under the rules of the Law of Entry, Buchner said, which state that those who foment trouble and who do not contribute to the welfare to the country may be deported. Glober later tried to enter Israel via the Allenby Bridge on the Jordanian border. Permission was denied.

The letters proved to be non-productive. They thereupon embarked upon a daring venture. On January 27, 1973, the Original Hebrew Israelite Nation of Jerusalem claimed to have opened an embassy at the home of a Mrs. Saudia Masaud at 852 St. Nicholas Avenue in New York City.

Mrs. Masaud, a Muslim by religion, denied the assertion. She assumed they had contacted her, she said, because she was active in freedom work. Sympathetic to their cause, she made her apartment available to them, but solely for a social gathering. Nothing occurred that even remotely resembled a business meeting, she emphasized. They attempted to persuade her to let them use her address as their headquarters, but she refused and never saw them again.

Eustace F. Beckles of 9 East 118th Street in New York City, who attended the gathering,[25] said he had no idea what the Original Hebrew Israelite Nation of Jerusalem was. Beckles speculated it might have been an organization associated with the Ethiopian Hebrew congregation in New York City to which he belonged.

On September 24, 1973, the Black Hebrews took to the pen again. They wrote to President Richard Nixon, Secretary of State Henry Kissinger, Kenneth Keating, United States Ambassador to Israel, and wrote again on November 30 to Nixon and Kissinger. Copies of the second letter were sent to Leonid Brezhnev in the Union of Soviet Socialist Republics and to Kurt Waldheim. They demanded that as the true representatives of the State of Israel they be invited to the peace conference being convened at Geneva on December 30, 1973, between Israel, Syria, Egypt, Jordan and Iraq. This matched Carter's earlier attack on Israeli officials for not soliciting his opinion and that of the Black Hebrews in March 1972 when King Hussein of Jordan proposed that an autonomous Palestinian state be established on the West Bank. The Kenesset, he said, should have come to Dimona to consult with him and his group. And again, when President Nixon gave Israel a $500 million loan in 1971, Carter and his people claimed that a share of the money belonged to them.

On December 31, 1973, the sect leaders wrote to all blacks in the United States Congress and to some black news organizations, condemning Israel for falsely arresting seven men and three women for "loitering" in Tel Aviv. After they had served their sentences, the Black Hebrews wrote, the judge "extended the sentences indefinitely without reason," causing their families undue hardships. They appealed to these black representatives and newsmen to right an injustice committed "against American blacks" (not Black Hebrews) in Israel. They said they wanted "the Black Community in America" to be aware that a great percentage of the billion dollars the United States allocated to Israel, came from "Black America's tax dollars." It "brought economic hardships on Black Americans and has reduced the Social programs geared toward the Black Communities' survival. In addition, the Eight Hundred

Million Dollars raised by the United Jewish Appeal for the recent Yom Kippur War of October 1973, was given primarily by Jewish Merchants in America whose businesses survive solely from the economic exploitation of the Black Community." Nevertheless, they asserted, Israel continued its "racist campaign against Black people from America."

The letter concluded with a call for:

1. A total economic boycott of all Jewish owned businesses.
2. A caucus lobby by black congressman for denial of further funds (tax dollars) to Israel for use against black Americans living in Israel.
3. An immediate and complete investigation and release of Hebrew Israelites (Black Americans) now jailed and held incommunicado in Ramla (Ramle) Prison in Israel.

Yet, while they appealed to black congressmen for assistance, Shaleak wrote that "Black Congressmen in Washington are obviously controlled by Jewish people." He saw no contradiction in attacking them.

The venom they spewed estranged even those in Israel who wanted to assist them. They were now attempting to influence American legislators against their country. Here again the blacks were in the contradictory position of seeking full acceptance by the State of Israel even as they aimed to undermine it.

Still unsuccessful, they became even more extreme in their statements. On April 15, 1974, Shaleak Ben Yehuda asserted[26] that Jewish slave merchants and slave-holders had become rich off the blacks. Utilizing the money their fathers acquired by this means, the children had become even wealthier and had invested this money in the State of Israel. Thus, he claimed, blacks were the source of this investment.

The American Jewish community "has manipulated itself into a solid and stable position in the black community," he wrote. "It is the Jewish community that has been in a position to profit the most financially from the black community. The Jewish community monopolized all real estate, food, loan institutions and all the inferior merchandise that was/is consumed in our communities."

Mouthing canards retched by virulent anti-Semites, Shaleak wrote, "white Christians in America have never been in control of the financial institutions in America. All finances in the world are controlled by white people of the religious faith of Judaism." To support this claim, he quoted a passage from Adolf Hitler's *Mein Kampf*. When questioned about using Hitler, the vicious anti-Semite responsible for the death of six million Jews, as a corroborating source, Shaleak replied, "Truth is truth no matter who it comes from."

In a surprising remark made in Dimona in 1974,[27] Shaleak Ben Yehudah said that one need not be black to be a Hebrew Israelite. "But doesn't this negate a fundamental premise of your group that white people cannot be Hebrew Israelites?" he was asked. "Anyone," he replied, "who lives in righteousness, regardless of race or nationality, can become an Israelite. Furthermore," he continued, "not all blacks are Israelites." Queried as to how one would differentiate between a black who was an Israelite and one who wasn't, he responded, "It is a spiritual feeling." As for themselves, he explained, "we just know that we are the true Israelites." Asked when this change in viewpoint came about, he replied, "We always believed this."

The Black Hebrews engaged in still another activity that militated against them in the eyes of the Israelis. They promoted illegal immigration by inviting friends and relatives and strangers, including the author, to come live with them permanently in Israel.[28] By swelling their numbers, they hoped to force government officials to yield to their demands.

On February 10, 1974, Shaleak Ben Yehudah mistakenly addressed a letter to the author as President of Johnson C. Smith University. Soon, the author was informed, he would be summoned to Jerusalem. "You must begin now even though you may not see your way, but it is a must that you make plans to make this journey." This refrain was repeated numerous times in a long correspondence.

With others, Shaleak's approach was more direct. On April 21, 1974, he wrote to a Los Angeles family spelling out precisely how they could circumvent the authorities once they arrived in Israel. "You do not need a visa to visit Israel," he wrote them. "It would be good if you could arange to be hooked up with a tour. You will check into the hotel with your tour group but you will wisely let your fellow tourists know that you plan to visit some friends in Israel. Take your luggage, get a cab and come to Dimona. The cost of the cab we will negotiate with (the driver?) when he arrives here with you. But let us not worry about that.

"But, here are some ideas so you will know when you talk to the cabdriver. From Lod Airport and Tel Aviv it will cost you 200 to 225 Israeli pounds to come to Dimona, which is 50 to 55 American dollars. From Jerusalem it will cost you around 40 American dollars. Do not stay but one day with the tour, just check into the hotel, relax and have dinner and come on down. Try to get a tour group that's going to stay in Israel for 10 to 14 days at least (we can always extend) so you can have time to look around before departing and enjoy yourselves and feel the land. If you do not get hooked up with a tour, by all means someone will be able to meet you. You will let us know in advance your flight number, name of airline, date and time of arrival, as soon as you can acquire this information.

"Above all things at this season you should use credit cards. Do not use cash for anything. The signs of the time indicate that when you get back to America you may not have the time to regroup yourselves with cash, just pay your monthly notes and hold to cash for your final exodus, if you have these intentions. To sum it all up, to flee anywhere is better than America."

Burdened with Jewish immigrants, the Israelis viewed this stratagem as a detriment to the country. Moreover, it frightened them personally.

Recognizing that their efforts were getting them nowhere, the blacks decided that to avoid deportation they would renounce their American citizenship. Being stateless, Israel would be unable to expel them unless another country was willing to accept them. So, on September 25, 1973, they started on a trek to the American Embassy in Tel Aviv to do this very thing. Enroute, Israeli police intercepted them. The blacks claimed they were mistreated by the police; the police denied it. Regardless, they were permitted to proceed to Tel Aviv. By the time they arrived, the Embassy had closed for the day. Thwarted, the blacks asserted that Ambassador Kenneth Keating had refused to see them. Embassy personnel contradicted this.[29]

They returned to the Embassy the following day and declared their intention to renounce their American citizenship. Before renunciation can take place, however, American law requires that its consequences must first be explained to the petitioner, and then a determination be made regarding his mental stability. If after re-thinking his decision he still wants to revoke his citizenship, the applicant is required to return to the Embassy.

Carter and two of his followers were pictured leaving the American Embassy after declaring their intentions.[30] Asked why he and his sect members had decided upon repudiation, Carter explained that they liked living in Israel. But far more compelling was their belief that their mission is to establish the Kingdom of God in Israel and to bring salvation to all men. Also, that the world would soon come to an end and they must be in Israel to welcome the Messiah prior to its destruction.

With all the grief the Black Hebrews have caused Israel, it is reasonable to assume that the country would be better off without them. It is unlikely, however, that they will ever be evicted from the country for various reasons. The first arrivals who came in December 1969 were handled in a peculiarly unorthodox manner. Given identification documents inscribed with "immigrant," it is hardly possible to oust them from the country.

In addition, more than 50 Black Hebrews have renounced their American citizenship and no other countries, despite earlier boasts by Arab nations, are ready to accept them. Furthermore, their recruitment of conscripts from abroad continues unabated.

An example of this is the case of two young black males who came to the American Vice-Consul in Tel Aviv on

August 8, 1975, to seek assistance in leaving the country. Black Hebrews had convinced them in Frankfort, Germany, to go to Israel, they said, but they were so disillusioned by the machinations of its leaders that their sensibilities were upset.[31] Asked how they managed to enter Israel without return tickets, they explained that their tickets were written in such a way as to give the appearance that they had paid for a round-trip. Apparently, this was another ruse devised by the Black Hebrews to outmaneuver Israeli authorities.

Of the approximately 100 to 125 blacks who either were deported or who left Israel voluntarily, some are reportedly organizing groups in the United States to encourage other blacks to move to Israel. It is a usual occurrence for black tourists in Israel to disappear from their hotels without discovering their whereabouts.

Black Hebrews are also circulating literature on black university campuses to promote immigration to Israel. When Asiel Ben Israel and Ben David visited the Johnson C. Smith University campus in Charlotte, North Carolina, on November 9, 1974, they were recruiting prospective candidates.

The effectiveness of all these efforts is uncertain, although the latest estimate of the number of Black Hebrews in Israel is put at between 750 and 1,000.[32] This is sizable growth from the 1974 figure of about 183 adults and an undetermined number of children. Much of the rise is believed to be due to natural growth with some seriously questioning the 1,000 figure.

Beyond this, deportation of the entire colony of Black Hebrews would probably foment a United Nations debate, arouse world opinion against Israel, and substantiate the Arab claim that Israel is a racist country. It is possible, though not predictable, that Israel's actions may be affected by these considerations.

Except for giving concerts at weddings and universities, playing basketball at army bases, and occasional articles in the newspapers about them as cutting a record,[33] little else is heard about them. There have been no new confrontations with the government and no new renunciations of American citizenship. Generally, the public has paid little attention to them, believing them to be either Falasha Jews from Ethiopia, or Cochin Jews from India, or blacks from New York who have undergone *halachic* conversion.

Then all at once, they were again catapaulted onto national headlines by Sansi Rona, an 8-year-old girl whose name was changed to Ahavah Bat Israel.[34] At the police department in Dimona, her mother, Soarah Jean Lee, charged Black Hebrew leaders with kidnapping her daughter. When Mrs. Lee was hospitalized in Tel Aviv, she left her daughter with the sect leaders in Dimona for safekeeping. When she was discharged from the hospital, Ahavah was not returned to her.

When Mrs. Lee located her daughter in Mitzpe Ramon, the leaders refused to surrender her. Thereupon, the police arrested four Black Hebrews there and brought them to Dimona for interrogation. Among them was the owner of the house in which Ahavah was last seen and Gabriel ha-Katan, the leader of the Black Hebrew community in Mitzpe Ramon.

The investigation that followed uncovered that the kidnapping was motivated by the Black Hebrew belief that the world, except for Israel, will be destroyed on September 22, 1977. Then, due to their efforts, the Kingdom of God will be in its glory in Jerusalem and they will assume control of the State of Israel.[35] Having learned that Mrs. Lee was contemplating returning to the United States with Ahavah, the leaders decided to "rescue" the child.

Gabriel Ben Israel, a Black Hebrew leader in Dimona, conferred with Gabriel ha-Katan in his cell at the police department. Gabriel ha-Katan agreed to reveal the whereabouts of the child only if Mrs. Lee would promise not to leave the country with Ahavah. With the pledge assured, Gabriel Ben Israel went to Mitzpe Ramon and returned Ahavah to her mother. The detained Black Hebrews were then released after posting bail.

The present attitude of Israeli officials toward the Black Hebrews is revealed in how they handled this situation. Although all the men involved in the kidnapping were in the country illegally, the government took no action against them. The officials have assumed a moderate stance toward them because they do not regard the Black Hebrews as a serious political or security threat, although their diatribes are assuming a more pronounced anti-Israel and anti-Semitic tone. In the meantime, as an Israeli official put it, "If they do not cause any disturbance, we will let the matter rest."

Chapter X

BLACK HEBREW IDENTIFICATION

The Black Hebrews adhere adamantly to the assumption that they are descendants of the ancient Hebrew patriarchs, Abraham, Isaac and Jacob—the premise that led some of them halfway around the world. To be black is a problem in America, where blacks have suffered for nearly four centuries. To be Hebrew as well compounds the problem where the dominant religion is Christianity, the wellspring of discrimination, persecution, pogroms and exile for Jews for almost two thousand years. Why would people whose skin color mitigates against them, knowingly undertake the burdens of an abhorred religious group? The search for additional ways to be disparaged and deprecated bears the earmarks of masochism. Their need lies in the history of black servitude in the United States and its parallels with Jewish history.

Slaveholding, as it developed in the United States, differed from servitude practiced in other countries. Americans used slavery to degrade and dehumanize blacks, stripping them of every vestige of human dignity, until the term "slave" and the slave system incorporated unprecedented racial doctrines.

Originally, the term "slaves" referred to white indentured servants. Indentured servitude was a contractual relationship in which the servant, compelled to surrender his freedom, bound himself to work for a master for a fixed period of time either as an apprentice, or to repay a debt or for some other reason. The master was obliged to provide life's necessities and "freedom dues"—either money or provisions—at the end of the indentured term to enable the servant to become independent and to guard against his becoming a public charge. He could sell the servant like a commodity to a new master for the remainder of the term, and the owner could demand whatever type of work he desired.[1]

It was in this manner that approximately half of the early white immigrants from England and other parts of Europe arrived in the American colonies. Many were not shipped directly to new masters but were sold at auction to the highest bidder by the ship's captain or the trading company. White servitude was introduced in Virginia in 1607 and flourished there until about 1676.[2] Where farming was the main source of income and labor was in short supply, scant attention was paid to the social status of workers or how and why they came there. Blacks were first introduced in August 1619 when twenty, who arrived on a Dutch man-of-war, were sold as servants. For the next half-century blacks continued to trickle into the colonies along with whites who were indentured. Their terms of service, like those of the white servants, were fixed by local custom and legislation. Slavery did not yet exist in the American colonies.[3]

At first it was simpler and cheaper to use white servants. There was no language barrier, some whites had technical skills, they knew the ways of Western civilization, sustained fewer losses crossing the ocean, and required less "seasoning." Blacks were imported mainly to do menial labor. Soon it became inappropriate to use the same term for both groups. By 1640, the status of the blacks underwent a transformation. Unlike the whites who could remain in America as free men with no evidence of their former servitude, the black indentured servants were seen by their masters as marked by their color with the stigma of servitude. Some masters began treating them as servants in perpetuity. Not only were they to render lifetime service, but the children of black servant women also became slaves for life. Thus was a racial distinction between black and white introduced. "Slaves" are mentioned in Virginia laws in 1656, and by 1662 mulatto children born of slave women were required to follow the status of their mothers.[4]

Although having white servants was still advantageous in that, once released, the master had no need to provide for their old age or be concerned about their health, the plantation system gave black servitude an economic advantage. Owning slaves was less expensive; slaves and their progeny furnished hereditary lifetime service; slaves were not given "freedom dues"; and, slaves were more completely under the master's control.[5] Slaves had no right to legal complaint; they were more tractable; they were not under contract as to what kind of labor they could perform; they had limited skills; and, should they escape they could be easily identified. Furthermore, slaveowners soon learned that there was no language barrier with native-born children of slaves and they were acclimatized to Western practices.

Whites, by comparison, posed problems to owners. They were generally on the same cultural level as their owners, were less submissive, and posed a moral problem in that they were Christians, while the Africans were heathens. Even when blacks were converted to Christianity, the moral problem was less acute because, it was argued, they were originally heathens and possessed an inherent racial inferiority.[6] Accordingly, as the demand for black slaves increased the need for white servants diminished.[7]

Black servants thus became chattel, and the principle of presumption arose among the colonists concerning them. Slavery was decreed hereditary, and blackness became the basis for assignment to the slave caste. All slaves were considered black and racially inferior, which led to the simplistic judgment that all blacks then must be slaves. Thus anyone judged to be a descendant of one or more black ancestors was assumed to be a slave, unless he could produce counterevidence.[8]

This principle of presumption differs from the Hebrew law of presumption. Whereas the colonists first decreed slavery was hereditary and then built a caste system based on it, Hebrew law states that in the absence of evidence that blacks had an association with Hebrew practices and institutions where they lived, it is presumed they are not Jewish.

The routine practice of dispersing family members coupled with the brutal manner in which they were brought to America, prevented slaves from knowing their origins. From diverse tribal and geographical backgrounds, the Africans had no common identity or common culture. In the deculturalization process that ensued, they first surrendered those elements of their African cultural heritage that conflicted with or differed greatly from prevailing custom and that was not essential for their survival in the new environment. Thus, little that was theirs remained with them, except where there were similarities between an African and a local institution. Then the African stamp was retained, but it manifested specific local features.[9] "They adapted part of their cultural heritage to the new environment, maintained elements, and created new methods to cope with their condition."[10] Then, a slave ethos emerged that provided them with cultural tools "necessary to develop a sense of peoplehood and to evolve their own mores and patterns of living."

Adrift from their moorings and compelled to discard features of their past to survive, inevitably they came to believe they had no past, no heritage, certainly none worth preserving. The blacks thus shared no real sense of history or historical identity, which are essential for the preservation of any minority group.

The separation of families detribalized the blacks, making it impossible for them to function as a group. In Africa, tribalism provided a sense of security and continuity and afforded sustenance through sharing. A hunter's kill was shared by all villagers; the children belonged to the village, with everyone concerned about them. Even the poorly endowed and least productive member of the tribe could feel a sense of identity in human relationships that were tempered with love and compassion. Tribal life was happy communal living; individualism was non-existent.

In America, the loss of tribal ties obliterated the slaves' culture. They were unable to construct an ethnic tradition, nor could they muster effective opposition to the institution of slavery. Attempts to revolt, like that of the Reverend Nat Turner in 1831 which resulted in the deaths of 57 whites and 100 blacks, only brought more severe restrictions in their wake.

Marriage as a legal institution was non-existent for American black slaves. Having no legal rights they were unable to enter into marriage contracts. Occasionally, however, marriage ceremonies, conducted by a white or black minister or by the master, were held for favored house slaves, although they were neither recognized nor binding. Field slaves might be married by either a black preacher or the master. On larger plantations, slaves devised other forms of marriage ceremonies.

"Jumping the broom"[11] was one of them. The slaves imposed the "ritual upon themselves because they needed some symbolism to bind them to one another." A broom was either laid on the floor or held a foot off the ground. When the man and woman jumped over it they were married. If either one stumbled on the broom, it was interpreted as a sign that trouble was ahead for them. As can well be imagined, they all jumped as high as they could, which amused the witnesses. If a couple wanted to divorce, they would jump backwards over the broom.

Another marriage procedure was the "blanket-wedding."[12] The slave community assembled in a hut where the bridegroom placed his blanket on the floor and awaited the bride. When she came and laid her blanket beside the groom's blanket, they were regarded as married. It is said that black preachers realistically married couples "until death and distance do us part."

Some slaves thus had socially, if not legally, recognized marriages, where father, mother and children lived together and apparently functioned as a nuclear family. Despite this development—and all slave marriages took place with the master's permission—no obstacle, except his own conscience, barred a slaveholder from selling his slave family to different people. Families were disrupted, and separations were especially common when the master died. His children would frequently sell some slaves.

Holding no legal or recognized status in the family, often

the father was more like a visitor and the amorphous family centralized around the mother or in her absence around the grandmother or some other female on the plantation. As a result, the lost tribal nurturing system was not replaced by a firm family structure. From infancy black children had no consistent male model after whom to pattern themselves and female models were frequently interchangeable.

The black male child was thus robbed of his manhood, for psychologists note that a child's identification with the parent of the same sex is the most important influence in his life prior to six years of age. Up to that age, a boy begins to imitate his father and eventually strengthens his masculine identification. The father's presence thus facilitates appropriate sex-role identification in his son.

When there is no father at home, studies indicate boys are less well-adjusted in peer relations, may imitate females or display exaggerated masculine behavior, and have lower IQ scores.[13] Studies among poor and lower middle-class black babies show that the more attention the father pays to his baby son, the brighter, more alert, more inquisitive and happier is the baby likely to be when he reaches his fifth or sixth month.[14]

The adult male behavior most visible to the boy born in slavery was his visit and then his departure. The male did not remain at home. Concomitantly, the adult male was denied the responsibility to fulfill the roles of provider-protector and discipliner of family members; these were assigned to the white master. And the female, often used sexually to satisfy the white man, might well have regarded womanhood as a peculiar phenomenon. From the family point of view, slaves had few cultural and social strengths to uphold them.

Although slavery legally came to an end after the Civil War, the physical, mental and emotional abuse blacks had suffered for 250 years in the United States continued to have the support of the social structure, and in the 1890s were once again enforced by law in the Southern states.[15] Segregation was then consciously and deliberately applied against the blacks in all areas of contact. They almost never walked with white people in public. When they met a white person on the street, they were expected, as in Richmond, Virginia, "to give the wall," and, if necessary, to get off the sidewalk into the street.[16] They were excluded from all developed culture, whether it be African or white Christian American. Emancipation did not enable the blacks to break these restraints nor did it resolve their resentments or satisfy their basic needs of peoplehood. Their lives were too animal-like for them to develop group pride and inner security. The granting of equality was like a dream that vanishes upon awakening to reality.

Freedom furthermore deepened their distress. Abruptly freed, many former slaves left the fields and farms only to be deluged by problems in a setting unfamiliar to many of them —urban life. Disoriented and totally lacking in social organization, individuals coped with their fears and frustrations as fully as they could.

Emancipation was not even hoped for by some slaves and only a relative few actually fought for it. But now that it was theirs, they accepted it, reluctantly yet with some measure of expectation. They were now to be active participants in the stream of history. Their first need was to establish some organized social structure among themselves to enable them to function with and within the larger society of which they were now a part. But they soon learned that their new condition did not really change things. While they were now a part of the social structure, they were a helpless fragment. Emancipated, they were in no position to contribute to history. In fact, they were not free to act. They were forbidden to work creatively within the social group of which they were now a segment. Paradoxically, they were expected to act responsibly, but did not share in responsible tasks. In reality, their freedom was no freedom.

Their situation was even more threatening than was that of the Hebrew slaves when they were liberated from Egypt. They had the greatest of leaders, Moses, to direct and guide them in their new circumstance. Yet, even with Moses, an entire generation had to pass away before they were regarded as competent to settle in the land of Canaan. How much more formidable were the difficulties the blacks had to deal with being essentially a rudderless mass.

As freedmen, the vast majority of blacks were denied the opportunity to develop personal and social self-concepts. Each individual must cope with both these spheres. The personal self-concept deals with how an individual sees himself. One's social self-concept relates to his perception of the degree of his success or failure in interacting effectively with the social environment. Interwoven with each other, these concepts serve as catalysts in the emotional growth of an individual. As he gains greater social competence, he develops a healthier self-concept, he functions successfully, and he helps shape society. The degree of his effectiveness is in direct proportion to the successes he scores. Each forward movement enables him to acquire general knowledge, techniques and skills which assure him of still further successes, and enables him to experience reality and to respond to the consequences. Should, however, an individual develop a poor opinion of himself, his low self-esteem will hinder his social competency.

The freed blacks were compelled to develop poor images of themselves in both these areas. Regarded as undesirables, they were barred from functioning as participating members of society and were accordingly consigned to subordinate positions. Unable to feel socially competent and to find a purpose in life, ingredients necessary for a meaningful life, their development—psychologically, politically, economically and socially—was stunted. They had to content themselves with observing others as they functioned, with a minimum of communication between themselves and the outside world. Helpless and alienated, they felt invisible and sensed their powerlessness and isolation.

Opinions differ with regard to the effect their degradation had on the development of their self-images. The general approach places the responsibility for all the inadequacies that beset the race onto the treatment accorded them by the white community. Others, however, disagree.[17] While they concede that some blacks have been overwhelmed by the unfortunate and inhuman circumstances to which they had been subjected, they maintain that the extent to which blacks have been affected inwardly by these conditions has been overestimated. Because blacks learned to behave subserviently in the presence of whites is no indication that they felt inferior within. Many harbored indomitable spirits that enabled them to overcome their predicament. Men like Booker T. Washington, George Washington Carver, Frederick Douglass and a host of others mentioned earlier seem to support this contention. One must admit, however, that they were a distinct minority.

Because the blacks were compelled to live separately, they organized themselves along ethnic lines. They lived as newly arrived immigrants do. Poverty was their lot, their labor was menial, and crime abounded. But unlike immigrants, their family structure was not stable.

Emancipation did not afford the erstwhile slaves religious equality either. During slavery, churches were not organized along color lines. Slaves were permitted to worship in white churches and to become members. But this practice led to complications. Masters and slaves were embarrassed in each other's presence, ministers were hard pressed to adapt their sermons to an audience so diverse in interests, backgrounds, needs and vocabularies, and the blacks were discriminated against. As a result, black congregations and Sunday Schools were established.

At first, the newly organized black congregations were housed in the white churches, but subordinate to them. Then, displeased by the domination of the white churchmen, blacks organized their own churches. They established the first Negro Baptist Church in 1773, the Protestant Episcopal Church for Negroes in 1787, and the African Methodist Episcopal (AME) Zion Church in 1820. Still other factors influenced them to separate themselves from whites. They had a special need for fellowship and fraternalization among themselves and some blacks had personal ambitions to become leaders. The churches they ran afforded them the only opportunity to assert authority.[18]

Despite the separation of the races, the heavy hand of white domination continued to circumscribe black church activities. Following the Nat Turner rebellion, laws were enacted that limited the freedom of Negro preachers. In 1831, black ministers were prohibited to preach in North Carolina. In 1832-33, Virginia and Alabama ordered that Negro preachers sermonize only in the presence of trustworthy whites. After 1834, Georgia legislators directed that black preachers needed licenses to preach. Securing a certificate from a white ordained minister was the first step in accomplishing this end.[19]

During Reconstruction, the number of black churches mushroomed. Assistance from the North stimulated their rapid growth, but worshiping by themselves made the blacks vulnerable to the influences of quacks and demagogues.[20] This susceptibility was not limited to the newly freed slaves. It is rampant today too in predominantly black neighborhoods in large cities where religious sects crop up with regularity in storefronts and apartments.[21] Often fly-by-night operations, these cults are led by "prophets" or other titled founders with personal motives. Anyone who could acquire a following, regardless of size, or claimed receiving a call from God, or who had an acquaintance with the Bible, could become a preacher. In addition to financial gain, it helped them attain status when every other avenue for such accomplishment was closed to them.

But while these pretenders are self-serving, they satisfy the needs of the cultists by adding meaning to lives devoid of content and by raising spirits sagging under the weight of insignificance. Unable to acquire meaningful experiences and feelings of self-importance in the established churches, the sects functioned for them as shells of protection and provided them with group identification.

Storefront churches are the usual religious institutions in Northern cities of people newly arrived from the South who have had a warm and satisfactory experience in small churches. City churches tend to be large and impersonal and do not provide warm, intimate settings the newcomers need. In storefront churches they are recognized, appreciated and can participate as persons.

The over-all situation that pervaded the Negro social structure after emancipation, left some unfinished tasks to be completed. The most overriding undertaking of all was their need to develop a sense of selfhood, because centuries of brainwashing had convinced them that they were racially inferior, culturally naked and devoid of worth as human beings. Products of their psychological environment, they lacked confidence in their basic abilities as persons.

Unsure of who they were and ashamed of what they were, the blacks experienced an identity-crisis. Seeing themselves through the eyes of the unfriendly majority, they identified with the aggressor and adopted toward themselves the hostility that prevailed toward blacks, which was the antithesis of group identification.[22] They hated their blackness because it separated them from the majority to which they yearned to belong. They did not seem to realize that their self-hatred resulted from their attitude toward themselves and their blackness, not from their individual personalities. When members of an underprivileged group seek to escape the consequences of a difficult situation, they leave the group. But for the blacks this was no solution because their skin color could not be rubbed off; blackness was theirs forever. Locked into an inescapable situation, they lived in a perpetual state of tension.

To compound their problem, the blacks were told that the United States is a democratic country, and in a democracy all citizens possess equal rights and are treated alike. But their personal experiences contradicted this claim. By no stretch of the imagination could it be argued that they were equal to the whites. Uncertain of their position in American society, adjusting was a difficult process. Displeased with existing conditions, they were frustrated seeing they were helpless to change them.

The problem of identity, a phenomenon as old as man, burdens many people. Basically, it is aroused by a lack of purpose in life and the concomitant search for meaning in existence. Following emancipation, blacks were deeply immersed in this problem, as are their descendants today.

How does one acquire a wholesome self-image? Some blacks felt that possessing a cultural and social structure would furnish them with feelings of worth and dignity and would enable them to relate to whites on a basis of equality. Others, to avoid confrontation with an unfriendly and often destructive environment, chose to remain in the background. Shunning open contact with the majority would be far less denigrating. Still others used devious tactics to bolster their egos in their own eyes. Speaking in Charlotte, North Carolina, Mayor Charles Evers of Lafayette, Mississippi, told that in his youth he worked in a restaurant. To "get back at the white folks," he would stir their coffee with his finger (one wonders how often he scalded it), and would sometimes spit in their food—in the kitchen, of course. His behavior was similar to that of children who, desiring to "get even" with their parents, would spit on their clothing as it hung in the closet.

Many of the newly freed blacks engaged in another strategy to circumvent the shortcomings imposed upon them. They would align themselves with an existing group already blessed with a well-established background and heritage. This approach would immediately add substance to their lives, would help them escape the reality of the present, and would elevate their status.

Affiliating with a conventional church was a path a vast majority of the erstwhile slaves took. It rankled many of them to associate with an institution that had justified slavery and had sided with their oppressors. Many white churchmen not only condoned slavery but were religious racists. They at first denied black slaves the opportunity to become Christians, because they did not regard Negroes as human beings. Not being Christian, they could not be admitted to the sacraments. And when the slaves were accepted into the faith, many colonies passed laws ruling that baptism did not confer freedom upon them.[23] Nevertheless, the blacks felt that in the long run the benefits of joining were promising. Once they identified with the church, they reasoned, their anxieties would disappear. Affiliation would serve for them as a defense mechanism. It would bolster their ego and engender within them qualities they sorely wanted to possess.

It is interesting to note how white Christian leaders vindicated the practice of slavery. Quoting Scripture, they interpreted the verse, "And as for thy bondmen, and thy bondmaids, whom thou mayest have: of the nations that are round about you, of them shall ye buy bondmen and bondmaids" (Leviticus 25:44), to mean that non-Christians may be kept in perpetual servitude. Another claim to support slavery was that it enabled the church to save the souls of the blacks. But what about slaves who had been converted to Christianity? Again turning to Scripture, Christian leaders devised an explanation based on race. All blacks are condemned to bondage, they argued, because they are the children of Ham (or Canaan) who was cursed by Noah to be "a servant of servants . . . unto his brethren" (Genesis 9:25).

Other blacks aligned themselves with divergent non-Christian religious sects. In this way, they rejected Christianity and asserted their independence of the white man and his paradoxical moral and religious principles.

Another group found an answer to their plight by making blackness work for them. Their basic premise was that the Hebrew Patriarchs, Abraham, Isaac and Jacob, were black. As blacks who were Jewish, they saw themselves as the direct descendants of the progenitors of the Children of Israel. Race thus became a decisive factor in acquiring an elevated status. A black skin was a basis for self-esteem. As the sole bearers of the Jewish heritage, they considered all others who made this claim imposters, usurpers who had to be dislodged. They even regarded themselves as superior to other blacks who did not make this claim of Jewishness.

Familiar with the Jewish Bible[24] and accepting it as the literal word of God, they moved from admiring the Patriarchs to adopting them as their own ancestors. From high esteem (or envy) of the modern Jew, the blacks began to imitate him and to identify with him.

This did not come about suddenly. Their identity crisis existed even before emancipation. While yet slaves, some of the more thoughtful ones wondered about their background. Who were they? Where did they come from? What did they have to look forward to? They felt alienated, suffered anomie, and saw no future for themselves as freedmen. They wanted something more for themselves and their children. By embracing a Jewish identity they added depth to their existence which challenged them to strive for higher achievement.

Thus, simultaneously they attained a sense of dignity and worth, and acquired a history, a people, a heritage and a culture. Possessing a defense against feelings of insignificance, they overcame anxiety. By associating themselves with a well established, highly revered and honored ancestry, they elevated their pride and entered Western society as equals in the Judeo-Christian tradition. It mattered little that this was an attempt at counterfeit self-esteem, since they knew perfectly well they did not have the remotest blood relationship with the Patriarchs. They had eagerly searched for an elevated self-image and now they had it.

They knowingly adopted Judaism because they did not view it as assuming an additional infirmity, but as upgrading their status. No, they were not masochistic. Rather, to be Jewish was more important to them than the inconvenience of any additional restrictions that might be directed against them. That no one took their claim seriously, not even the Jewish community, did not disturb them. It was just another manifestation of cruelty directed against them. What mattered most was that they believed it, and accepting it gave them inner peace.

As a result of this action, a number of small black Jewish sects began to appear in New York City after World War I. None had historical links to the Jewish people, but reflected rather the religious cults and charismatic entrepreneurs among blacks. Still retaining Jesus as Savior, they adopted certain Jewish practices. The sects celebrated the Festival of Passover as the most important holy day of their religious year, because it commemorated for them two liberations—from Egyptian bondage and from American slavery. From these groups black Jews spread to other metropolitan cities such as Chicago, Boston, Philadelphia and Cincinnati. The blacks who left for Liberia undoubtedly were offshoots of one of these Harlem groups.

The soul-searching pretense of being Jewish fortified them to face the morrow with dignity. Perceiving themselves as Jews gave them an identity that was understood and recognized by all civilized people. It especially made an impression upon the Christian who, in the Bible Belt of the South, was well-versed in Scripture, but often remarkably uninformed about Jews and Jewish practices.

Assuming a Hebrew identity was to know who one was. As God's blessed chosen people, they were the bearers of a special revelation. It was their ancestors who received the Torah with its Ten Commandments on Mount Sinai. Being a Hebrew was a privilege that carried with it a responsibility. It didn't matter that they were mistreated and maligned and despised, for soon everyone would know the truth about them. Eventually God would redeem them as His suffering servants. They now had stature and this enabled them to walk with straight backs and heads upraised. Calling themselves Jews was especially meaningful after having been taught for years that the Negro "is a beast," is "akin to the monkey," and is a member of "an ignorant, debased and debauched race."[25] Their new identity washed all this away.

What may further have encouraged them to pursue this approach was that blacks had frequently been urged by such leaders as Benjamin Tucker Tanner, editor of the *African Methodist Episcopal Church Review*, 1864-1884, and Booker T. Washington, the noted black American educator, to emulate the Jews, especially with regard to inner pride and mutual supportiveness. The implication was that this would lead to their financial success and social acceptance; that it would serve as an antidote to the disorganization that was rampant among blacks; that it would promote a cohesiveness among them and strengthen their emotional and structural bonds. Like the Jewish people, the blacks would develop a social structure that would redound to their welfare.[26]

Washington spoke of the Jew's "unity, pride, and love of race." "Unless," he said, "the Negro learns more and more to imitate the Jew in these matters, to have faith in himself, he cannot expect to have any high degree of success."[27] He frequently used the Biblical expression that refers to the Jewish people as "a peculiar people," to describe the black race in the United States.

It was essential for them to have these deep, firm roots because black Americans were unlike other minorities in the United States. Other groups could identify themselves with a heritage and a culture; blacks could not. Italians, Irish and Orientals, for example, could point to a particular country as their place of origin. Blacks could not. They may claim a continent but it is not sufficiently specific to be meaningful. An individual who says he comes from Family X has a more marked and more comforting identity than one who says, "I belong to the human race." This may explain partially why the back-to-Africa movements, as tantalizing as they were, were unable to attract large numbers of blacks. Although such movements date back to 1714, the number of blacks who emigrated to Africa was minimal.

The slaves felt a particular affinity to the Children of Israel because of their attachment to the Jewish Bible. The section of Scripture they saw as most relevant to them was the enslavement of the Jews in Egypt and the story of the Exodus—the miraculous deliverance of the Hebrews from the hands of Pharoah. Similarities between their own plight and that of the Israelites abounded. Both were in bondage to harsh taskmasters; both suffered through no fault of their own; both knew how it felt to be despised and mistreated in the same intolerant and bigoted ways; both were involved in migrations; both could sympathize with the other's minority status; both were excluded from effective participation in and contribution to American society; and, both turned inward to strengthen their emotional and structural bonds of cohesion.

This parallelism intensified the identification between their plight and that of the Jews whose God battled for them and swept their enemies away before them. Did not their God enable them to withstand the unremitting hostility of Christians throughout centuries of hatred? They could believe in a God who showed such intense and immense interest in His believers. Coupled with the concepts of election and the promise of the possession of a land, the entire package captured the imagination of black religious people. Negro spirituals, replete with Biblical names and places, are poignant expressions of this identification.

The Jewish Bible served the blacks in yet another way. As a result of Biblical allusions, they initiated a number of revolts. For example, Gabriel Prosser, a slave in Virginia and a student of the Bible, led an insurrection by slaves out of religious conviction. Identifying with Samson, his favorite Biblical hero, he wore his hair long as Samson had and was convinced that God had selected him to deliver His people. As the black

Samson, he would shatter the slave system and establish a nation of free blacks in America. It is reported that his was probably the first of many well-planned revolutionary attempts. The night the attack was to take place, a violent storm erupted and his followers, estimated in the thousands, disbanded in confusion believing it to be a sign from the Lord that He did not look favorably upon the plan.[28]

The preacher Nat Turner claimed he was moved by the spirit of the Jewish prophets and the words of Jesus to foment his great insurrection.[29] And Psalms 68:32, "Nobles shall come out of Egypt; Ethiopia shall hasten to stretch out her hands unto God," became the "ultimate fulfillment of the black man's spiritual yearning."

Others perceived similar intimations. Denmark Vesey saw in Joshua's siege of Jericho a parallel between the Jews and the American slaves. After the Hebrews crossed the Jordan River, the walled cities barred them from settling in their land. The blacks who came to the New World were likewise prevented from attaining their freedom by the rich and powerful cities that dominated the country.[30]

The Bible came to mean different things to black preachers. It became "the cornerstone for missionary emigrationism in the Black church," and "the Black church in the United States" came to symbolize "the ark of safety for the regenerate children of Ham."[31]

How different this was from what Christian ministers had taught them. The Christianity that was preached to them aimed to keep them enslaved, to perpetuate their inferior and intolerable status. The Christian God made a virtue of accepting meekly the suffering and persecution to which they had been subjected. Their disillusionment with Christianity ran deep as it was expressed decades later by Ben Ammi Carter. "The Christians have dealt treacherously with us and have sold us for 400 years." No black could be a Christian without betraying the cause of black manhood and black liberation.

Furthermore, Christianity could not supply them with the roots they sought. It did not possess a proud culture that reached as far back into the ancient past as did Judaism. In fact, without Judaism Christianity had no foundation on which to base its claims about Jesus' messiahship and the historicity of its founding. With Judaism, they instantly established an unbroken tie with the distant past and with a proud culture 4,000 years old, and entered into a direct relationship with God Himself. "It is with Israel that God made the covenant and it is Israel who will be resurrected when the Messiah comes . . . We are the elect of Israel," said Rabbi Wentworth Matthews.

The deliverance of the Jews from slavery captured the imagination of religious leaders generally. The American colonists likewise applied the simile of Egyptian bondage to their treatment at the hands of Great Britain, and their efforts at freedom as similar to the Jewish struggle against tyranny and enslavement.

Despite the attachment blacks had to Africa, it was not the solution to the race problem. It is much easier to identify with a particular piece of real estate, as the Jewish people do with *Eretz Yisrael*, than with a large mass of land. Even with Israel, no voluntary mass exodus has taken place from countries with large Jewish populations. *Aliyah* (immigration to Israel) is a continuing struggle for The Jewish Agency. The 20-year period from 1948 to 1968 saw only 8,800 American Jews emigrate to Israel and of them, a significant number has returned to the United States.[32]

This trend was evident among blacks as well. Even when black leaders selected particular areas in which to establish colonies, their movements were still referred to as "back-to-Africa" adventures and not as "back-to-Ghana" or "back-to-Liberia" projects.

The black Jews in Chicago had reached a point where they saw no future for themselves in the United States. So they journeyed to Africa to rid themselves of their "negrotism"— their feelings of servility. But this venture also proved to be a failure. Deciding to capitalize on their Jewishness, they went to Israel and sought to be recipients of all the benefits given to Jewish immigrants. The United States had failed them; Liberia was a misguided undertaking; Israel would pay off. With the mood of the world favorably disposed toward blacks, they reasoned, Israel would be compelled to treat them with deference and take their claim seriously lest it be described as racist and incur unfavorable world opinion.

Israel did extend itself on their behalf, but did not surrender to their demands. The blacks could enter the country as American citizens, but they would need to comply with state law. The State of Israel tried to cooperate with them, but they stubbornly insisted that Israel conform to their demands. This is where they made their greatest mistake. Not only did they muff the ball; they struck out. Their many attempts to harm the State and to inconvenience private citizens removed whatever leverage they may have had. The insistence that the State belongs to them was a disaster. It will be Israel's way or no way—and the blacks know it. Usurping a heritage availed them nothing, nor did all their letter writing.

Asked whether or not his group would accept Israeli citizenship if it were offered to them, Shaleak Ben Yehudah was quick to reply in the affirmative.[33] The Black Hebrews would like to become Israeli citizens, but it will not be offered to them unless they ask for it and conform to the laws of the State.

At some time, every black person concludes that he has been penalized because of his skin color, and occasionally his assumption is correct. Blackness keeps some from attaining their goal. The Black Hebrews, however, failed to accomplish their objectives because of their own obtuseness, not because of their group identity.

Despite their protestations, the Black Hebrews are more obsessed with the problem of identity than with accepting the tasks and responsibilities of the State of Israel. Being able to call a land their own would have a beneficial effect upon them. It would normalize their lives and serve as a constructive force. And Israel might well have been the place where this could have taken place. The Holy Land is part of what may be called the Promised Land syndrome. Regardless of how meager an education people may have, they are acquainted with the Bible. To them, this small parcel of land has special significance. Other places may better serve the purposes of the American blacks, but they have heard of Jerusalem and the assurance of redemption. Thus, Israel represented to the Black

Hebrews a political or national solution, not a religious or cultural one.

The Black Hebrews have never truly identified with the Jewish people. To identify means to adopt Jewishness thoroughly and meaningfully as a way of life. It means to assume the responsibilities that being Jewish demands; to accept the advantages and disadvantages of the Jewish people; to feel themselves a part of the Jewish heritage. It means to model themselves after the people with whom they seek to identify. The blacks have done none of this.

The Black Hebrews are still in the oedipal stage. They are attempting to kill the father (the State) and to possess the mother (the land). They have not yet achieved identification, for if they had, they would have a love and a respect for the Jewish people. Instead, they have criticized them and attempted to embarrass the State in many ways. To justify their assertions, they have even used Hitler's *Mein Kampf*. Fleeing prejudice, they have been willing to use it for selfish purposes. Identification means to be identical with the model, not to destroy it.

Eventually, the Black Hebrews may make peace with Israel because they have a need to identify with a country. Also, people will usually identify with a successful rival and the State has proven itself to be just that. The government has demonstrated that it is too powerful for them and they realize that it is both an effective punisher and an effective provider. Recognizing the futility of their provocations, they may wholly cease their hostile and aggressive actions against the State and come to terms with its requirements to achieve full acceptance. Then will they be able to clarify their clouded and contradictory notions concerning their relationship with the Jewish people.

Almost as long as they have been in Israel, they have conducted themselves as lower-class children who commonly hold few positive attitudes toward adult authority figures because they have often experienced rejection. Their behaving coldly and indifferently may in reality be their way of concealing a yearning for a warm relationship.

When they left the United States, the Black Hebrews took

their first painful steps as free men. Their failures have been the failures of people who have not yet learned the techniques of social organization. In Liberia, they floundered for lack of leadership. And Carter, their one strong leader, was himself operating in a vacuum. There was no system for making decisions as a community, no authority except his personal magnetism. Nor could the Liberian government provide a workable pattern to emulate. With only a brief history, a borrowed constitution, and a conception of humanity limited by a reverse racism, it was not yet strong enough to withstand the threat of internal dissension.

In the brief span of time that the Black Hebrews have been in Israel, they have taken a leap across centuries of social evolution. Almost without realizing it, they have followed the advice of Booker T. Washington. By living among Jews in a Jewish nation, they have unwittingly initiated some of the patterns the Jewish people evolved over centuries of self-discipline. They have confronted the unyielding first commandment, "I am the Lord thy God." They are not (or not yet) prepared to commit themselves to it wholly by renewing the covenant through conversion, but they have emulated the Jews in many strange and sometimes amusing and illogical ways. If the Jews, the People of the Book, cite Biblical authority for their position, the Black Hebrews support their own in similar fashion. If Jews, escaping from the holocaust, entered Palestine illegally, the Black Hebrews escaping white oppression could find a way to enter Israel, legal or not. If the Israelis speak of deportation, the Black Hebrews threaten the same when they come to power; if the Israelis insist upon conversion, the Black Hebrews warn they will require everyone to follow their ways when they take over; if the Jews point to their history of persecution, the Black Hebrews cry "Jim Crow." Their response is not always appropriate, but they have demonstrated the determination to survive—the will to persist—that is the strength of the Jewish people.

Gradually, the Black Hebrews have learned to adjust to external pressures. They have begun to focus their attention on themselves, to find their weaknesses and their strengths. They have begun to recognize that there is strength in community. They have instituted their first form of self-government, the Council of Twelve Princes, and invested it with authority. They have made the partial sacrifice of individual freedom to achieve stability, and they have taken the awesome responsibility of enforcing conformity with the threat of expulsion from the group. And they have enforced it.

Whether or not the Black Hebrews will abandon their preoccupation with terminology and revert to the identity of Black Jews, whether or not they will convert or remain pseudo-Jews, whether or not they will remain in Israel or move on—these are all possible and all unknowable. There is no doubt, however, that unless they do formally adopt Judaism, their future in Israel is precarious. Surrendering their American citizenship does not assure them longevity in the country or acceptance by Israeli citizens.

NOTES TO CHAPTER I

1. Jews generally feel it improper to use the King James Version of Scripture for various reasons. It contains Christian headings, and to support Christian Messianic interpretations its translations are inexact. For example, to bolster the Christian claim of the Virgin Birth, Isaiah 7:14 is translated as "a virgin shall conceive." The literal translation is "the young woman shall conceive."
2. Rolner, Murray, "Black and Being Jewish," *The National Jewish Monthly*, (October 1972) 43.
3. *Hatzaad Harishon* was founded in 1964 by Jacob Gladstone, a white Hebrew teacher, who aimed to build an organized black Jewish community that would establish lines of communication between black and white Jews for the purpose of bringing them into a common relationship.
4. Ploski, Harry A. and Warren Marr, *Negro Almanac: A Reference Work on the Afro American*, New York: Bellweather Co., 1976, p. 969.
5. *Christianity Today*, December 7, 1973, p. 53.
6. Borsten, Joan, "Sect Problems," *The Jerusalem Post International Edition*, December 7, 1976, p. 9.
7. Asiel Ben Israel, International Ambassador of the Original Hebrew Israelite Nation, told the author at Johnson C. Smith University on November 19, 1974, that not Greer, but Gavriel Ben Israel was appointed to the committee. Greer's name, however, has come up too frequently not to accept it. It should be noted that there is much contradiction in the information supplied by different members and spokesmen of the group.
8. Ajala, Adekunle, *Pan-Africanism*, London: Andre Deutsch, Ltd., 1973, p. 1-4; Legum, Colin, *Africa: A Handbook to the Continent*, New York: Prager Publishers, 1968, p. 413.
9. Carmichael, Stokely, "Pan-Africanism—Land and Power," *The Black Scholar*, November 1969, p. 7.
10. "Meredith Now Looks to Future in Africa," *The Charlotte Observer*, June 6, 1976, p. 4A.
11. Aptheker, Herbert, editor, *A Documentary History of the Negro People in the United States*, New York: The Citadel Press, 1951, p. 648-9, 713.
12. Moses, Wilson J., "Marcus Garvey: A Reappraisal," *The Black Scholar*, 4:3 (November-December 1972) 40; Adams, Russell L., *Great Negroes Past and Present*, Chicago: Afro-Am Publishing Co., 1972, p. 108.
13. Aptheker, H., *Op. Cit.*, p. 648-9, 653; Moses, W. J., *Op. Cit.*, p. 40.

14. Meier, August, *Negro Thoughts in America 1880-1915*, Ann Arbor: University of Michigan Press, 1964, p. 66.
15. Tindall, George B., "The Liberian Exodus of 1878," *South Carolina Historical Magazine*, 53:3 (July 1952) 139; Moses, W. J., *Op. Cit.*, p. 40.
16. Lynch, H. R., *Op. Cit.*, p. 16f.
17. *Ibid.*, p. 60f.
18. *Ibid.*, p. 250.
19. Rudwick, Elliott M., *W. E. B. DuBois: A Study in Minority Group Leadership*, Philadelphia: University of Pennsylvania Press, 1960, p. 208, 210.
20. Washington, Booker T., *The Future of the American Negro*, New York: The New American Library, Inc., 1969; p. 159-160; ——, *Up From Slavery*, New York: Dodd, Mead and Co., 1965, p. 181.
21. Wilmore, Gayraud S., *Black Religion and Black Radicalism*, New York: Doubleday and Co., 1972, p. 203.
22. *Ibid.*, p. 207.
23. Vincent, Theodore C., *Black Power and the Garvey Movement*, Berkely: Rampart Press, 1971, p. 134f.
24. Cronan, Edmund D., *Black Moses*, Madison: University of Wisconsin Press, 1968, p. 199f; Rose, Arnold M., *The Negro's Morale*, Minneapolis: The University of Minnesota Press, 1949, p. 43-45.
25. Conrad, Earl, *Harriet Tubman*, New York: Paul S. Eriksson, Inc., 1943, p. 49.
26. Cronan, E. D., *Op. Cit.*, p. 181.
27. Polos, Nicholas C., "Black Anti-Semitism in Twentieth Century America: Historical Myth or Reality," *American Jewish Archives*, 27:1 (April 1975) 14-15.
28. Ottley, Roi, *New World A-Coming*, New York: World Publishing Co., 1943, p. 149-150.
29. Rose, A. M., *Op. Cit.*, p. 22, 123, 134f.
30. Weisbord, Robert G., *Ebony Kinship*, Westport, Connecticut: Greenwood Press, 1973, p. 93.
31. Buch, Saul, "Falasha: The Black Jews of Africa Revisited," *The American Zionist*, 64:1 (September 1973) 18.
32. Brotz, Howard M., *The Black Jews of Harlem*, New York: Schocken Books, 1970, p. 12, 49; ——, "Negro 'Jews' in the United States," *Phylon*, 13 (1952) 329.
33. Brotz, H. M., *The Black Jews of Harlem*, p. 12; Lincoln, C. Eric, *The Black Muslims in America*, Boston: Beacon Press, 1961, p. 11.
34. Samuel X, "A Brief History of the Messenger," *Muhammad Speaks*, Special Issue, no date, p. 4; *Muhammad Speaks*, March 21, 1975, p. S-4.
35. Lincoln, C. E., *Op. Cit.*, p. 10f.
36. Waitzkin, Howard, "Black Judaism in New York," *Harvard Journal of Negro Affairs*, 1:3 (1967) 17-18.
37. King, Kenneth J., "Some Notes on Arnold J. Ford and New World Black Attitudes to Ethiopia," *Journal of Ethiopian Studies*, 10:1 (January 1972) 81.
38. *Ibid.*
39. *Ibid.*, 81, 85.
40. Waitzkin, H., *Op. Cit.*
41. Scheer, Robert, *Eldridge Cleaver: Post-Prison Writings and Speeches*, New York: Rampart Books, 1969, p. 67-69.
42. Blitzer, Wolf, "Arabs are the World's Worse Racists, Says Eldridge

Cleaver," *The Jerusalem Post Weekly*, January 20, 1976, p. 14.

43. Isaacs, Harold R., *The New World of Negro Americans*, New York: The John Day Co., 1963, p. 304.

44. "Arrest Sect Leader, Seize Arms Cache," *Chicago American*, May 25, 1968.

45. Brodie, Fawn M., *Thomas Jefferson: An Intimate History*, New York: W. W. Norton and Co., Inc., 1974, p. 159.

46. *Ibid.*, p. 441. The first half of the statement reads, "Nothing is more certainly written into the book of fate, than that these people are to be free."

47. Redding, Saunders, *They Came in Chains*, Philadelphia and New York: J. B. Lippincott Co., 1973, p. 76.

48. Young, James C., *Liberia Rediscovered*, New York: Doubleday, Doran and Co., 1934, p. 5f. In Charles M. Wilson's *Liberia*, New York: William Sloane Associates, 1947, p. 11, his name is given as Robert Goodlowe Harper.

49. Constitution of Liberia, Article 1, Section 3.

50. Liberian Code of Laws of 1956, Miscellaneous Provisions, Article 5, Section 13.

51. The author was given this information at the Firestone Plant outside of Monrovia.

52. Isaacs, H. R., *Op. Cit.*, p. 119f.

53. *Ibid.*, p. 117f.; Harris, Sheldon H., *Paul Cuffe*, New York: Simon and Schuster, 1972, p. 70; Garvey, Amy Jacques, *Philosophy and Opinion of Marcus Garvey*, New York: Arno Press & The New York Times, 1969, p. v.

54. Harris, S. H., *Op. Cit.*, p. 64.

55. Garvey, A. J., *Op. Cit.*, p. iii-vii.

56. Weisbord, R. G., *Op. Cit.*, p. 15f.

57. Garrison, William Lloyd, *Thoughts on African Colonization*, New York: Arno Press & The New York Times, 1968, p. vi, xi; Harris, S. H., *Op. Cit.*, p. 70.

58. Garrison, W. L., *Op. Cit.*, p. xiif.

59. Meier, August and Elliott M. Rudwick, *From Plantation to Ghetto*, New York: Hill and Wang, 1966, p. 80.

60. *Ibid.*

61. Golden, Harry, *Only in America*, Cleveland and New York: The World Publishing Co., 1958, p. 121f.

62. Meier, A. and E. M. Rudwick, *Op. Cit.*, p. 134f.

63. Garrison, W. L., *Op. Cit.*, Part II, p. 35.

64. "American Colonization Society," *Encyclopedia Americana*, New York: American Corporation, 1975, Vol. 1, p. 681.

65. Fisher, Miles M., *The Evolution of Slave Songs of the United States*, dissertation, University of Chicago, December 1948, p. 214-216 .

66. Meier, A. and E. M. Rudwick, *Op. Cit.*, p. 111.

67. *Ibid.*, p. 109-110.

68. Jones, Reginald L., ed., *Black Psychology*, New York: Harper and Row, Publishers, 1972, p. 315-6.

69. "Jewish Negroes From Chicago Settle in Liberia," *The New York Times*, January 18, 1968, states that they paid $1.00 an acre. A statement circulated by the group quotes the price as 50 cents per acre.

70. Liberian Code of Laws of 1956, Miscellaneous Provisions, Article 5, Section 12.

NOTES TO CHAPTER II

1. "Ex-Chicagoans Struggle in Liberia," *Chicago Tribune*, January 18, 1968.
2. King Craig, one of the emigrants, said this interview should have been attributed to Eliyahu Buie, since he was a religious leader of the group, not Moses Buie. "Moses is no spokesman," said Craig. "I should know. He's my step-father."
3. Price, Larry, "Black Jews in the Promised Land," *Chicago Today Magazine*, November 8, 1970, p. 9; Har-Shefi, Joela, "Black Tidings," *Maariv*, December 31, 1971.
4. Thompson, Era Bell, "Are Black Americans Welcome in Africa?" *Ebony*, 24:3 (January 1969) 45.
5. Isaacs, H. R., *Op. Cit.*, p. 120.
6. The names of the recipients are listed in the Appendix.
7. Letter to the author, April 15, 1974.
8. Barnes, John, "Into the Wilderness," *Newsweek*, January 27, 1969, p. 52.

NOTES TO CHAPTER III

1. The Jewish people do not use the letters B.C. (before Christ) and A.D. (anno Domini—the year of the Lord) because they do not accept Jesus as their Messiah or Lord. Instead, the Jewish people substitute the letters B.C.E. (before the common era) for B.C. and C.E. (common era) for A.D.
2. Tomaschoff, Baruch, "Herzl's Family Background: A Far Cry From Assimilated," *The Jerusalem Post Weekly*, October 12, 1976, p. 9.
3. Bein, Alex, *Theodore Herzl*, Philadelphia: Jewish Publication Society, 1940, p. 94f.
4. *Ibid.*, p. 111.
5. *Ibid.*, p. 115f.
6. In an interview published in *Maariv*, December 12, 1971, Carter said Blackwell was accompanied to Israel by a second person who disappeared upon arrival there. Prince Asiel Ben Israel, International Ambassador of the Original Hebrew Israelite Nation, contradicted Carter when he told the author at Johnson C. Smith University in Charlotte on November 19, 1974, that Carter was the one who accompanied Blackwell. In Chicago, Levi Israel, a present-day leader of Carter's sect in that city, assured the author that the second man was Mikael Ben Yehuda, who is supposedly residing in Jericho, Israel. The author is inclined to accept the Prince's statement because of the unhesitant certainty with which he made it and Levi Israel's difficulty in recalling facts.

NOTES TO CHAPTER IV

1. Manheimer, Aron, "The Black Jews of Dimona," *Davka*, 2:3 (May/June 1972) 7.
2. "Chicago Blacks Happy in Israel," *Chicago Sun-Times*, February 4, 1970.

NOTES TO CHAPTER V

1. Windsor, Rudolph, *From Babylon to Timbuktu,* New York: Exposition Press, 1969, p. 24-25, 35-36.
2. Gaskell, G. A., *Dictionary of All Scriptures and Myth,* New York: The Julian Press, 1960, p. 825.
3. Rolner, M., *Op. Cit.,* erroneously calls him Crowley.
4. Clark, Elmer A., *The Small Sects in America,* Nashville: Cokesbury Press, 1937, p. 188f.
5. Brotz, H. M., *Op. Cit.,* p. 9, lists him as H. Z. Plummer as does Rolner, M., *Op. Cit.;* Clark, E. A., *Op. Cit.,* p. 190.
6. Spear, Allan H., *Black Chicago: The Making of a Negro Ghetto, 1890-1920,* Chicago: University of Chicago Press, 1967, p. 193.
7. Fauset, Arthur H., *Black Gods of the Metropolis,* Philadelphia: University of Philadelphia Press, 1944, p. 34f.
8. Mathison, Richard R., *Faiths, Cults and Sects in America,* Indianapolis: Bobbs-Merrill Co., 1960, p. 245-6.
9. It should be noted that no black has ever been formally ordained as Rabbi by any Jewish seminary.
10. Brotz, H. M., "Negro 'Jews' in the United States," p. 326.
11. Cleage, Albert B. Jr., *The Black Messiah,* New York: Sheed and Ward, 1969, p. 38f., 41, 53, 111.
12. From a tract entitled "The Truth About Our Black African Heritage," published by the group.
13. Wilmore, G. S., *Op. Cit.,* p. 237.
14. Rogers, J. A., *Op. Cit.,* 2 volumes.
15. Rolner, M., *Op. Cit.,* p. 40.
16. Mannix, Daniel P. and Malcolm Cowley, *Black Cargoes: A History of the Atlantic Slave Trade,* New York: The Viking Press, 1962, p. 32.
17. *Ibid.,* p. 30.
18. Howard, Richard, *Black Cargo,* New York: G. P. Putnam's Sons, 1972, p. 28.
19. Franklin, John H., *From Slavery to Freedom,* New York: Alfred A. Knopf, 1967, p. 31.
20. Mannix, D. P., and M. Cowley, *Op. Cit.,* p. 40-45; Owen, Robert D., *The Wrong of Slavery: Their Right of Emancipation,* Philadelphia: J. B. Lippincott & Co., 1864, p. 40-43.
21. Howard, R., *Op. Cit.,* p. 92; Mannix and Cowley, *Op. Cit.,* p. 197.
22. Howard, R., *Op. Cit.,* p. 93; Hodgkin, T., *Nigerian Perspectives,* O. U. P , 1968, p. 245.
23. Cleage, Albert B., *Black Christian Nationalism,* New York: William Morrow and Co., 1972, p. 97.
24. Howard, R., *Op. Cit.,* p. 36-37; Cameron, V. L., *Across Africa,* New York: Johnson Reprint Corp., 1971, Vol. 2, p. 136.
25. Howard, R., *Op. Cit.,* p. 17-18; Mannix D. P. and M. Cowley, *Op. Cit.,* p. 36.
26. Howard, R., *Op. Cit.,* p. 29.
27. *Ibid.,* p. 20.
28. Meier, A. and E. M. Rudwick, *Op. Cit.,* p. 30.
29. Williams ,Joseph J., *Hebrewisms of West Africa,* New York: The Dial Press, 1931.

30. Yaffe, Richard, "A Black 'Rabbi' in New York Jungle," *Jewish Chronicle*, March 2, 1973, p. 7.
31. July 11, 1974, addressed to the author.
32. Ottley, R., *Op. Cit.*, p. 140; *Encyclopaedia Judaica*, Vol. 6, p. 1143-1154.
33. Bleich, J. David, "Black Jews: A Halakhic Perspective," *Tradition*, 15:1-2 (Spring-Summer 1975) 50.
34. "Chief Rabbi Yossef Officially Recognizes Falashas as Jews," *Jewish Chronicle*, March 23, 1973.
35. "Ethiopia," *The Universal Jewish Encyclopedia*, Vol. 4, p. 182-5.
36. Gerard, A. S., *Four African Literatures*, Berkely: University of California Press, 1971, p. 274; "Ethiopian Literature," *Encyclopaedia Brittanica*, 1970, Vol. 8, p. 791b.
37. *Ibid.*, p. 326.
38. Rogers, J. A., *World's Great Men of Color*, New York: The Macmillan Co., 1972, Vol. 1, p. 33. She is also known by the name Bilkis.
39. Wendt, Herbert, *It Began in Babel*, Boston: Houghton Mifflin Co., 1962, p. 107.
40. Bruce, James, *Travels to Discover the Source of the Nile*, Dublin: William Porter, 1791, Vol .3, p. 583, 622, 670, et passim.
41. Ullendorf, Edward, *The Ethiopians*, London: Oxford University Press, 1960, p. 52-3, 110-12, 154; Meisler, Stanley, "Black Jews of Africa: An Identity Crisis," *The Los Angeles Times*, February 15, 1973.
42. Mannix, D. P. and M. Cowley, *Op. Cit.*, p. 243.
43. Bleich, J. D., *Op. Cit.*, p. 51, where he quotes the Radvaz.
44. Chouraqui, Andre N., *Between East and West*, Philadelphia: Jewish Publication Society, 1968, Introduction, Chapter 1.
45. Ben Ammi Carter betrayed his ignorance of these factors when he insisted that Ashanti, the name and language of the British protectorate on the Gold Coast, is Hebrew. The Hebrew word *ashan* means "smoke," and *ti* is a suffix referring to the first person singular. To claim that this proves that Ashanti is Hebrew is foolish. It is only a further indication of the relationship between Hamitic and Semitic languages.
46. Hershkovits, Melville J., *The Myth of the Negro Past*, Boston: Beacon Press, 1958, p. 137.
47. Rawick, George P., *The American Slave: A Composite Autobiography*. Westport, Conn.: Greenwood Publishing Co., 1972, p. 32f.
48. Hershkovits, M. J., *Op. Cit.*, p. 233f.
49. Wilmore, G. S., *Op. Cit.*, p. 34.
50. Frazier, E. Franklin, *The Negro Church in America*, New York: Schocken Books, 1974, p. 19.
51. *Ibid.*, p. 15.
52. Frazier, E. Franklin, *The Negro Family in the United States*, Chicago: University of Chicago Press, 1939, p. 30.
53. Wilmore, G., *Op. Cit.*, p. 36.
54. Frazier, E. F., *The Negro Church in America*, p. 3.
55. Rawick, G. P., *Op. Cit.*, p. 33-34.
56. Hershkovits, M. J., *Op. Cit.*, p. 207.
57. Korn, Bertram, W., *Jews and Negro Slavery in the Old South 1789-1865*, Elkins Park, Penna.: Reform Congregation Keneseth Israel, 1961, p. 49.
58. Marcus, Jacob R., *Early American Jewry*, Philadelphia: Jewish Publication Society, 1953, Vol. 2, p. 224; Elzas, Barnett A., *The Jews of South Carolina*, Philadelphia: J. B. Lippincott Co., 1905, p. 153.

59. Bleich, J. D., *Op. Cit.*, p. 61f.
60. Korn, B. W., *Op. Cit.*, p. 49.
61. Marcus, J. R., *Op. Cit.*
62. Hershkovits, M. J., *Op. Cit.*, p. 137.
63. Cheek, William F., *Black Resistance Before the Civil War*, Beverly Hills, Calif.: Glencoe Press, 1970, p. 60f.
64. *Ibid.*, p. 13; Lincoln, C., *The Black Experience in Religion*, New York: Anchor Press/Doubleday, 1974, p. 260.
65. Rawick, G. P., *Op. Cit.*, p. 39-43.
66. Barnes, J., *Op. Cit.*
67. *The New York Times*, September 20, 1967; January 18, 1968; *Chicago Tribune*, January 18, 1968.
68. Isaacs, H. R., *Op. Cit.*, p. 130f.
69. *Ibid.*, p. 306.
70. Isaacs, Harold R., *American Jews in Israel*, New York: The John Day Company, 1967, p. 16f.
71. *Ibid.*
72. Isaacs, H. R., *The New World of Negro Americans*, p. 297f.
73. P. 17f.
74. *The Europa Yearbook 1975 A World Survey*, London: Europa Publications, Ltd., 1975, Vol. 2, p. 936.
75. *Encyclopaedia Britannica,* Macropaedia, Vol. 10, 1974, p. 855.
76. Buell, Raymond L., *Liberia: A Century of Survival 1847-1947*, Philadelphia: University of Pennsylvania Press, 1947, p. 35.
77. Gunther, John, *Inside Africa*, New York: Harper and Brothers, 1955, p. 861-64.
78. Personal interview, June 1973.

NOTES TO CHAPTER VI

1. "Negroes Win Israel Stay of Three Months," *The Chicago Tribune*, December 23, 1969.
2. Price, L., *Op. Cit.*, p. 9; Manheimer, A., *Op. Cit.*, p. 8.
3. *The Sentinel*, January 8, 1970, p. 3; Arba, Abu, "The Black Jews of Dimona," *The Jewish Digest*, 16:9 (June 1971) 54.
4. "Negroes Win Israel Stay of Three Months," *Op. Cit.*

NOTES TO CHAPTER VII

1. Raymist, Malkah, "Jewish Negroes From Chicago Settle Into New Life in Israel," *Chicago Tribune*, May 31, 1970.
2. Price, L., *Op. Cit.*, p. 10.
3. Goldfarb, Harold, "Blacks and Conversion to Judaism," *The Jewish Digest*, March 1972, p. 32-34.

4. Coleman, Robert, "A Black Jew Speaks," *The Jewish Observer,* 7:1 (November 1970).
5. Cale, R., *Ibid.; The Jerusalem Post International Edition,* November 23, 1976, p. 15.
6. Coleman, Robert, "Black and Jewish—And Unaccepted," *Sh'ma,* 4:70 (March 22, 1974).
7. Spiegler, Samuel, "Who is a Black Jew?" *Journal of Jewish Communal Service,* 47:3 (Spring 1971) 269-270.
8. Bleich, J. D., *Op. Cit.,* p. 48f.
9. Gallob, Ben, "Black Converts Majority in New Interracial Congregation in Brooklyn," *Intermountain Jewish News,* December 26, 1975, p. 4.
10. Purim is the Feast of Lots and is based on the narrative in the Biblical Book of Esther.
11. Arba, Abu, *Op. Cit.,* p. 54-56.
12. Ha-Elyon, Jacob, "The Righteous Teacher Says No," *Maariv,* May 22, 1970, p. 22-23.
13. Rabbi Ralph Simon of Chicago, who worked with Carter and his group, told the author that Carter went to Israel from the United States. In Liberia, the author was told by King Craig that he saw Carter in Monrovia the day before he left for Israel.
14. Borsten, Joan, "Sect Problems," *The Jerusalem Post International Edition,* December 7, 1976, p. 9. Some of the data in this article do not agree with earlier published material in Israeli newspapers.
15. *The Jerusalem Post,* May 22, 1970; Ha-Elyon, J., *Op. Cit.*
16. Raymist, M., *Op. Cit.*
17. In a personal interview.
18. "America's Black Jews in Israel," *Israel Magazine,* 3:1 (1970) 43.

NOTES TO CHAPTER VIII

1. Ha-Elyon, J., *Op. Cit.*
2. *The Jerusalem Post,* December 23, 1969.
3. "America's Black Jews in Israel," *Israel Magazine,* p. 35.
4. *The Jerusalem Post,* December 29, 1969.
5. Constitution of Liberia, Bill of Rights, Article 1, Section 3.
6. *The Jerusalem Post,* December 29, 1969.
7. "America's Black Jews in Israel," *Israel Magazine,* p. 36.
8. *Ibid.*
9. The author was unable to decipher his name.
10. Givon, Shlomo, "The Blacks in Dimona," *Maariv,* October 7, 1971.
11. Manheimer, A., *Op. Cit.,* p. 9.
12. Cale, Ruth, "Israel Grapples With a 'Black Hebrew' Problem, *Baltimore Sun,* November 6, 1971.
13. Mitchell, Grayson, "Barred From Israel, Blacks Return Home," *Chicago Sun-Times,* October 8, 1971.
14. *The World Book Encyclopedia,* 1973, Vol. 16, p. 52f.
15. Letter to author April 15, 1974.
16. *Chicago Defender,* August 28, 1973.
17. Lynne, Edward, "Sons of Cush Get the Push," *Jewish Observer and Middle East Review,* 20:42 (October 15, 1971) 12.

18. Cale, R., *Op. Cit.*
19. Givon, S., *Op. Cit.*
20. Har-Shefi, J., *Op. Cit.*
21. Givon, S., *Op. Cit.*
22. Price, L., *Op. Cit.*
23. Givon, S., *Op. Cit.*
24. Har-Shefi, J., *Op. Cit.*
25. Cale, R., *Op. Cit.*
26. Givon, S., *Op. Cit.;* Har-Shefi, J., *Op. Cit.; The Sentinel,* September 2, 1971.
27. Ayil, Aylee, "Dynamite in Dimona," *Maariv,* October 8, 1971.
28. *Ibid.*
29. Manheimer, A., *Op. Cit.,* Part 2, p. 52.
30. Weisbord, Robert G., "Israel and the Black Hebrew Israelites," *Judaism,* 93:24 (Winter 1975) 44, footnote 44.
31. Cheatham, Thomas, "Blacks Cite Racism in Israel," *Chicago Defender,* February 8, 1972.
32. Givon, S., *Op. Cit.*
33. " 'Black Hebrew' Sentenced for Break In," *Maariv,* October 19, 1971.
34. Manheimer, A., *Op. Cit.,* p. 11.
35. Ayil, A., *Op. Cit.*
36. Manheimer, A., *Op. Cit.,* p. 9.
37. Kent, Clark, "Dashikis in the Promised Land," *Israel Horizons,* May-June 1972, p. 11.
38. Lynne, E., *Op. Cit.*
39. Jewish Telegraphic Agency Daily News Bulletin, October 6, 1971, p. 3.
40. Personal interview.
41. Mitchell, G., *Op. Cit.*
42. Lewis, Larry, "Black American Soldier in the Israeli Army," *Sepia,* 24:10 (October 1975) 18-24.
43. Letter to author May 16, 1976.
44. *Ibid.*
45. Friedman, David, "Black Psychologist Finds Israel Not Racist," *The Jewish Advocate,* October 9, 1975.
46. Letter from Larry Lewis, May 16, 1976.
47. "Chief Rabbi Yossef Recognizes Falashas as Jews," *The Jewish Chronicle,* March 23, 1973; Rapoport, Louis and Judy Siegel, "Ethiopian Falashas Recognized as Jews Under Law of Return," *The Jerusalem Post Weekly,* April 15, 1975; Kessel, Yoram, "Must the Falashas Face Extinction?" *The Jewish Advocate,* July 26, 1973.
48. Rapoport, L. and J. Siegel, *Op. Cit.*
49. Meisler, S., *Op. Cit.*
50. "Rabbi Yosef Converts 40 Falashas," *Jerusalem Post Weekly,* December 26, 1972.
51. Griggs, Tony, "Angry Blacks Return Here," *Chicago Defender,* September 27, 1972.
52. *Christianity Today,* December 7, 1973, p. 53.
53. Lynne, E., *Op. Cit.,* p. 12.
54. Ayil, A., *Op. Cit.*
55. Leona Clark and Others, Petitioners, v. Minister of the Interior, Respondent (H.C. 482/71).

56. Bushinsky, Jay, "Blacks Appeal to Stay in Israel," *Chicago Daily News*, November 26, 1971.
57. Lynne, E., *Op. Cit.*
58. Har-Shefi, J., *Op. Cit.*
5ς Cheatham, T., *Op. Cit.*
60. Har-Shefi J. *Op. Cit.*

NOTES TO CHAPTER IX

1. Manheimer, A., *Op. Cit.*, Part 2, p. 50.
2. A UPI report from Israel in *The Chicago Defender*, September 27, 1972 erroneously reported that Kirkpatrick tried to settle 20 blacks from Arad and Mitzpe Ramon in Dimona. Givon, Shlomo, "Kirkpatrick Died from Axe Beating," *Maariv*, February 22, 1972, presents still another version.
3. *The Chicago Sun-Times*, Kup's Column, February 10, 1972.
4. "Black Israelites Seek a Promised Land," *The Jewish Monitor*, March, 1972, p. 11; *The Jerusalem Post*, February 21, 1972.
5. The *menorah* is an ancient Jewish religious symbol. One with seven branches was placed in the tabernacle the Jewish people built in the wilderness following their liberation from Egyptian bondage. King Solomon later erected ten *menorot* in the Temple he constructed in Jerusalem. An 8-branched *menorah* is used by the Jewish people during the celebration of *Chanukah*, the Festival of Lights. The 7-branched *menorah* is the emblem of the State of Israel.
6. Ben-Adi, Herbert, "Black Hebrews on Trial," *The Jerusalem Post*, February 21, 1972.
7. "Witness, 17, Describes Black Hebrews Fight," *The Jerusalem Post*, February 22, 1972.
8. "Key Witness in Black Hebrew Trial Arrested," *The Jerusalem Post*, February 23, 1972.
9. The judges were Shlomo Elkayam, Avraham Mallul and Meir Wolinsky.
10. "Ex-Chicagoans Sentenced," *The Chicago Tribune*, June 13, 1972.
11. Cale, R., *Op. Cit.*
12. *The Jerusalem Post*, November 21, 1972.
13. Goldberg, Hillel, "View from Jerusalem," *Intermountain Jewish News*, February 14, 1975, p. 4.
14. Weiss, Charles, "Israel Gradually Closing Door to Black Hebrews," *Chicago Tribune*, September 16, 1973.
15. Har-Shefi, J., *Op. Cit.*
16. Glazier, Douglas, "Israel Rebuffs Black Sect as Immigrants," *The Detroit Sunday News*, October 20, 1974, p. 11B.
17. *Ibid.*
18. *The Jerusalem Post*, October 8, 1971.
19. *The Liberian Star*, November 14, 1969.
20. "300 Blacks Label Israel as Racist," *The Chicago Tribune*, December 31, 1971.
21. Lankin, Doris, "Black Hebrews and Israel," Law Report, *The Jerusalem Post*, January 9, 1973, p. 9.
22. He was joined by Justices Moshe Landau and Eliyahu Mann.

23. King Craig disputed this contention during an interview in Monrovia.
24. August 21, 1973.
25. In a conversation with the author
26. Sent to the author.
27. Personal interview.
28. Of course the author, a Jew, would be welcome under the Law of Return.
29. Interview with American Embassy personnel, June 6, 1974.
30. *Chicago Defender*, October 2, 1973.
31. Personal interview, American Embassy, Tel Aviv, August, 1975.
32. Givon, Shlomo, "Visas of Most Black Hebrews Expired," *Maariv*, December 8, 1975; Borsten, J., *Op. Cit.*
33. Harshunsky, Yose, "The Fiesta of the Dimona Messengers," *Maariv*, September 23, 1975; "The Rhythm and Soul of the Dimona Messengers," *Maariv*, December 31, 1975.
34. Givon, Shlomo, "Search for Kidnapped 8-year-old of Black Hebrew Sect," *Maariv*, December 4, 1975.
35. Borsten, J., *Op. Cit.*

NOTES TO CHAPTER X

1. Moore, Wilbert E., *American Negro Slavery and Abolition*, New York: The Third Press, 1971, p. 6.
2. *Ibid.*, p. 8.
3. Brown, Richard D., editor, *Slavery in American Society*, Lexington, Mass.: D. C. Heath and Co., 1969, p. 15; Moore, W. E., *Op. Cit.*, p. 9.
4. Moore, W. E., *Op. Cit.*; Brown, R. D., *Op. Cit.*, p. 14.
5. Elkins, Stanley M., *Slavery*, Chicago: University of Chicago Press, 1969, p. 48.
6. Moore, W. E., *Op. Cit.*, p. 82-86; Brown, R. D., *Op. Cit.*, p. 20.
7. Elkins, S. M., *Op. Cit.*
8. Moore, W. E., *Op. Cit.*, p. 94f.
9. Bascom, William, "Acculturation Among the Gullah Negroes," *American Anthropologist*, 43 (1941) 44.
10. Harris, Robert L., Jr., "The Heart of the Slave: Attitudes Toward Bondage in America," *Black Lines*, 2:2 (Winter 1972) 30.
11. Rawick, G. P., *Op. Cit.*, Chapter V.
12. Bracey, John H., Jr., August Meier and Elliott Rudwick, editors, *The Black Sociologists: The First Half Century*, Belmont, California: Wadsworth Publishing Co., 1971, p. 111.
13. McCandless, Boyd R., *Children: Behavior and Development*, New York: Holt, Rinehart and Winston, Inc., 1967, p. 164f.
14. Papalia, Diane E. and Sally W. Olds, *A Child's World: Infancy Through Adolescence*, New York: McGraw-Hill Book Co., 1975, p. 251.
15. Vander Zanden, James W., *American Minority Relations*, New York: The Ronald Press Co., 1972, p. 414.
16. Bracey, J. H., A. Meier and E. M. Rudwick, *Op. Cit.*, p. 112.
17. Baughman, E. Earl, *Black Americans*, New York and London: Academic Press, 1971, p. 41.

18. Moberg, David O., *The Church as a Social Institution,* New Jersey: Prentice-Hall, Inc., 1962, p. 448f.
19. Meier, A. and E. M. Rudwick, *Op. Cit.,* p. 75-78.
20. Rose, A. M., *Op. Cit.,* p. 74.
21. "An Interview With C. Eric Lincoln," *Black Enterprise,* 3:5 (December 1972) 34.
22. Lewin, Kurt, *Resolving Social Conflicts,* New York: Harper and Brothers, 1948, Chapter 12.
23. Mannix, D. P. and M. Cowley, *Op. Cit.,* p. 59-60.
24. Christians call the Jewish Bible Old Testament.
25. Woodward, C. Vann, *Origins of the New South, 1877-1913,* Baton Rouge: Louisiana University Press, 1951, Vol. 9, p. 352.
26. Lincoln, C. E., *Op. Cit.,* p. 255f.
27. Quoted in Ehrman, Albert, "Black Judaism in New York," *Journal of Ecumenical Studies,* 8:1 (Winter 1971) 109f.
28. Wilmore, G. S., *Op. Cit.,* p. 74f.
29. *Ibid.,* p. 91.
30. *Ibid.,* p. 80.
31. *Ibid.,* p. 166f.
32. *Time Magazine,* March 10, 1975, p. 23.
33. Personal Interview.

BIBLIOGRAPHY

Adams, Russell L., *Great Negroes Past and Present*, Chicago: Afro-Am Publishing Co., 1972.

Ajale, Adekunle, *Pan-Africanism*, London: Andre Deutsch, Ltd., 1973.

"America's Black Jews in Israel," *Israel Magazine*, 3:1 (1970) 34-43.

Aptheker, Herbert, ed., *A Documentary of the Negro People in the United States*, New York: The Citadel Press, 1951.

Arba, Abu, "The Black Jews of Dimona," *The Jewish Digest*, 16:9 (June 1971) 54-56.

Ayil, Aylee, "Dynamite in Dimona," *Maariv*, October 8, 1971.

Barnes, John, "Into the Wilderness," *Newsweek*, January 27, 1969.

Bascom, William, "Acculturation Among the Gullah Negroes," *American Anthropologist*, 43 (1941) 44.

Baughman, E. Earl, *Black Americans*, New York and London: Academic Press, 1871.

Bein, Alex, *Theodore Herzl*, Philadelphia: Jewish Publication Society, 1940.

Ben-Adi, Herbert, "Black Hebrews on Trial," *The Jerusalem Post*, February 21, 1972.

Bittle, William E. and Gilbert Geis, *The Longest Way Home: Chief Alfred C. Sam's Back to Africa Movement*, Detroit: Wayne State University 1964.

Bleich, J. David, "Black Jews: A Halakhic Perspective," *Tradition*, 15:1-2 (Spring-Summer 1975) 48-79.

Blitzer, Wolf, "Arabs Are the World's Worst Racists, Says Eldridge Cleaver," *The Jerusalem Post Weekly*, January 20, 1976.

Borsten, Joan, "Sect Problems," *The Jerusalem Post International Edition*, December 7, 1976.

Bracey, John H., Jr., August Meier and Elliott Rudwick, eds., *The Black Sociologists: The First Half Century*, Belmont, California: Wadsworth Publishing Co., 1971.

Brodie, Fawn M., *Thomas Jefferson: An Intimate History*, New York W. W. Norton and Co., Inc., 1974.

Brotz, Howard M., *The Black Jews of Harlem*, New York: Schocken Books 1970.

———, "Negro 'Jews' in the United States," *Phylon*, 13 (1952) 324-337.

Brown, Richard D., ed., *Slavery in American Society*, Lexington, Massachusetts: D. C. Heath and Co, 1969.

Bruce, James, *Travels to Discover the Source of the Nile*, Dublin: William Porter, 1791.

Buch, Saul, "Falasha: The Black Jews of Africa Revisited," *The American Zionist*, 64:1 (September 1973) 17-20.

211

Buell, Raymond L., *Liberia: A Century of Survival*, Philadelphia: University of Philadelphia Press, 1947.

Bushinsky, Jay, "Blacks Appeal to Stay in Israel," *Chicago Daily News*, November 26, 1971.

Cale, Ruth, "Israel Grapples With A 'Black Hebrew' Problem," *Baltimore Sun*, November 6, 1971.

Cameron, V. L., *Across Africa*, New York: Johnson Reprint Corp., 1971, Vol. 2.

Carmichael, Stokely, "Pan-Africanism—Land and Power," *The Black Scholar*, November 1967.

Cheatham, Thomas, "Blacks Cite Racism in Israel," *Chicago Defender*, February 8, 1972.

Cheek, William F., *Black Resistance Before the Civil War*, Beverly Hills, California: Glencoe Press, 1970.

Chouraqui, Andre N., *Between East and West*, Philadelphia: Jewish Publication Society, 1968.

Clark, Elmer A., *The Small Sects in America*, Nashville: Cokesbury Press, 1937.

Cleage, Albert B., Jr., *Black Christian Nationalism*, New York: William Morrow and Co., 1972.

——, *The Black Messiah*, New York: Sheed and Ward, 1969.

Coleman, Robert, "Black and Jewish—And Unaccepted," *Sh'ma*, 4:70 (March 22, 1974).

——, "A Black Jew Speaks," *The Jewish Observer*, 7:1 (November 1970).

Conrad, Earl, *Harriet Tubman*, New York: Paul S. Eriksson, Inc., 1943.

Constitution of Liberia.

Cronan, Edmund D., *Black Moses*, Madison: University of Wisconsin Press, 1968.

Ehrman, Albert, "Black Judaism in New York," *Journal of Ecumenical Studies*, 8:1 (Winter 1971) 103-114.

Elkins, Stanley M., *Slavery*, Chicago: University of Chicago Press, 1969.

Elzas, Barnett A., *The Jews of South Carolina*, Philadelphia: J. B. Lippincott Co., 1905.

Encyclopaedia Brittanica.

Encyclopaedia Judaica.

Encyclopedia Americana.

The Europa Yearbook 1975: A World Survey, London: Europa Publications Ltd., 1975, 2 volumes.

Fauset, Arthur H., *Black Gods of the Metropolis*, Philadelphia: University of Philadelphia Press, 1944.

Fisher, Miles M., *The Evolution of Slave Songs in the United States*, dissertation, University of Chicago, December 1948.

Franklin, John H., *From Slavery to Freedom*, New York: Alfred A. Knopf, 1967.

Frazier, E. Franklin, *The Negro Church in America*, New York: Schocken Books, 1974.

——, *The Negro Family in the United States*, Chicago: University of Chicago Press, 1939.

Friedman, David, "Black Psychologist Finds Israel Not Racist," *The Jewish Advocate*, October 9, 1975.

Gallob, Ben, "Black Converts Majority in New Interracial Congregation in Brooklyn," *Intermountain Jewish News*, December 26, 1975.

Garrison, William Lloyd, *Thoughts on African Organization*, New York: Arno Press and The New York Times, 1968.

212

Garvey, Amy Jacques, *Philosophy and Opinion of Marcus Garvey*, New York: Arno Press and The New York Times, 1969.

Gaskell, G. A., *Dictionary of All Scriptures and Myths*, New York: The Julian Press, 1960.

Gerard, Albert S., *Four African Literatures*, Berkeley: University of California Press, 1971.

Givon, Shlomo, "The Black Jews in Dimona," *Maariv*, October 7, 1971.

———, "Kirkpatrick Died From Axe Beating," *Maariv*, February 22, 1972.

———, "Search for Kidnapped 8-Year-Old Girl of Black Hebrew Sect," *Maariv*, December 4, 1975.

———, "Visas of Most 'Black Hebrews' Expired," *Maariv*, December 4, 1975.

Glazier, Douglas, "Israel Rebuffs Black Sect as Immigrants," *The Detroit Sunday News*, October 20, 1974.

Goldberg, Hillel, "View From Jerusalem," *Intermountain Jewish News*, February 14, 1975.

Golden, Harry, *Only in America*, New York: The World Publishing Co., 1958.

Goldfarb, Harold, "Blacks and Conversion to Judaism," *The Jewish Digest*, (March 1972) 32-34.

Griggs, Tony, "Angry Blacks Return Here," *Chicago Defender*, September 27, 1972.

Gunther, John, *Inside Africa*, New York: Harper and Brothers, 1955.

Ha-Elyon, Jacob, "The Righteous Teacher Says No," *Maariv*, May 22, 1970.

Harris, Robert L., Jr., "The Heart of the Slave: Attitudes Toward Bondage in America," *Black Lines*, 2:2 (Winter 1972) 28-38.

Harris, Sheldon H., *Paul Cuffe*, New York: Simon and Shuster, 1972.

Har-Shefi, Joela, "Black Tidings," *Maariv*, December 31, 1971.

Harshunsky, Yose, "The Fiesta of the Dimona Messengers," *Maariv*, December 31, 1975.

Hershkovits, Melville J., *The Myth of the Negro Past*, Boston: Beacon Press, 1958.

Hodgkin, T., *Nigerian Perspectives*, O. U. P., 1968.

Howard, Richard, *Black Cargo*, New York: G. P. Putnam's Sons, 1972.

"An Interview With C. Eric Lincoln," *Black Enterprise*, 3:5 (December 1972) 31-34, 56.

Isaacs, Harold R., *American Jews in Israel*, New York: The John Day Co. 1967.

———, *The New World of Negro Americans*, New York: The John Day Co., 1963.

Jones, Reginald L., ed., *Black Psychology*, New York: Harper and Row, Publishers, 1972.

Kent, Clark, "Dashikis in the Promised Land," *Israel Horizons*, May-June 1972.

Kessel, Yoram, "Must the Falashas Face Extinction?" *The Jewish Advocate*, July 26, 1973.

King, Kenneth J:, "Some Notes on Arnold J. Ford and New World Black Attitudes to Ethiopia," *Journal of Ethiopian Studies*, 10:1 (January 1972) 81-87.

Korn, Bertram W., *Jews and Negro Slavery in the Old South 1789-1865*, Elkins Park, Penna.: Reform Congregation Keneseth Israel, 1961.

Lankin, Doris, "Black Hebrews and Israel," Law Report, *The Jerusalem Post*, January 9, 1973.

Legum, Colin, *Africa: A Handbook to the Continent*, New York: Prager Publishers, 1968.

213

Lewin, Kurt, *Resolving Social Conflicts*, New York: Harper and Brothers, 1948.

Lewis, Larry, "Black American Soldier in the Israeli Army," *Sepia*, 24:10 (October 1975) 18-24.

Liberian Code of Laws.

Lincoln, C. Eric, *The Black Experience in Religion*, New York: Anchor Press/Doubleday, 1974.

———, *The Black Muslims in America*, Boston: Beacon Press, 1961.

Lynch, Hollis R., *Edward Wilmot Blyden: Pan Negro Patriot, 1832-1912*, New York: Oxford University Press, 1971.

Lynne, Edward, "Sons of Cush Get the Push," *Jewish Observer and Middle East Review*, 20:42 (October 15, 1971) 12.

Manheimer, Aron, "The Black Jews of Dimona," *Davka*, 2:3 (May-June 1972).

Mannix, Daniel P. and Malcolm Cowley, *Black Cargoes: A History of the Atlantic Slave Trade*, New York: The Viking Press, 1962.

Marcus, Jacob R., *Early American Jewry*, Philadelphia: Jewish Publication Society, 1953, 2 volumes.

Mathison, Richard R., *Faiths, Cults and Sects in America*, Indianapolis: Bobbs-Merrill Co., 1960.

McCandless, Boyd R., *Children: Behavior and Development*, New York: Holt Rinehart and Winston, Inc., 1967.

Meier, August, *Negro Thoughts in America 1880-1915*, Ann Arbor: University of Michigan Press, 1964.

——— and Elliott M. Rudwick, *From Plantation to Ghetto*, New York: Hill and Wang, 1966.

Meisler, Stanley, "Black Jews of Africa: An Identity Crisis," *Los Angeles Times*, February 15, 1973.

Mitchell, Grayson, "Barred From Israel, Blacks Return Home," *Chicago Sun-Times*, October 8, 1971.

Moberg, David O., *The Church as a Social Institution*, New Jersey: Prentice-Hall, Inc., 1962.

Moore, Wilbert E., *American Negro Slavery and Abolition*, New York: The Third Press, 1971.

Moses, Wilson J., "Marcus Garvey: A Reappraisal," *The Black Scholar*, 4:3 (November-December 1972) 38-49.

Ottley, Roi, *New World A-Coming*, New York: World Publishing Co., 1943.

Owen, Robert D., *The Wrong of Slavery: The Right of Emancipation*, Philadelphia: J. B. Lippincott and Co., 1864.

Papalia, Diane E. and Sally W. Olds, *A Child's World: Infancy Through Adolescence*, New York: McGraw-Hill Book Co., 1975.

Ploski, H. A. and W. Marr, eds., *The Negro Almanac: A Reference Work on the Afro American*, New York: Bellweather Co., 1976.

Polos, Nicholas C., "Black Anti-Semitism in Twentieth Century America: Historical Myth or Reality," *American Jewish Archives*, 27:1 (April 1975) 8-31.

Price, Larry, "Black Jews in the Promised Land," *Chicago Today Magazine*, November 8, 1970.

Rapoport, Louis and Judy Siegel, "Ethiopian Falashas Recognized as Jews Under Law of Return," *The Jerusalem Post Weekly*, April 15, 1975.

Rawick, George P., *The American Slave: A Composite Autobiography*, Westport, Conn.: Greenwood Publishing Co., 1972.

Raymist, Malkah, "Jewish Negroes From Chicago Settle Into New Life in

Israel," *Chicago Tribune*, May 31, 1970.

Redding, J. Saunders, *They Came in Chains*, New York: J. B. Lippincott and Co., 1973.

Rogers, J. A., *World's Great Men of Color*, New York: The Macmillan Co., 1970, 2 volumes.

Rolner, Murray, "Black and Being Jewish," *The National Jewish Monthly*, (October 1972) 38-43.

Rose, Arnold M., *The Negro's Morale*, Minneapolis: The University of Minnesota Press, 1949.

Rudwick, Elliott M., *W. E. B. DuBois: A Study in Minority Leadership*, Philadelphia: University of Philadelphia Press, 1960.

Samuel X, "A Brief History of the Messenger," *Muhammad Speaks*, no date.

Scheer, Robert, *Eldridge Cleaver: Post-Prison Writings and Speeches*, New York: Rampart Books, 1969.

Spear, Allan H., *Black Chicago: The Making of a Negro Ghetto, 1890-1920*, Chicago: University of Chicago Press, 1967.

Spiegler, Samuel, "Who is a Black Jew?" *Journal of Jewish Communal Service*, 47:3 (Spring 1971).

Thompson, Era Bell, "Are Black Americans Welcome in Africa?" *Ebony*, 24:3 (January 1969) 44-50.

Tindall, George B., "The Liberian Exodus of 1878," *South Carolina Historical Magazine*, 53:3 (July 1952) 133-145.

Tomaschoff, Baruch, "Herzl's Family Background: A Far Cry From Assimilated," *The Jerusalem Post Weekly*, October 12, 1976.

Ullendorff, Edward, *The Ethiopians*, London: Oxford University Press, 1960.

The Universal Jewish Encyclopedia, 10 volumes.

Vander Zanden, James W., *American Minority Relations*, New York: The Ronald Press Co., 1972.

Vincent, Theodore G., *Black Power and the Garvey Movement*, Berkeley: Ramparts Press, 1971.

Waitzkin, Howard, "Black Judaism in New York," *Harvard Journal of Negro Affairs*, 1:3 (1967).

Weisbord, Robert G., *Ebony Kinship*, Westport, Conn.: Greenwood Press, 1973.

———, "Israel and the Black Hebrew Israelites," *Judaism*, 93:24 (Winter 1975) 23-38.

Weiss, Charles, "Israel Gradually Closing Door to Black Hebrews," *Chicago Tribune*, September 16, 1973.

Wendt, Herbert, *It Began in Babylon*, Boston: Houghton Mifflin Co., 1962.

Williams, Joseph J., *Hebrewisms of West Africa*, New York: The Dial Press, 1931.

Wilmore, Gayraud S., *Black Religion and Black Radicalism*, New York: Doubleday and Co., 1972.

Wilson, Charles M., *Liberia*, New York: William Sloane Associates, 1947.

Windsor, Rudolph, *From Babylon to Timbuktu*, New York: Exposition Press, 1969.

Woodward, C. Vann, *Origins of the New South, 1877-1913*, Baton Rouge: Louisiana University Press, 1951.

World Book Encyclopedia.

Yaffe, Richard, "A Black 'Rabbi' in New York Jungle," *Jewish Chronicle*, March 2, 1973.

Young, James C., *Liberia Rediscovered*, New York: Doubleday, Doran and Co., 1934.

215

APPENDIX

Abercrombie, Lafayette
Abercrombie, Lydia
Alexander, Hazel
Alexander, Ruby
Arnold, Charlotte
Arnold, Sheila
Banks, Harman
Bey, Barbara Washington
Blackwell, Charles
Blackwell, Mary
Blackwell, Rupert
Boyd, John
Brooks, Cauzet Clay
Buie, Alice M.
Buie, Landar Jr.
Buie, Landar Sr.
Buie, Mattie
Buie, Moses
Burton, James T.
Butler, Janice
Butler, Shirley
Butler, Willie
Carter, Alice J. S.
Carter, Ben
Carter, Patricia
Craig, King E.
Davis, James
Davis, Joan
Dean, Mildred
Dean, Walter
Dixon, Catherine Steward
Ellis, Clarence
Ellis, Mellones
Figgares, Odessa
Fouch, Freddie L.
Fouch, Inez
Fouch, William
Freeman, Joan
Gilland, Dora

Gillie, Kittie
Gordon, Darwin
Greer, James T.
Harris, Melvin
Holmes, Lillian
Holmes, Theodore
Humphrey, Elnora
Jackson, Claddie
Jefferson, Dorothy
Jefferson, Larry
Little, Lannie
McCaskill, Annie
McCaskill, Jesse
Miller, Joyce
Moore, Annie
Moore, Barbara
Moore, Travis
Murray, Harbey
Parker, Carl
Potter, Larry
Readers, Ernestine
Rollison, Bartha
Smith, Stanley
Sutton, Hazel
Vernia, Gloria
Ward, Minnie
Washington, Cardian
Washington, Drewy
Whitfield, Thomas
Williams, Columbus
Williams, Lenetta
Williams, Mas Ella
Williams, Senella
Williams, Mertis R.
Winters, Isaiah
Winters, Mattie
Winters, Ophelia
Wolfold, Mattie
Wolfolk, Louise

* The names of the people in this Appendix were submitted by J. Newton Garnett, secretary of the commission appointed by President William V. S. Tubman to investigate the needs of the black Americans who moved into Liberia. They were the beneficiaries of a $50 monthly stipend from the Liberian government for a period of three months.

216

INDEX

217

218

Ford, Joseph 16
Ford, Mignon 16
Forten, James 26
France, French 24, 50, 52, 167
Freedom dues 177, 178
Freedom's Journal 24
French Equatorial Africa 12

Gabriel 58, 60, 61, 87, 88, 92, 103, 105, 107
Gabriel (Gavriel) Ben Israel 174, 199
Gabriel (ha) Katan 137, 174
Gad 77
Garcia, Sandra A. 147-150
Gardner, Newport 25
Garnett, J. Newton 38, 94
Garrison, William Lloyd 25, 27, 28
Garvey, Marcus (Garveyism) 12-17, 20, 24, 32, 49, 70, 98
Gbatala 31, 34, 37, 38, 40-44, 53, 54, 95
Gedara 51
Gehazi 67, 68
Geneva 168
German Southwest Africa 12
Germany 50, 138, 167, 173
Georgia 33, 83, 185
Gershom, Mar 104-115
Geva, Joseph 123
Ghana 11, 74, 99
Giyur Chelki 91, 92, 123
Giyur Chumri 92
Gladstone, Jacob 199
Glober, Thomas 157, 166, 167
Golden, Harry 26
Gondor 80
Goren, Shlomo 150
Great Britain 15, 108, 193
Greaves, Milt 134, 135, 166
Greenberg, Chaim 58-60
Greer, James T. 9, 20, 23, 29, 31, 33, 39, 42, 46, 49, 96, 199
Guryea Clan 34

Halachah Halachic 90, 91, 93, 121, 122, 127, 149, 174
Halevy, Israel 80
Ham, Hamites 67, 78, 188, 192
Hamitic language 82, 204
Harlem Renaissance 17
Harper, Robert Monroe (Goodlowe) 22, 201
Harris, Israel Lee 145, 156-158
Har-Shefi, Joela 153
Hatsheput 73
Hatzaad Harishon 7, 199
Hebrews 2, 13, 14, 17, 19, 20, 33, 36, 37, 42, 47, 49, 50, 55, 57, 59, 62, 65-71, 73, 74, 78, 79, 81, 82, 88, 91, 100, 104, 109, 117, 119, 120, 122-124, 128, 129,

138, 152, 157, 164-166, 176, 178, 179, 182, 188-192, 204
Hebrew Israelites 2, 124, 126-128, 131, 144, 153, 164, 169, 170
Henry, Hubert 52
Herod the Great 60
Herzl, Theodore 13, 14, 51-53
Herzog, Isaac 149
Higginson, Thomas Wentworth 85
Hitler, Adolph 170, 195
Hodges, James 7
Holy Land 55, 57, 164, 194
House of Israel Hebrew Cultural Center 30, 99
Hungary 116
Hunt, H. L. 167
Hussein, King 168

Identification, identify 135, 181, 191, 195
Identity, identity-crisis 69, 179, 186, 188, 194
Illinois 33
Imhotep 73
Immigrant Adjustment Board 38
Immigrants' rights 59, 89, 105, 112, 123, 124, 152
Indentured servant (servitude) 176-177
Independent Episcopal Church 13
India 114, 116, 118
International Peace and Brotherly Love Movement 70
Isaac 2, 5, 15, 48, 55, 65, 70, 100, 106, 138, 152, 176, 188
Isaacs, Harold R. 97
Isaiah 50, 68, 199
Islam 72
Israel, Israeli 2, 7, 10, 11, 18, 19, 48-50, 53, 54, 56-63, 67, 69, 71, 73, 81, 87, 88, 90, 93, 98-100, 102, 105, 107-111, 113-120, 123, 125, 127-130, 133-153, 157-159, 161-166, 168, 169, 171-175, 188, 193-197, 206, 208
Israel Independence Day 133
Israel, Levi 8, 147, 202
Israel, Tziona 58, 60, 87, 88, 92, 103, 105, 107
Israelite(s) 20, 66-68, 79, 86, 128, 136, 139, 170
Italian (Italo)-Ethiopian War 16, 77
Itzoch, Henry 70

Jacob 2, 5, 16, 48, 55, 65-67, 70, 100, 106, 138, 153, 176, 188
Jaures, Jean 52
Jefferson, Thomas 21
Jeremiah 66, 78
Jericho 133, 141, 144, 158, 192
Jerusalem 58, 79, 100, 108, 112, 115, 134,

219

220